RICH DAD'S
PROPHECY

Why the Biggest Stock Market
Crash in History Is Still Coming...
and How You Can Prepare
Yourself and Profit from It!

RICH DAD'S
PROPHECY

Why the Biggest Stock Market
Crash in History Is Still Coming...
and How You Can Prepare
Yourself and Profit from It!

PLATA®
PUBLISHING

Published by Plata Publishing, LLC

CASHFLOW, Rich Dad, B-I Triangle, knowledge: the new money and CASHFLOW Quadrant are registered trademarks of CASHFLOW Technologies, Inc.

   are registered trademarks of CASHFLOW Technologies, Inc.

Plata Publishing, LLC
4330 N. Civic Center Plaza
Suite 100
Scottsdale, AZ 85251
(480) 998-6971

Visit our websites: PlataPublishing.com and RichDad.com
Printed in the United States of America
072013

First Trade Edition: January 2004
First Plata Edition: June 2013
ISBN: 978-1-61268-025-5

Best-selling Books
by Robert T. Kiyosaki

Rich Dad Poor Dad
What the Rich Teach Their Kids About Money –
That the Poor and Middle Class Do Not

Rich Dad's CASHFLOW Quadrant
Guide to Financial Freedom

Rich Dad's Guide to Investing
What the Rich Invest in That the Poor and Middle Class Do Not

Rich Dad's Rich Kid Smart Kid
Give Your Child a Financial Head Start

Rich Dad's Retire Young Retire Rich
How to Get Rich and Stay Rich

Rich Dad's Prophecy
Why the Biggest Stock Market Crash in History Is Still Coming...
And How You Can Prepare Yourself and Profit from It!

Rich Dad's Success Stories
Real-Life Success Stories from Real-Life People
Who Followed the Rich Dad Lessons

Rich Dad's Guide to Becoming Rich
Without Cutting Up Your Credit Cards
Turn Bad Debt into Good Debt

Rich Dad's Who Took My Money?
Why Slow Investors Lose and Fast Money Wins!

Rich Dad Poor Dad for Teens
The Secrets About Money – That You Don't Learn In School!

Escape the Rat Race
Learn How Money Works and Become a Rich Kid

Rich Dad's Before You Quit Your Job
Ten Real-Life Lessons Every Entrepreneur Should Know
About Building a Multimillion-Dollar Business

Rich Dad's Increase Your Financial IQ
Get Smarter with Your Money

Robert Kiyosaki's Conspiracy of the Rich
The 8 New Rules of Money

Unfair Advantage
The Power of Financial Education

Why "A" Students Work for "C" Students
Rich Dad's Guide to Financial Education for Parents

CONTENTS

CONTENTS

Acknowledgments

I acknowledge and thank the Rich Dad community. I am humbled
by the messages I receive from people who have taken control of their
financial lives and are teaching others financial literacy.

Keep learning and teaching!

NOTHING HAS CHANGED

Question: What is the job of a prophet?

Answer: To be wrong.

When *Rich Dad's Prophecy* was published in 2002, over a decade ago, I hoped my rich dad was wrong.

To test the accuracy of my rich dad's predictions—predictions made many years ago—we have made no material changes to the content of this book for its re-release.

I continue to hope that my rich dad was wrong…although I am afraid he was right.

– Robert Kiyosaki

NOAH AND THE ARK

My rich dad often said, "If you want to be a rich business owner or investor, you need to understand the story of Noah and the ark." Although rich dad did not see himself as a prophet, he did work diligently to improve his ability to see the future. As he trained his son and me to be business owners and investors who could also see the future, he would often say, "Do you realize how much faith it took for Noah to go to his family and say, 'God told me there is a great flood coming, so we need to build an ark?'" He would then chuckle and say, "Can you imagine what his wife, kids, and investors must have said to him? They might have said, 'But Noah, this is a desert we live in. It does not rain here. In fact, we are in the middle of a drought. Are you sure God told you to build an ark? It's going to be tough to raise capital for a boat-building company in the middle of a desert. Wouldn't building a hotel, spa, and golf course make more sense than an ark?'"

For nearly 30 years, starting when we were just nine years old, rich dad trained his son and me to be business owners and investors. He regularly used very simple teaching tools, such as the game of *Monopoly*®, to teach us the principles of investing. Rich dad also used common everyday fables, such as the story of "The Three Little Pigs," to convey the importance of building financial houses made out of bricks rather than straw or sticks. He also used stories from the Old Testament, such as "David and Goliath", to teach his son and me the power of leverage—in this case, the leverage represented by David's slingshot. This is the lesson of how a little guy can beat a big guy. In teaching us the importance of having a vision of the future, rich dad would often say, "Always remember that Noah had vision. But more than vision, he had the faith and courage to take action on his vision. Many people have vision, but not everyone has the sustainable faith and courage as Noah did—the faith and courage to take action on their vision—so their vision of the future is the same as their vision of today." In other words, people without faith, courage, and vision often do not see the changes that are coming, until it is too late.

My rich dad was very concerned about a 1974 law known as ERISA. He said, "At the time of its passage, most people were not even aware of ERISA. Even today, many people have never even heard of this act passed by Congress and signed into law by President Ford. The full impact of this law change will not be felt for 25 to 50 years, long after I am gone. I wish I could tell them to prepare now, but how do I tell them about the future?"

In January of 2002, the people of the United States, still reeling from the events of September 11, 2001, began hearing of the bankruptcy of Enron, one of the biggest blue-chip companies in America. But more than the bankruptcy, the news that sent chills through many people of my generation—the baby-boom generation, the generation born between 1946 and 1964—was the realization that many of the employees of Enron had lost their entire retirement savings. For the first time, millions of baby boomers began to realize that a 401(k), IRA, and other such plans filled with mutual funds and company stock, were not as safe as they thought or had been told by their financial planner. Millions of baby boomers shared something in common with the thousands of people who worked for Enron. The demise of Enron was sounding a personal alarm, a fear, a realization that their own retirement might not be as secure as they may have once thought. Rich dad's prophecy was coming true.

A local television station called and asked if I would come in and comment on the impact of the bankruptcy of Enron, a one-time oil-and-gas industry leader. The attractive young TV commentator asked me, "Is this Enron bankruptcy an isolated event?"

My reply was, "The Enron bankruptcy is an extreme case, but not an isolated case." Continuing, I said, "I am surprised that the media is not mentioning Cisco, Viacom, Motorola, and other giants. Although not as dramatic as Enron, there are many companies similar to Enron where employees have a significant percentage of their retirement tied up in their employer company's stock."

"What do you mean?" asked the TV host.

"I mean this Enron disaster should be a wake-up call for people— a wake-up call letting them know that their 401(k) is not bulletproof, that it is possible to lose everything just before you retire, that mutual funds are not safe even if you do diversify."

"What do you mean, 'Mutual funds are not safe even if you diversify'?" she asked with a hint of shocked anger. I sensed that I was now stepping on her toes even though she did not work for Enron.

Rather than getting into a debate on mutual funds and diversification, I said, "I retired at the age of 47 without any stocks or mutual funds. To me, mutual funds and stocks are too risky, even if you do diversify. There are better ways to invest for your retirement."

"Are you saying not to invest in stocks or mutual funds and not to diversify?" she asked.

"No," I replied. "I am not telling anyone to do anything. I am simply saying that I retired early in life without a single share of stock or mutual fund or any diversification within funds. If you want to invest in stocks and mutual funds and diversify, that might be right for you, but not for me."

"We need to go to a commercial break," said the young woman. "Thank you for being a guest on our show." She shook my hand and quickly turned to the camera and began talking about the advantages of a new wrinkle cream.

The interview was over earlier than expected. It seemed that when the interview strayed from Enron to the likely personal investment strategies of the TV hostess, wrinkle cream became a more pleasant subject to discuss—not only for the TV host, but also for the thousands of viewers. The subject of retirement was not a comfortable one.

One of the intended results of ERISA was to encourage individuals to save for their own retirement. This would encourage a three-pronged approach to retirement funding:

1. Social Security

2. A worker's own savings

3. A company pension plan paid out of money the company set aside for a defined-benefit pension plan for their employees.

On May 5, 2002, an article in the *Washington Post* titled "Pension Changes Pose Challenges" compared this three-pronged approach to a three-legged stool:

> *Last time we looked, the first leg, Social Security, was still standing, though shuddering a bit as its guarantees are pecked away at—ever-increasing taxable income, a raised retirement age, taxation of some benefits, and so forth.*

> *All the lettered and numbered savings plans blessed by Congress—the 401(k)s, 403(b)s, IRAs, SEP-IRAs, Keoghs—were arguably intended to bolster the second leg, workers' savings, needed to meet an ever*

longer and ever more expensive retirement. The corporate tax benefits attached to the company-sponsored plans, made up largely of a worker's own cash, have been nudged over to bolster or even replace the third leg of the stool. Instead of rewarding thrift in employees, they have enabled companies to ditch or severely curtail traditional pension plans.

All of which means: Look, Ma, a three-legged stool with only two legs!

So as a result of ERISA, people suddenly became responsible for their own retirement planning, transferring the responsibility from the employer to the employee—without the financial education needed to help the employee plan successfully. Suddenly there were thousands of quickly trained financial planners educating millions of people to "invest for the long term, buy and hold, and diversify."

Many of these employees still do not realize that their income during retirement will be totally dependent on their ability to invest wisely now. If rich dad's prophecy comes true, the problem will only get worse for millions of people over the next 25 years—and rich dad's prophecy seems to be coming true.

Gloom and Boom

This is not a gloom-and-doom book. It is really a gloom-and-boom book. All through the late 1970s and into the 1980s, rich dad reminded his son and me about ERISA. He would say such things as, "Always watch for changes in the law. Every time a law changes, the future changes. If you will prepare to change with the changes in the law, you will lead a good life. If you do not pay attention to changes in the law, you may find yourself behaving like the driver of a car who fails to see the sign warning him of a sharp turn in the road up ahead. If, instead of slowing down to prepare to make the turn, the driver instead reaches over to turn on the radio, he will drive the car off the road and into the woods."

For those of you who have read my other books, you may recall me mentioning the Tax Reform Act of 1986. This law change was another change in the law that rich dad cautioned me to pay attention to. Many people did not pay attention to this change, and the price tag for their lack of awareness was measured in the billions of dollars. In my opinion, this 1986 law change was a major contributor to the crash of the savings-and-loan industry—one of the biggest crashes of the real estate market and the reason why well-educated professionals such as doctors, lawyers, accountants, and architects cannot use many of the tax benefits that businesspeople enjoy. Again, as rich dad said, "Always watch for changes in the law. Every time a law changes, the future changes."

Because of ERISA, this little-known change in the law will negatively affect the financial lives of millions of people. For others, this law change will be the best thing that ever happened to them. That is why I state that this is not a doom-and-gloom book, but a gloom-and-boom book. For those who delude themselves into thinking that the future will be the same as today, I am afraid that they may find themselves in the same predicament as many Enron employees did at the end of their working careers—without any money left for retirement. For those who are vigilant and are aware that the future always changes and are prepared for the changes coming, the future is very bright—even if the biggest stock-market crash in history does occur, a crash caused by this change in the law.

One of rich dad's main lessons from the story of Noah and his ark was not that any of us try to become prophets. Instead of training us to have crystal balls and become professional fortune tellers, rich dad used the story of Noah and the ark as a lesson in vigilance and preparation. He would say, "Just as a sailor constantly watches for signs of changing weather ahead, a business owner and investor must be vigilant and prepared for anything that lies ahead. Business owners and investors must think like sailors, guiding their tiny boat on a giant ocean, prepared for anything."

This book is not written to say that rich dad's prophecy will come true. This book is written to make six main points:

1. *To remind all of us to be vigilant and to point out some of the warning signs that rich dad said we needed to pay attention to.* In this book, you will find out about the flaw in ERISA. In other words, inside this little-known law is an even less-known flaw—a little flaw that rich dad said would trigger the biggest stock-market crash in the history of the world.

2. *To see the world today with a true financial perspective .* Rich dad took his cues from solid facts, such as changes in the law and the flaws in the law. He also used statistical realities, such as the fact that 75 million baby boomers—83 million if you count immigrants legal and illegal—are getting older and most will live longer than their parents. Rich dad would then ask the question: How many of these baby boomers have enough assets set aside to retire on? Conservative estimates show that less than 40 percent of today's baby boomers have enough.

   If the U.S. government must raise taxes to pay for these aging baby boomers' financial and medical needs in old age, what happens to the U.S. economy? Can it sustain its leadership role in the world? Can we afford to remain competitive if the government raises taxes to pay for the aged? When taxes are raised, companies may leave in search of countries with lower taxes. And what happens if China passes the United States as the world's largest economy? Can we afford to keep wages high when a Chinese worker will do the same job for less? Rich dad trained his son and me to base our prognostications of the future on today's facts.

3. *To ask yourself if you're truly ready for the future.* I am not saying that rich dad's prophecy will come true, since rich dad did not see himself as a person with special psychic

powers or a crystal ball or a special connection to God. This point is to ask you the question: Are you prepared *if* rich dad's prophecy does come true? In other words, *if* the biggest stock-market crash in history does occur, sometime between now and the year 2020, how will you do financially? Will you be better off or worse off? If this market crash does occur, will you be prepared for it, or will you be devastated by it?

4. *To offer some ideas on what you can do to prepare for the biggest stock-market crash in history.*
   Although some of the ideas have been mentioned in my previous books, I will go into greater detail on what you can do *now*—and more importantly, why it is essential to take proactive steps *now*.

5. *Finally, to let you know that you will probably be better off financially, if you actively prepare.*
   In other words, if you plan now, take action, and prepare, your financial future may be much brighter even if the biggest stock-market crash in the history of the world does not occur. Being proactive, educated, and prepared is much better than the financial strategy most people have when it comes to their investments—the passive strategy of "buy, hold, and pray" that the stock market will always boom and never bust. Of course, people who believe that the stock market only goes up and never comes down probably also believe in the Easter Bunny.

The story of Noah and the ark is a great story of a great prophet with tremendous vision, faith, and courage. This book will not teach you to be a prophet, but I believe it will give you great faith that a brighter financial future is available to you and your loved ones, regardless if the biggest stock-market crash in history does or does not occur.

This book is not intended to be a crystal ball, but it is intended to teach you to be more of a person who is vigilant and prepared for whatever happens, good or bad—in other words, to give you more control over your financial future. As rich dad said, "The point of the story of Noah and the ark is not that Noah was right, but that Noah had the faith, the courage, and was prepared for anything that happened, even a giant flood in the middle of the desert that wiped out the rest of the world."

NOTE: ERISA helped create the infamous 401(k) plan, as well as other retirement plans in America. Other countries have similar plans. They just go by different names. For example:

- *In Australia, it is called superannuation.*
- *In Canada, it is called the RRSP.*
- *In Japan, the plan is also called 401(k).*

SECTION ONE
IS THE FAIRY TALE OVER?

Once upon a time, all a person had to do was go to school, get good grades, find a safe secure job, be a loyal employee, retire, move to a smaller house on a golf course, and live happily ever after.

Today, most of us know that any story beginning with *once upon a time* and ending with *they lived happily ever after* is a fairy tale. The problem is that today there are many modern-day fairy princes and princesses who are hoping the fairy tale is not over, hoping that their financial planner's advice of "invest for the long term, buy and hold, and diversify," will keep the fairy tale alive for as long as they live.

Unfortunately, as most professional investors know, fairy tales attached to the stock market do not always have happy endings.

What Is More Important Than Becoming a Rich Investor?

When I was a kid in the 1960s, investing was an activity only for the rich or for those who wanted to become rich. Today, we all need to invest for something far more important than simply to become rich.

Today, how intelligently you invest will determine your future— your future standard of living, your future financial security, and maybe even how long you will live. In other words, when medical care is factored in, how intelligently you invest today will ultimately determine how well you live and if you can afford to live. That is far more important than simply investing to become rich.

Chapter One

A CHANGE IN THE LAW, A CHANGE IN THE FUTURE

Both my rich dad and my poor dad were very concerned about the overall well-being of their employees. My real dad, as the superintendent of education for the State of Hawaii, had tens of thousands of workers who counted on him to take care of them. My real dad, the man I call my poor dad, was so concerned about his teachers that when he was no longer the superintendent of education, he became the leader of HSTA, the Hawaii State Teachers Association. As head of the teachers' union, he again negotiated for the well-being of his teachers.

My rich dad was also very concerned about his employees. In fact, in many ways, he was much more concerned about his employees than my real dad was. The reason he was more concerned was because my poor dad's employees had the financial support of the government and the protection of the local and national teachers' unions.

My rich dad's employees did not have the government support and union protection. He would often say, "I wish I could tell my workers what I know and what I see coming in the future. I wish I could, but I am afraid I would frighten them too much. Besides, the main problem is that most of them lack the basic financial education to understand what I am saying and then to be able to take corrective action. How do I tell my loyal, hardworking employees that today, being loyal and hardworking is not enough? How do I explain to them that long-term job security does not ensure long-term financial security? How do I tell them about a change in a law that has changed their future forever?"

How do I tell them without frightening or depressing them? How do I tell people about what I think might happen, but I am not certain will happen?"

As I said, both my poor dad and my rich dad were very concerned about their workers. The difference was that my poor dad had the power of the government and the teachers' unions to help his workers. My rich dad knew that his workers were at a disadvantage, and this concerned him greatly.

In 1974, there was a major law change in America that was reportedly designed to help workers who worked for people like my rich dad. While many people thought the intent behind the new law was a great idea, rich dad could see its inherent flaws. He knew that, in many ways, most of his workers would not be better off in the long run. He could see a growing threat of financial disaster looming in the future, a financial disaster caused by the passage of this act into law.

In 1979, I was 32 years old and struggling to keep my business above water. My nylon-and-Velcro surfer-wallet business had taken off faster than expected. In only a few years, we were a big company with a sales force of over 380 independent sales reps in the United States alone. Worldwide, we never really did figure out how many salespeople we had selling for us. The problem was that we had a worldwide product, but we were a small-time company with a young and incompetent management team. When success and incompetence meet, disaster is not far away.

It has been said, "You cannot learn to swim from a textbook." I would also add, "You cannot learn business from a textbook or from business school." My partners and I had limited textbook knowledge and very little real-life business experience. At an early age, we were learning some simple yet tough lessons about business—lessons that can only be learned from front-line experience.

Besides the lesson that "success can kill you," some of the other lessons I was learning were:

- Friends do not always make good business partners.

- A company can be profitable and still be in serious financial trouble.

- Little things, like not having enough thread, can stop the whole business.

- People do not always pay their bills, which means you cannot always pay *your* bills. People do not like you when you do not pay your bills.

- Patents and trademarks are important aspects of a successful business.

- Loyalty can be fleeting.

- It is essential to have accurate financial records and accounting.

- You need a strong management team and a strong team of professional consultants, such as lawyers and accountants.

- It costs a lot of money to build a business.

- It's not just the lack of money that kills a business. It's the lack of business experience and the lack of personal integrity that kill a business.

The actual list of lessons is much longer. The experience of worldwide success and worldwide failure was priceless. I went through such experiences not once, but twice. Although I do not want to go through it all again, I am ready to because the lessons are priceless, if you are willing and humble enough to learn from your mistakes. Each business failure showed me what I did not know and what I needed to learn, and each learning experience led to the next success.

In 1979, I was up to my ears in learning experiences. I was over my head in mistakes, buried by my own personal incompetence, and

I did not want to learn anything more. I had more than enough stupidity to learn from, yet rich dad had more to point out to me. I walked into his office for our regular meeting and showed him my company's financial statement. Looking over the statement, rich dad shook his head and said, "Your company has financial cancer, and I'm afraid it's terminal. You boys have mismanaged what could have grown into a rich and powerful company."

Mike, rich dad's son, was not a partner in my business, yet he did sit in on most of the mentoring meetings I had with his dad, the man I call my rich dad. Mike and I had been best friends all through high school, but after I returned from college and the Vietnam war, it was difficult to maintain a close friendship since we were in completely different business and financial leagues. In 1979, Mike was in the process of taking over his father's multimillion-dollar empire, and I was in the process of losing a multimillion-dollar business. As Mike looked over my company's financials, I felt shame and embarrassment when Mike also shook his head.

"What is this?" asked rich dad, pointing to a section of my financial statement.

Looking at where he was pointing, I said, "It's the amounts we owe the employees and the government for the employees' payroll and payroll taxes."

"Now look at your cash position. There isn't any money there," said rich dad sternly. "How are you going to make payroll and pay the taxes?"

I sat there quietly, saying nothing. "Well," I began feebly, "when we collect on some of our back accounts receivables, we'll have enough to pay them."

"Oh, come on," said rich dad. "Don't give me that jive. I'm not your college professor. I can see from your financials that much of your accounts receivables are over 120 days delinquent. You and I know that these people you have sold product to are never going to pay you. Tell me the truth. Tell yourself the truth. You're broke. You're broke, and now you're about to default on paying your employees and their taxes. You're using your employees' money to keep your company afloat."

"But it is only a short-term credit problem. We have money coming in. We have sales coming in from all over the United States and the world," I replied in my defense.

"Yes, but what good are sales if you cannot build product and cannot deliver on those sales? I can see from these financial statements that people owe you money and you also owe money. You owe money to the people who supply the materials to produce your products. What makes you think that your suppliers will give you any more credit?"

"Well… " I began, but was cut off again by an angry rich dad.

"Your suppliers won't give you any more credit. Why should they?"

"Well, I'll go talk to them again."

"Good luck," said rich dad. "Look, why don't you just face the truth? You and the three clowns you call partners have mismanaged your business. You don't know what you're doing, you're incompetent, and worst of all, you don't have the guts to admit any of this. You guys are pretending to look like businesspeople, but when I look at your financials, you boys are either crooks or clowns. I hope you're clowns, but if you don't make some changes, you clowns will become crooks." Rich dad said this pursing his lips and slowly moving his head from side to side. "Borrowing money from your employees is bad enough. Just look at the back taxes you owe. How are you going to pay them?"

Rich dad had been my teacher since I was nine years old. He was a very loving and caring man, but when he was angry, he was not a polite man. This particularly heated lesson in business management went on for hours. Finally, I agreed to shut the business down, liquidate the remaining assets, and use the money to pay the taxes and the employees.

"There is nothing wrong with admitting you're incompetent," said rich dad, "but there is plenty wrong with lying and pretending you know what you're doing. Lying and pretending you know what you are doing is a bad habit, and I want you to stop that habit now. If you want to be rich and successful, you need to learn to tell the truth quicker, ask for help quicker, and be more humble. The world is filled with arrogant poor people, educated and uneducated, people who cannot admit they do not know something. The world is filled with people who go through life pretending they are smart, and that makes them stupid. If you want to learn quickly, the first step is to admit quickly you do not know something.

"Remember the lesson from Sunday School that goes, 'Blessed are the meek for they shall inherit the earth'? The passage does not go, 'Blessed are the weak,' or 'Blessed are the arrogant,' or 'Blessed are the well educated.' It says, 'Blessed are the meek,' for the meek shall learn. And if you learn, you shall inherit the abundance of life that God or nature has placed in front of you. You boys are arrogant, conceited, cocky, and ignorant—not meek. You think that, just because your product is a success, you are also a success. You boys are not yet businessmen. You boys got lucky, but you do not have the skill and experience to turn your luck into a business. No one becomes a successful businessperson overnight. You have a lot more to learn. And the lesson you must learn today is that if you owe money, pay the bill. People hate people who do not pay their bills. Friends, families, and businesses have broken apart because money owed was not repaid. From your company's financial statements, I can see that you owe money to the government, to your suppliers, to your landlord, and most importantly, to your employees. Pay those bills, and pay them now. Don't do anything else until those bills are paid. Don't come back here until you've paid your taxes and *all* your employees. You're becoming a sloppy businessman, and sloppy businesspeople do not become rich and successful businesspeople. Now get out of here, and don't come back until you have done what I have just told you to do."

As I said, rich dad had chewed me out many times over the years, but this lesson from rich dad was especially memorable. As I closed the door behind me, I could feel this particular lesson sinking into my soul and becoming a lesson I would never forget. Although I hurt, I knew that the lesson was an important one. If it were not important, rich dad would not have gotten so angry or been so brutally forthright. At 32 years old, I was old enough to take this strong, emotionally charged lesson, and I was wise enough to know that I had something important to learn.

Over the years, rich dad had a lesson on truth and honesty he repeatedly taught. He often said to his son and me, "Many people ask young people, 'What do you want to be when you grow up?' When they ask that question, they are usually asking what profession the child wants to pursue. Personally, I don't care what you want to do when you grow up. I don't care if you become a doctor, a movie star, or a janitor. But I do care that you grow up to become more and more truthful and more honest. Too many people grow up becoming more polite, but not necessarily more truthful. Even worse, if they told lies as kids, they become bigger liars as adults." As I walked down the street to where my car was parked, I knew it was again time for me to become more truthful and more honest with myself, my partners, and my employees.

Climbing into my car, I could hear rich dad saying, "Any coward can tell a lie. Telling the truth takes courage. As you boys grow up, grow up to become people who have more and more courage to tell the truth quicker—even if the truth hurts, even if being honest makes you look bad. It is better to look bad telling the truth than to be a good-looking, lying coward. The world is filled with good-looking, lying cowards." As the engine came to life and I put my car into gear, I felt terrible and I knew that I probably looked as bad as my financial statements. Driving away, I also knew that I had two choices. One was to continue lying to myself and never see rich dad again. The other was to begin finding the courage to face the truth, to clean up the mess I made, and then look forward to seeing rich dad again.

At 32, I realized I still had a lot of growing up to do. I knew that if I wanted to become a richer, more successful person and a better human being, I had to be able to hear a more refined truth, even if it was a little tougher truth. As part of my growing up, I also had to be able to tell the truth better. As I pulled up into my company's parking lot, I knew the time to begin telling that truth was now, and it would begin with my partners—the partners rich dad called "clowns."

Approximately four months later, I returned to rich dad's office with a new set of financial statements in hand. Rich dad and Mike looked them over for what seemed to be an extra-long period of silence. Finally rich dad said, "So all your back taxes and your employees are paid?"

"That is correct," I said. "If you notice, I also cleaned up a lot of my old accounts receivables."

"You got them to pay?" asked rich dad.

"Either they paid, or I took them off the financial statement and sent a collection agency after them."

"That's good," said Mike. "A customer who does not pay is not a customer. A customer who does not pay is a thief."

"I understand that now," I replied. "But I was doing the same thing."

Rich dad looked up at me, paused, and then slowly nodded and quietly said, "Thanks for admitting that."

"It wasn't easy," I replied. "I had this image of myself as a successful person, but in reality, I owed a lot of people a lot of money."

Mike and rich dad sat silently, nodding ever so slightly. Finally rich dad said, "The truth does set you free. Hopefully, now you are free to clean up your mess and begin building your next business on more solid ground. So many people attempt to build their financial empire upon a mess of lies, and lies never seem to support much of an empire."

Now it was my turn to sit silently and just let the crystal-clear silence fill the room. After a long pause, Mike asked, "So what condition is your company in? Your financial statement is a lot more honest, but a financial statement can never tell the whole story."

"The company is finished," I replied. "We still have sales and the actual business is strong, but the four of us who started this business are finished. We'll probably never be partners or friends again. Truthfully, the truth tore us apart."

"So when you returned to your company, you had a heart-to-heart talk?"

"Well, it started out as heart to heart, but it soon became face to face. We almost came to blows, but thankfully, that did not happen. It has not been pleasant at work, but I do give my partners credit for being willing to stick it out and clean up the mess, as you suggested."

"Now what happens?" asked Mike.

"Well, we are turning over the remains of the company to one of our suppliers, and we are all going our separate ways. We will soon begin letting our employees go, and they will have all the money we owe them. Our investors will get some, but not all, of their money back, but we have talked to them and they understand the risk they took. Several have said they would invest with me again. And our taxes are paid."

Mike and rich dad just sat silently. It was like being at a funeral—a lot of emotion, but little to say. The winding down of a business is like the ending of anything. Good or bad, there were parts of the experience that forever changed our lives, our future, and who we would become. I was dreading turning out the lights and closing the office door for the last time, even though I was also glad it was going to soon close. Finally, rich dad broke the silence and said, "Well, I'm proud of the way you handled the loss of your business. I know it isn't pleasant, and I know you could have handled it differently. You could have taken the remaining money and run, but you chose a better way of ending things. That will give your next venture a little better ground to start from. Have you learned a lot?"

"Massive learning," I said. "I'm still digesting the lessons."

"You will for years," said rich dad. "But someday this experience and the mistakes and experiences yet to come will become the basis for your success and fortune. Most people avoid mistakes. Most people spend their lives playing it safe and avoiding such lessons. That lack of life's experience limits their future financial success. Always remember that business experience can never be gained from a textbook or a classroom. Although painful, because of the way you chose to handle this business failure, this painful short period of time will someday become the basis of your long-term financial wealth. If you had run and lied, your financial future would probably be a coward's future. If you had run, you would have been letting the coward in you determine your future."

I simply sat quietly and nodded. There was not much to say. I had heard this talk and this lesson before, but on this day, this simple lesson had much more meaning and a deeper impact. Rich dad often said to his son and me that inside each of us is a cast of characters. Inside each of us is a kind person, a mean person, a greedy person, a rich person, a poor person, a coward, a crook, a hero, a liar, a cheapskate, a lover, a loser, and more. He constantly reminded us that growing up is a process of choosing which person we want to become, which person we want to draw out of all the cast of characters available. As stated earlier, when he asked us what we wanted to be when we grew up, he was asking which character we were choosing to become—not if we were going to be a doctor, lawyer, or firefighter. To rich dad, a person's choice of character was far more important than a person's choice of profession.

"When it comes to money, the world is filled with cowards," said rich dad. "Money has a way of bringing out the coward more than the hero, and that may be why there are so few truly rich people. Money also has a way of bringing out the cheat and the crook in some people, and that is why our jails keep filling up. Money also has a way of bringing out the betrayer, the person who will steal from those who love and trust them. When you 'borrowed' from your employees, that is the character you were choosing to become, and that is why I was especially tough on you. Crooks and cowards are one thing, but becoming a person who betrays those who trust you is one of the most despicable of all characters, and you were choosing that character."

There was not much for me to say. The internal pain was intense. Truth and honesty are not always pleasant, and this dose of truth and honesty was very unpleasant, yet necessary. I realized that in my desperation to save my company, I had chosen to betray those who trusted me.

"Have you gotten your lesson?" asked rich dad. "Have you gotten the lesson in character choices?"

I just nodded my head again. I had understood the lesson—a deep, painful lesson, a lesson I would always remember. I had always thought of myself as a good, honest person. Yet under pressure, the character that emerged was the person who betrayed those who trusted me.

"Good," said rich dad. "A lesson in character is far more important than a lesson in reading a financial statement, yet the financial statement did reflect your character. Your financial statement told me the story of the betrayer in you taking over your business. That is another lesson in the importance of accounting, accountability, and being able to read financial statements. The numbers tell me a story of which character is in charge of the money. When you and your partners started your business, you started off as gamblers. You got lucky and became clowns, thinking your luck was skill. When the money came pouring in, you became fools buying Porsches and Mercedes sports cars. And when you got into financial trouble, you became people who betrayed your suppliers, your government, and your workers. Your financial statements tell a better story than most novels."

"That's enough, Dad," Mike said, as he jumped in to protect me from any more of the lesson. "I think you have made your point."

"Okay," said rich dad. Turning to me, he then asked, "Have you got the lesson?"

"Right between the eyes," I replied.

"Good. Let's go get some lunch," said rich dad. "There is a far more important lesson I want you to learn, a very important lesson, a lesson that begins with the question: Why did your employees not know what you were doing with their money?"

When the elevator finally arrived, we found it crowded with people also going to lunch. Packing into the elevator, rich dad said, "Sometime in the future, long after I am gone, millions of hardworking people will find out that clowns like you and your partners have been playing games with their money—their retirement money, their financial future, their financial security. The government has made changes in the law to protect workers, but I do not think this law change will solve the problem. In fact, I think the law change will make things worse for many people. I am afraid something terrible is going to happen."

Chapter Two

THE LAW THAT CHANGED THE WORLD

Rich dad, Mike, and I went to one of our favorite Chinese restaurants for lunch. As usual, the place was packed because the food was good, the service fast, and the prices fair. We had to wait a few minutes before a table opened. Our favorite waiter cleaned it as we took our seats.

As we looked through the menu, rich dad said to me, "Most people will not have enough money set aside for their retirement. In fact, I would be willing to bet that most of the people sitting in this restaurant will never be able to retire, simply because they have nothing in their retirement plans."

"You mean the workers here?" Mike asked. "People like our waiter and those who cook and wash dishes in the back?"

"Not only the restaurant workers, but many of the executives in suits and ties who are dining here will have nothing, or will not have enough money to retire on. Most of the people in this room will never be able to afford retirement."

"Most?" I asked in surprise. "Wouldn't it be more accurate to say *some* rather than *most*?"

"No," said rich dad. "I believe the more accurate word is *most*, not *some*."

"How can that be?" I asked. "Most seem to have good jobs. They dress well and appear to be rather intelligent."

"Do you remember me telling you about ERISA?" asked rich dad.

"Yes, vaguely," I replied. "You've mentioned it on several occasions. I just have not fully understood what you were saying or why this law change was so important."

"Most people don't realize its importance," said rich dad. "It may be years before people begin to wake up to the ripple effects this law change will have in the future."

"What is this law change and why was it passed?" I asked.

"Good question," said rich dad. "First of all, ERISA stands for Employee Retirement Income Security Act. It was the act that made 401(k)s possible. I did not pay much attention to its passage either, but soon my accountants and my attorneys began advising me on changes I needed to make in my businesses. Once that began to happen, I began asking more in-depth questions."

"And what did you find out?" I asked.

"It seems the act was passed to help protect employees' retirement money from abuse by their business owners," said rich dad.

"What kind of abuse?" I asked.

"There have been many kinds of abuses of retirement plans. Even in some large blue-chip companies, pension plans are empty or underfunded. Many times a company would buy another company, not because of the business, but because they wanted the business's retirement money. Some of the more responsible businesses had tens of millions of dollars in their employee retirement funds, and that pool of money was often more valuable than the business. So the raiding company would buy the business and bleed the employee retirement fund."

"They would take over the company just for the retirement money?"

Rich dad nodded his head. "But that was not the only abuse. There were more. It was because of these abuses that ERISA was supposedly passed."

"Why do you say 'supposedly'?" I asked.

"Well, the act was passed as a benefit for employees, a way to protect employees from these abuses. But as we all know, nothing is only good for only one group of people. The company also benefited from the act, but the benefits to the company were not really mentioned in the press."

"So how did it benefit the businesses?" I asked.

"Well, now that you've had your first business, let me ask you this question: How expensive is an employee retirement plan to the company?"

"You mean Social Security payments plus adding money to the employees' retirement plan?" I asked.

Rich dad nodded his head, saying, "Yes. How expensive is it?"

"Very expensive," I replied. "I often wished I could pay my workers more, but the hidden taxes that employees are often not even aware of are so high, I could not afford to pay much more. Every time I gave my employees a raise, the government also got a raise."

"So while ERISA was passed as a benefit to employees, it was in many ways more of a benefit to the employer. In many cases, the expense of retirement was transferred from the employer to the employee."

"But doesn't the employer have to match the amount the employee puts in?" I asked.

"They can if their plan allows it, but the key word is *match*," said Mike. "In other words, the dollar amount the employer has to pay is now significantly reduced. That is like taking the cost of your mortgage payment and cutting it in half. Wouldn't you want to reduce your mortgage payment by half?" Mike was very well versed in this new retirement plan because rich dad put him in charge of understanding it. "And on top of that, many employees elect not to contribute anything, so the employer has nothing to match."

"So if the employee does not put any money into his or her fund, the employer pays nothing. The cost of that employee's retirement just went to zero. Is that why we're going to have the problem of people without any retirement savings?" I asked.

"That is one of the problems, and it's a very big problem. But in my opinion, it is not the person who has nothing in their retirement plan who will ultimately cause the biggest problem. The biggest problem will come from those employees who have diligently put money into their retirement accounts. Those who have faithfully put money into their retirement plans will cause the biggest stock-market crash in history."

"In history?" I asked skeptically. "And the crash will not be caused by those employees who have nothing? It will be caused by those who have set money aside?"

Rich dad nodded his head. "Think about it. Can someone with nothing cause the stock market to crash?"

"I don't really know. I've never really thought about it," I replied.

"The biggest stock-market crash of all will be caused by millions of people with their money tied up in mutual funds and other types of shares in the stock market, not by those without any shares or money," Mike added. "It's just common sense."

"This change in the law will bring about many problems, and one of the problems will be this giant stock-market crash," said rich dad, as our food arrived.

"Why is that? How can you be so sure?" I asked.

"Because the people putting money into the market are not investors. As you already know, most of your workers cannot read a financial statement. So how can you invest if you cannot read a financial statement?" asked rich dad. "The resulting impact started by ERISA is not only leaving millions of people without a retirement plan, but it is also forcing people to trust their financial future to the stock market. And we all know that all markets go up and all markets go down."

Rich dad looked directly at me. "I've been training you and Mike to be investors who can make money in an up market and in a down market, but most employees do not have that mental and emotional training. When the big crash begins, I believe they will react as most untrained investors react. They will panic and begin selling to save their lives and protect their future."

"When do you think this will happen?" I asked.

"I don't know," said rich dad. "No one has a crystal ball with 20/20 vision. But between now and the biggest crash of all, I predict there will be smaller, but growing booms and busts in the stock market. These smaller booms and busts will come before the biggest of all booms and biggest of all busts."

"So there will be warning signs?" Mike asked.

"Oh yes," smiled rich dad. "There will be plenty of them. The good news is that you boys will have plenty of time to practice gaining experience and skill through these smaller booms and busts. Just as you two practice surfing on the smaller waves of summer in preparation for the larger waves of winter, I would recommend you do the same with your investing skills. As the booms and busts get bigger and bigger, you'll find it easier to become richer and richer."

"But others will become poorer and poorer," I said quietly.

"Unfortunately, that is true. But always remember the story of Noah and the ark. Noah could not get all the animals on board, and I am afraid the same is true for the coming stock-market crash."

"So it is survival of the fittest?" I asked.

"It will be survival of the financially fittest and the financially smartest," said rich dad. "It will be survival for those who are prepared, just as Noah prepared for the future by building an ark. I have been training you boys to build an ark also."

"We're building arks?" I chuckled. "Where is it? I don't see one."

"The ark I have been helping you build is inside your head."

"An ark inside my head," I said cynically. "That's a new thought."

"Look," said rich dad, as he reached for a serving of food, "if you don't want to prepare, then tell me now. Don't waste my time. Do you think I like scolding you for mismanaging your business and your personal finances? Have I been wasting my time and my faith in you? If I have, tell me now."

"No, no, no," I pleaded. "It's just the ark. I have a hard time with this building-an-ark concept—especially in my head."

"Well, where do you think money, investing, and business take place? They take place in your head. If money is not found in your head, it will not be found in your hands," said rich dad angrily.

"Okay, okay, okay," I said apologetically.

"Look," said rich dad. "There may or may not be this giant stock-market crash, but I can assure you that there will be booms and busts. There always have been booms and busts in the past, and there will always be booms and busts in the future. Predicting that booms and busts are coming is not much of a prediction. You boys are in your early thirties. You have a good financial foundation, and you're gaining great business experience. You are now old enough to face the real world. Just as you practice surfing nearly every day, riding the ups and downs of the waves, I ask you to practice riding the ups and downs of financial markets and financial cycles. If you do that, your skills will improve."

"So markets boom and bust just like the waves on the ocean," I said.

"Correct," said rich dad. "They're called business cycles."

"And you think that ERISA is like a storm out at sea that will soon be sending waves crashing on shore, altering business cycles for a long time," said Mike.

"In surfer terms, the answer is yes. That is what I think," rich dad said, as he finished his meal. "There have always been booms and busts, but I believe this law change will lead to the biggest boom and biggest bust of all."

"But what if you're wrong?" I asked.

"If I am wrong and if you do what I suggest, at a minimum you will get richer and richer. You'll get richer and richer because you will be building your ark, a financial ark in your head, and that alone will make you rich in a good economy and in a bad economy."

"Okay," I said. "I'll keep this ark idea in my head and think about it. I'll think about it as preparation and planning for the future, preparing as Noah did for something that might or might not happen. But what makes you think this change in the law will have such a big impact and cause such a large market crash?"

"Because changes in the law change the future," rich dad replied. "For example, if the government changed the speed limit on this small street in front of this restaurant from 25 miles per hour to 100 miles per hour, we would see some immediate changes. Immediately there would be more traffic accidents and more fatalities. That is how law changes change our future, good and bad."

"And this law change, what has it changed? Why can't we see the changes? Why aren't these executives sitting all around us as concerned as you are?"

Rich dad took a fresh paper napkin and wrote the following letters on it:

DB

DC

"The reason the executives around us and the workers who work here are not concerned is because we are now in the transition period between DB pension plans and DC pension plans."

"What?" I asked. "DB to DC plans?"

"DB pension plans to DC pension plans," said Mike. "Most people are like you, unaware of the differences between the two plans—and there are massive differences. Most of the executives sitting around us are still thinking in terms of DB pension plans, and that is why they are not concerned. They are not aware of the changes or the future consequences."

"When will these executives start becoming aware of the differences?" I asked.

"The lag time is pretty long," said rich dad. "I predict that it will take 25 to 50 years before people become aware of the full impact of this law change."

"You mean we should begin to notice the changes sometime around the year 2000?" I asked.

"Oh, you will begin to notice the changes way before that year," said rich dad. "Although people will notice the changes, such as smaller booms and busts in the stock market, I don't think people will be aware of the frightening consequences of this law change until the year 2000 or later, maybe much later."

The bill was paid. As we stood up from the table, our favorite waiter was already wiping it off, getting it ready for the next group of hungry diners. "And what are you doing to prepare for these coming changes?" I asked rich dad.

"I'm already prepared. I've already built my ark," smiled rich dad as we stepped out on the street. "The problems will not be my problem, but they will be your problem. I will not be around when the real impact of this law change hits. Your dad and I will be gone and buried before the tidal wave hits shore."

"So this law change is almost like your generation passing on your problems to our generation," I said, testing rich dad's receptivity to the idea of intergenerational passing of the buck—or the passing on of the problem.

"I'd say that is pretty accurate," said rich dad. "It's the World War II generation passing on the problem to the baby-boom generation and future generations. It's a problem my generation has benefited from."

"Your generation benefited, and now my generation pays for your benefits?" I asked. "That is the legacy we inherit?"

"That is part of the story," said rich dad with a sly smile. "First let me explain the difference between a DB pension plan and a DC pension plan."

Rich dad went on to explain that a DB, or defined benefit, pension plan was a retirement plan that defined the benefit or the dollar amount a retired person would receive. For example, if an employee worked for 40 years for a company and retired at 65, a defined benefit might pay that employee, let's say, $1,000 a month for as long as he or she lived. If that employee lived to 66, the company actually did well because the company only had to pay the defined benefit for a year. If the ex-employee lived to 105, the company paid the $1,000 a month for 40 years. In that case, the employee was much better off, but at the expense of the company. Social Security is a government DB plan.

Subsequent changes to ERISA will allow companies to switch to DC, or defined contribution, plans. The difference between a DB and DC plan is found in the difference between the definitions of the words *benefit* and *contribution*. A DB plan defines the *benefit*. A DC plan defines the *contribution*. In other words, a worker's retirement is only as good as the contribution—if there is a contribution.

A worker might retire with nothing because he or she contributed nothing. In addition, if a worker retired with $2 million in their plan and that $2 million was gone by age 85—either through distribution or by mismanagement or a market crash—then at 85, this worker would be out of retirement funds and out of luck. The worker could not go back to the company and demand more financial benefits.

Simply put, the responsibility, expense, and long-term consequences of retirement will pass from the employer to the employee. Although the difference between the letters DB to DC is small, the long-term consequences are, and will continue to be, large. As rich dad said, "It's the World War II generation passing on the problem to the baby-boom generation, and future generations. It's a problem my generation has benefited from." In other words, they got the benefit, and now we get the bill. And it will be a very big bill.

Returning to rich dad's office, I gave both of them a hug and thanked them for the lesson. I was starting over again, without any money, without a job, but with a wealth of knowledge and experience. Although a little worried and nervous, I was ready to get back to work, looking for a new business opportunity to begin building a new company.

"I have one more question," I said, looking at rich dad. "Many of those executives in that restaurant are not aware of the difference between a DB and DC pension plan?"

"No, I would say most aren't," said Mike, stepping in for his dad. "And that is going to cause bigger problems in the future. Because they are not aware, they are not preparing for the future. They still think that after retirement, there will be plenty of money for as long as they live."

"I'm afraid that many of your generation will be forced to live at a lower standard of living after they retire," said rich dad. "Most of my generation still have DB pension plans. They can retire to the golf course community and play golf and bingo all day. Many of your generation will never be able to retire. Many, in fact I would say most, will work all their lives—some because they want to, but most because they have to."

"I hope they love what they do," I said with a smile.

"That is short-term thinking," said Mike. "I've looked into this, and statistics show that 25 percent of all workers are disabled at one time or another after retirement. Some are permanently disabled and some are just temporarily. That is why it's shortsighted to just believe that doing what you love is a solution. Our generation and future generations need to think long term, because we will live longer. The question is: Can we afford to live longer, and can we afford the rising costs of health care? And what happens if we are one of the 25 percent that is disabled and cannot work and do what we love? Those are more pertinent questions you and I need to ask ourselves, our families, and our workers."

"And right now, we are not asking those questions," I said, looking at rich dad.

"No, I am afraid not," rich dad replied, checking his watch. "The problem with most of the executives in that little Chinese restaurant is that most of them think they have the same DB pension plans their parents had. They may think that way because they work for large corporations. But in the near future, large corporations will switch to DC pension plans and most workers, even the executives, will not be aware of the long-term consequences of these changes."

"Working for a large corporation is like working on board a large cruise ship," said Mike, jumping back into the conversation. He had done a lot of research and was very concerned about the future. "In the old days, once a worker was through working, the corporation gave the worker a stateroom in the back of the ship. The retired worker joined the other passengers and enjoyed the benefits of working for the good ship SS *Good Corporation*. The retired worker danced the night away, listening to Benny Goodman music, sipping champagne, and playing shuffleboard all day. But that was the past. The SS *Good Corporation* may now throw the retired worker over the side with a small life preserver known as a defined-contribution plan."

"And what if there is nothing in the defined-contribution plan?" I asked.

"Not the ship's problem," said Mike.

"Try building an ark out of a life preserver," smirked rich dad sarcastically. "Most people are not trained to build arks, so most people will spend their later years of life clinging to tiny little life preservers and handouts from family and the government. That is why I want you two boys to begin building your arks now. If you do, when the changes come, you will have your own large ship, your own ark, that will be big enough and strong enough to withstand any storm at sea. And trust me, there is a storm coming, a big one."

Thanking rich dad and Mike for lunch, I turned and headed for the elevator. I was 32 and had no money and no job, but this time I was starting over again with a wealth of knowledge and experience. I knew that the building of my next business would be easier and faster. So even though I was out of money, I was filled with excitement about the future, even though I knew there was a very large storm brewing at sea. To me, building an ark made more sense than building a life preserver known as a defined-contribution plan (or whatever financial life preservers are called in other parts of the world).

Chapter Three

ARE YOU READY TO FACE THE REAL WORLD?

The streets of Waikiki were busy with tourists either going to the beach or returning from the beach. Most were dressed in swimsuits and rubber slippers covered with sand. They seemed happy just to be taking some time off from their regular lives from wherever they came.

As I crossed the street to get to the bus stop, I glanced at the waves breaking a few hundred yards offshore and wondered if I had time for an evening with my friends who surfed out there. The breaking waves, the warm water, and the gently sinking sun were calling to me. I stood envious, looking out on the ocean at a way of life I grew up in, surfing until the sun and my energy were gone, but I knew today it was best for me to head home. Sadness came over me as I realized that I wasn't a kid anymore, and it was time for me to clean up the mess from my past so I could have a better future. The lunch with rich dad and Mike was painful yet beneficial. Going over my financial statements was painful yet truthful. Those simple documents told the story of the lies up to this point, and it was time to change the story. I tucked the brown manila envelope that contained my company's financial statement under my arm as the bus arrived and headed back to a home that I would soon have to give up as well.

Many people ask me today, "How did you start over again?" They are very curious about how you pick yourself up after losing everything and begin again. Many of those who ask have good jobs or established careers and seem to be hesitant at losing what they have already established. One young man from Japan asked me, "After you lost everything, did you not feel shame?" Laughingly I said, "I felt many things, and shame was definitely one of the emotions." I then asked him a few more questions and found out that his job did not pay enough and he hated it. But his job was secure and he would rather suffer for the rest of his life than risk shame and disgrace. I reassured him that his feelings were not limited to him. Many people would rather have some money and happiness than risk shame and embarrassment going for all that life has to offer.

"How did you get started without a job or without any money?" That's another frequently asked question about this period of my life. There is not one solid or convincing answer to those types of questions. Words alone are limiting, so the answers I normally give are:

- "I did it because I had no place else to go. I had nothing to fall back on."

- "I took it one day at a time."

- "Those were some of the worst days of my life. I would not want to repeat them, but in retrospect they were some of the best days of my life because they changed the direction of my life. Those days also changed who I became in the process of changing my life."

- "I had to choose between my past and my future, whether my past would be the same as my future or whether my future would be much better than my past."

That last puzzling statement crinkles a few brows, but what I am saying is that most people afraid of change or risk will wind up doing the same thing tomorrow as they are doing today. For many people, surviving one day at a time is better than risking today for a better future. I understand that strategy for life. Today, I occasionally see my friends who are still beach boys on Waikiki Beach and I envy their life—especially when I'm sitting in a 747 flying from London to New York or Los Angeles to Sydney. I, too, often wonder if I have made the right decisions in life. As I am sitting on a plane eating airline food, my three friends who have been beach boys now for 35 years go to the same spot on Waikiki Beach every day. They rent surfboards, meet young coeds that flatter their aging male egos, and they sing and play Hawaiian songs for tips. Tomorrow they will do the same thing at the same spot. In many ways, so will I. I believe the difference is that we wanted different ends to our lives. I wanted a different tomorrow. They want the same tomorrow.

I believe most people fall into one of those two categories. That will determine who will take the risk for the best of life or settle for the same life today and the same life tomorrow. I risked everything because I wanted a much better tomorrow. That is the best answer I have for explaining how I stood up again after I lost everything. I risked, lost, and stood up because I still wanted the same thing—a better tomorrow. Most people stay where they are, like my beach-boy friends, because today is safe and they want tomorrow to be safe. Unfortunately, most of us know that today will eventually come to an end, and tomorrow will begin. Even my beach-boy friends know that.

Rich dad knew how big a financial hole I had blown in my financial statement and in my personal life. As he said when he looked at my business's financial statement a few months earlier, "Your company has financial cancer." Although he knew I was out of money, had no place to live and no job to go to, he never offered me a job or any financial support, and I did not want or expect any such support. I had been studying with him for over 20 years, and I knew what was now expected of me.

My poor dad was very understanding. He offered several times to give me money, but I was aware of his financial position and knew he was in very bad financial shape. He was not much better off than I was. He had his house, but now in his late fifties, he was almost totally dependent upon a small early-retirement pension from the teachers union. What little savings he did have, he lost on a failed ice-cream franchise. That was my dad's first foray into the real world of business and the world of business pounded him, not for his academic brilliance, but for his lack of real-world experience. He was also having trouble finding a job because of his age and because of his ego. Having once been the boss, the superintendent of education, I believe he found it tough asking for a job from much younger people.

He also got very angry when told that his experience in state government did not transfer over to the business world. He was often told, "You have great work experience and are definitely successful, but your skills are not what we need. We cannot use what you have spent your lifetime learning." He then did what many men at his age and in his predicament do, he became a consultant. I do not know if anyone hired him, but the title seemed to quell a pain inside of him.

One of the things that really kept me going was a vow I made at that time: "I will never let my own ignorance, arrogance, or fear get in the way of the life I know I can have." I saw what age, arrogance, lack of practical real-world skills, lack of financial intelligence, lack of up-to-date information, and dependence upon a government handout was doing to my dad, and I vowed I would use his example as a lesson of what I would *not* become. At that moment, I vowed to become a student again. My education began with first cleaning up my personal financial statement—a statement that reflected the mess my financial ignorance and arrogance had gotten me in. I then vowed to listen to rich dad and begin to study what most people do not study.

Since the age of nine, rich dad had been an important mentor to me. Now at the age of 32, I vowed to learn more from him as an adult. I knew that my surfing and rugby days were coming to an end. As sad as that thought was, I was also looking forward to the future, a new and different future that gave me more control over the subject of money and the rest of my life. I say this because I did not want to grow up to be like my poor dad, a man who was now a consultant still looking for work as he neared his sixties because he realized his pension was inadequate. I did not want to wait until I was 60 to make the changes I was making in my thirties. I did not want to wait until

I was 60 to find out that there was not enough money in my retirement plan for me to live on for the rest of my life. My vow at 32 was to clean up my financial life, get educated, and take care of my future today—not tomorrow.

As I was preparing to move out of my apartment, which I could no longer afford, and wondering where I was going to live next, a friend called. He was moving to California for four months on a job assignment and asked me if I would care for his house, water his plants, and feed his dog. That solved my housing problem—at least temporarily. Money seemed to come in different forms. Checks would appear in the mail, just in the nick of time, from overpayments, refunds, and money from the bill collectors who had finally collected some of the money owed the business. But even though the checks came in, they were infrequent, and there were days when I could not eat simply because there was not any money. As tough as things were at times, the reason I say this period of time was a good one is because it gave me time to find out who I was and what I was made of.

Another friend called soon after I moved into the temporary house. This friend was a headhunter, someone who looks for management-level employees. "I have a company that is very interested in you. I told them you were the top salesman for Xerox and for the last four years you have run a national and international sales team of hundreds of salespeople. They're looking for someone just like you. The pay is great. Lots of travel, big expense account, generous benefits, and who knows—you could someday be president of the company. You don't have to relocate. They want you to be the bridge between their Asian and California accounts right here in Hawaii. Are you interested?"

Let me tell you, being broke and desperate, that phone call was like a phone call from heaven. I was higher than a kite. The needy and desperate part of me could feel the call of a high-paying job, prestige, title, benefits, a car, and the corporate ladder. Most importantly, I felt loved and wanted again. I too knew I was perfect for the job because I was educated in New York and I also understood the culture of the Japanese since I was a fourth-generation Japanese-American. I accepted immediately.

Four weeks later, I was one of only three remaining out of 16 candidates the company had selected from resumes. I even purchased a new suit for each interview, trading food money for clothes. On the final days of interviewing, I found myself sitting outside the regional vice president's office. But instead of feeling good, I began to feel bad. Something was wrong. My stomach began to turn as I realized that I was doing the same thing my poor dad was doing—interviewing for jobs. The only difference was that I was 32, and my dad was 59. The offer of money, security, title, promotion, and benefits had called to me and I found out which character inside of me was responding.

For a very long ten minutes, I sat outside the vice president's office and had a conversation with myself. At the end of the ten minutes, I wrote a note that said, "Thank you for your interest in me. I greatly appreciate your time and consideration. It has been good for my self-esteem, but I must move on with my life and that is why I am removing my name as a candidate as a possible employee with your company. Thank you." I handed the note to the secretary and closed the door behind me. That was the last time I ever applied for a job.

Rich dad was always more interested in what character I chose to become rather than the profession I chose. During this period of time, the two characters I had to choose between were the *wimp* and the *warrior*. After facing the real world with nothing, for about two weeks, the wimp in me was winning. Then one day, the warrior won and I felt good for a whole day. Then the wimp took over again. By the fourth week, the battle was tied. I was a wimp for half the time and a warrior for the other half.

Things finally began to change in my life when I became comfortable with my status of being a person with no money, no job, and no professional status. In other words, I was becoming comfortable with being a nobody. I was no longer a kid, a student, a ship's officer, a military pilot, or an entrepreneur. I had nothing, and I kind of liked it. It wasn't that bad. I was facing nothing with nothing, and the more I could do that, the more the warrior inside of me was growing stronger. One of the reasons I turned down the possibility of the job as national sales manager was because I was in the middle of my own personal experiment and I simply wanted to find out which character would win.

Rich dad often asked this question of his son and me: "If you had nothing—no money, no work, no food, no shelter—what would you do?"

If we answered with, "I'd go find a job to make a few dollars," rich dad would say, "You boys are programmed to be employees."

If we answered with, "I'd look for a business opportunity and build or buy a business," rich dad would say, "You boys are programmed to be entrepreneurs."

If we replied with, "I'd find an investment and then look for investors," he would say, "You boys are programmed to be investors and entrepreneurs."

Rich dad also said, "Most people are programmed from birth to go and look for a job. They go to school to reinforce that programming. If you want to be able to respond with the latter two answers, you will need a different form of education—education for the real world."

In my quiet time alone, I remembered rich dad's little quiz, and now in my moment of nothingness, I began to choose which answer I wanted to be the answer for the rest of my life.

Rich dad called me about six weeks after our Chinese luncheon and asked if I would join him for lunch. Of course I accepted. This time we met at an expensive downtown Honolulu restaurant, the place where the movers and shakers meet to have lunch. Almost everyone there was in business attire. I arrived by bus, dressed in shorts and a bright red Aloha shirt, doing my best to pretend I was a man who was rich and no longer needed to dress like everyone else. I doubt if I fooled anyone or if anyone cared. I was having lunch with rich dad and no one else. A suit would not have impressed rich dad because he knew my financial status. Standing to greet me and shake my hand, rich dad asked, "How are things going?"

"Pretty good," I replied, as I took my seat. "I'm getting used to having nothing and being a nobody."

Rich dad chuckled and said, "It's not that bad, is it?"

"No, it isn't," I said. "Things only get bad when the self-doubt creeps in and I begin to beat myself up for all the stupid things I've done. But I am getting stronger. The wimp in me is losing his grip and the warrior is getting stronger. I'm about ready to face the real world."

After I told him about pursuing a high-paying national sales manager's job and then turning it down, a broad smile came across rich dad's face. "That is the best thing I've heard you say in months. You have really decided to change your future. And most importantly, I'm glad you're finding the courage to face the real world."

Puzzled, I squinted and asked, "Doesn't everyone want to face the real world?"

"Most think they do," said rich dad, "but if the truth be told, most people today do their best to hide from the real world."

The waiter came, handed us our menus, filled our water glasses, and quickly told us the specials of the day. "People hide from the real world? How do they do that? Is it only by job security?" I asked.

Rich dad handed his menu back to the waiter and said, "The usual."

He then looked at me and said, "There are many ways people hide from the real world. Most people today spend their lives running from sanctuary to sanctuary—sanctuaries that protect them from the real world. For example, many people leave the sanctuary of home and go to the sanctuary of college. After graduation, many run to the sanctuary of a job or profession. If they get married, they then create a sanctuary for their family, and the process continues with people running from safe sanctuary to safe sanctuary. When people lose their job, they often dust off their resume and run in search of another sanctuary. Or if they get divorced, many run in search of another person to create a new home sanctuary with."

"Is there anything wrong with that?" I asked.

"No, not necessarily—as long as there is always another sanctuary," said rich dad, taking a sip from his glass of water. "But problems do arise when a person leaves one safe sanctuary and then cannot find the next sanctuary. That is what happened to your dad."

"My dad?" I replied with a little surprise.

"Yes, your dad," said rich dad. "Your dad is facing the real world today just as you are facing the real world today, and I wonder which of the two of you will do better. The difference is your dad began facing the real world after he was 50, and you are only in your thirties. Both of you are out of work. I find it all very interesting to observe."

"Explain to me the real world you see my dad facing today."

"Your dad left the sanctuary of his parents' home, went to a good school, got a good job, and climbed the ladder to success. Is that correct?"

"Yes," I replied.

"So your dad went from safe sanctuary to safe sanctuary until he reached the position and title of superintendent of education. He left home and went to school, got married, and never left the school system. Isn't that correct?"

I nodded my head, saying, "He was a great student so he stayed in a system, or a sanctuary, as you say, that fed his ego and allowed him to achieve. Are you saying he should have left the sanctuary of higher education?"

"Why should he?" said rich dad. "He was smart, a great student, class president, soon head of the system, so he should have just stayed in a system that he did well in. If I were in his shoes, I would probably have done the same thing. But then he chose to leave the system at age 50, and the world outside the school system is the real world. When it came to finances, your dad was not mentally or emotionally ready for the real world."

"You mean when he decided to run for lieutenant governor of Hawaii?" I asked.

"Yes. Your dad, being an honest man, runs against a corrupt political system and finds that honesty is not the best policy. He runs into the real world when he runs for lieutenant governor and loses. After the loss, he then finds himself outside the system he grew up in, the system he did well in, the only real system he knows, and suddenly he must face the real world—and he is not surviving well. On top of that, as soon as he lost his job, your mom dies of an early heart attack. I suspect that she could not stand the embarrassment that comes with any loss or the fact that your dad was now out of work, because the two of them were now outside the system that once protected them."

"My mom did take it harder than my dad. Many of her phony socialite friends in government stopped calling her or going to lunch with her once my dad lost the election. That included many of her closest friends. The world can be very cruel to people they perceive as losers. They love you when you're on top and forget you when you're down. I believe my mom took my dad's fall from the top harder than anyone else, and I believe that is why she died before she was 50."

Rich dad sat silently as I talked about my mom. He could tell I missed her very much. After an appropriate length of time, he continued, saying, "After your dad finishes his grieving, he marries again, of course to a schoolteacher. Then he purchases that ice-cream franchise and loses his life savings. He then gets divorced because I think the pressure of no sanctuary, no safe harbor, is terribly stressful on couples, young or old. So today, your dad is like an orphan. His parents are gone, his wives are gone, his kids can't support him, and the sanctuary he grew up in, the educational system, won't let him back in. Now he takes odd jobs trying to stay alive, trying to find the door to the next sanctuary so he can find protection from the real world."

"If not for his teacher's pension, the real world would crush him," I said. "He might even be homeless."

Rich dad agreed. "You kids might have to take him in, which many kids do. The sanctuary of last resort is family, if the family can afford him," rich dad said, looking directly at me. "You can't afford to take care of him right now, can you?"

"It would be tough, but I would find a way," I replied. "But why are we discussing this real world versus sanctuary stuff?"

"Because your lessons continue," said rich dad with a smile. "Just because you are in your thirties does not mean you can't learn more. The financial situation you are in is a horrible situation, but thank God you're facing it at age 32. Now, you can choose to make this bad experience an even worse situation, which is what losers do, or you can turn this bad situation into the best situation of your life so far. Millions of people are stuck in offices, on farms, in sales jobs, in professions, living in terror of what you are facing today. Many would sneer at you and treat you like a pariah. A few might envy you because at least you've gone through the pain of losing it all."

"That sounds ridiculous," I said. "Why would anyone envy me having nothing?"

"Because a few people out there do have vision that others do not have or do not want to see," said rich dad. "Some people are beginning to realize that the challenges facing your generation are greater than the challenges facing my generation. After the year 2000, many of your generation will realize that they will be facing the same financial situation you are facing today. A few of those people with vision would envy you, because you are facing nothing, facing the real world, a world without sanctuaries, today, not tomorrow. Just because your peers have money and success today, does not mean they will have money and success tomorrow. Those who realize it will envy you."

"I'm still not totally clear why they would envy me," I said.

"Because you're halfway through the process. Most people are clinging to a false sense of security, knowing there is less and less job and financial security today," said rich dad. "So you've screwed up early, and now you have time to clean it up and grow from the experience. Are you willing to go forward rather than go backward?"

"I may as well," I replied. "I'm in the middle of this mess. I'm already facing what you call 'the real world,' and it's not that bad."

"Good," smiled rich dad. "You see, the best thing that happened to me was I faced the real world when I was 13 years old."

"When your dad died and left you in charge of the business and the family?"

Rich dad explained, "At 13, while your dad was in school learning about the ABCs of job security, I was facing the real world, the world he faces today. As a young teenager, I had no education, no money, a brokenhearted and sick mother, a family to take care of, a failing business, and no one to fall back on. In retrospect, it was the best thing that could have ever happened to me. The reason I have so much money today is because I had no sanctuary to hide in, and that is why I won't give you a hand right now. If I gave you a hand and offered you sanctuary, I would be delaying the inevitable. If you were of my generation, I would give you a job because for my generation, job security was all you needed. Your generation needs financial security more than job security. Your generation has lots of jobs. The fast-food restaurants are always looking for help. Your generation lacks the financial education required to achieve true financial security, and that lack of education will be the cause of the inevitable."

"The inevitable?" I asked.

"Yes, the inevitable," said rich dad. "Chances are, your generation will not have the safe sanctuary of Social Security or Medicare, or enough of it, to fall back on, as your dad and I do. Millions of people in your generation will not have any or sufficient retirement money to fall back on. Millions of your generation will not have a DB pension plan or a union pension plan to protect them from the real world. So what you are facing today is what millions of your generation will begin facing sometime after the year 2010, long after I am gone."

I sat there silently as the waiter placed our meals in front of us. I was beginning to understand why both my dads had been such advocates of their employee retirement plans. After the waiter had gone, I said, "So your generation has DB pension plans and my generation may not. And to you, that is a big difference."

"A monstrous difference," said rich dad. "You see, the employees who worked for your dad have the government and the unions backing their retirement. My employees only have themselves backing them, and most of my employees are not putting any money into their retirement plans. They do not know what they are. Some think they are the same as DB pension plans, the same plans their parents have. Because of this false sense of DB security, most of my employees do not have any savings. They have nice homes, nice cars, and nice TV sets, but nothing else. That worries me. I talk to them about investing, but nice cars and nice TVs mean more to them. Besides, they do not know the difference between saving and investing. They think they are the same thing. That is why I am worried for you and your generation. Most of my generation has some protection from the real world. Most of your generation will eventually face the real world, a world that they are not prepared to face and many will be too old to face. There is this massive problem brewing and no one seems to worry about it."

"So millions of my generation will someday have to face what I am facing today—the real world with nothing?"

"Yes, that's exactly what I am saying," rich dad said sternly. "That is precisely what I am saying. The difference is that you are facing the real world in 1979 at the age of 32 and many of your peers will face the real world after 2010 when they turn 62 or 72 or 82 or, heaven forbid, older. But they will face the real world."

"So my generation's pension plan could run out of money, if they do not contribute enough money to it."

"More than that," said rich dad. "Your generation's pension plan could run out of money even if a person puts a lot of money into it, because your generation's pension plans can be wiped out by a massive stock-market crash, a crash I predict is coming."

"So a DB pension plan has protection from a stock-market crash and a DC plan does not?" I asked.

Rich dad nodded. "In most cases, but even DB plans have been known to crash due to mismanagement. But the risks are greater for DC pension plans. The problems are brewing, and soon the moment of truth will arrive. Soon your generation will find out if this new DC plan works or not. The problem is, your generation will only find out if the plan worked after they retire."

"You mean my classmates may find out at age 65 that their DC plan was inadequate or insufficient?" I asked. "The only way they are going to know is after they retire, when it might be too late to work and replenish it to make up the shortfall?"

Rich dad nodded and continued, saying, "Not only are many of your generation not contributing anything to their plans, but many who are contributing are not contributing enough, and very few are aware how risky stocks and mutual funds are. Mutual funds can fall all the way to zero in a market crash. Sometime in the future, your generation will get the wake-up call that their DC retirement is not safe and their retirement sanctuary is at risk. Once your generation realizes that, they will begin to get out of the market, a panic will set in, and the market will crash. If the panic is large, the crash will be the biggest in the world. The problem is, too many amateur investors are entering the market, and it is these amateur investors who are the problem—a problem far greater than the flaws in pension reform. That is why I predict most of your generation will face the real world you are facing today. The only question is: How old will they be when they face it?"

"Most of my generation?" I asked, questioning the statement.

"Yes, most of your generation. I would say at least 80 percent of your generation will not have enough money to retire on. And millions will be out of money and out of support after the year 2020, after this massive stock-market crash occurs. The U.S. government will not be able to afford over 150 million people needing government support just for financial and medical survival."

"Over 150 million people?" I said again, questioning rich dad's numbers. "There are only 75 million baby boomers."

"Yes, the number will be well over 150 million because there will be members from my generation still alive and still needing support, as well as millions of immigrants who will add to the numbers, as well as the millions of poor people who already exist. By the year 2030, simply because of medical breakthroughs that extend life, half the U.S. population could be requiring more and more government support because they are not prepared financially to face their old age."

"And that does not include the millions of federal and state employees who will also be expecting the government to take care of them as promised," I added. "Lifelong government employees just like my dad."

"That's correct," rich dad said as he nodded. "Too many people have been taught to expect the government to take care of them, to be the safe sanctuary that protects them from the real world. And that is why this problem will only grow."

"So many of the kids of the baby boomers will have to support their parents," I said.

"More than their parents," said rich dad. "The kids of the baby boomers, those born after 1970, may be asked to support double families. In other words, if a young couple has two kids, through various taxes, they may have to support an additional four people who cannot afford to support themselves."

"You mean a family of four is really a family of eight?" I asked.

"It's possible. It could lead to a battle for money and life support between the different generations, young and old. And if the old control the government, the young will definitely be taxed to pay for the old," rich dad suggested. "If the young win in politics, there will be millions of old people, your baby-boom generation, complaining that young people no longer respect their elders." Rich dad chuckled at that thought.

"Why do you chuckle?" I asked.

Still chuckling, rich dad said, "Respect for elders is an idea whose time has passed. I think the coming generations will have less respect for their elders, not more. But I could be wrong. Maybe the children of the baby boomers will be glad to open their wallets and give their elders all the money they want. Who knows? Stranger things have happened."

We spent the next few minutes eating and not really saying much. I sat there thinking about the bus trip home, wondering if I should walk or splurge on a bus ride. I dared not ask rich dad for a ride. Besides, I did not want to waste this opportunity to face the real world and face it with nothing, or in this case, very little. I had begun to feel lucky about facing the real world at 32 instead of at 72, 82, or 92 years of age.

As the bill came and rich dad picked it up, I asked him, "How did we get into this mess? How come we have so many millions of people who need a safe sanctuary from the real world?"

Security vs. Freedom

"Good question," responded rich dad as he handed the waiter his credit card. "I think the big difference came when people began seeking security instead of freedom."

"Don't we all have freedom?" I asked. "After all, this is America, land of the free and home of the brave."

"Yes, it is America and that is an old song," smirked rich dad. The problem is, most people think security and freedom are the same word. They are not. In fact, in many ways, security and freedom mean exactly the opposite things."

"Security and freedom mean the opposite things?" I asked. "Explain that."

"Look, in 1773, the year of the infamous Boston Tea Party, what were the American rebels protesting?" asked rich dad.

"Taxes," I replied. "We wanted freedom from taxes. Those brave men risked jail or prison by performing a criminal act against Mother England."

"Good," said rich dad. "So they did not throw the tea overboard in the name of greater job security?"

"No, they were willing to fight for freedom, not job security."

"And what do we teach in school today?" asked rich dad. "What is the main reason parents and teachers fearfully insist their kids study hard and get good grades? Is it for freedom?"

"No," I said quietly. "Parents and teachers want their kids to get good grades for job security, hopefully a high-paying job."

"And what happened to our founding fathers' focus on freedom— the freedom brave men and women fought for hundreds of years ago? It's been shoved aside for a focus on job security. The fear of not having enough money to put food on the table has replaced freedom as a priority in our society.

"So school is not really about freedom. It's about job security and DB pension plans. That is what teachers have, but their students will not," said rich dad. "That is only one reason why there is less and less relevance between school and the real world. Most of the real world will not have DB pension plans, but schoolteachers do.

Rich dad went on, "And what did you fight for in Vietnam, even though you did not have to go, even though you were draft-exempt? Didn't you fight for freedom?"

"Yes, but that is because both you and my dad explained that it was a son's duty to fight for his country. I do not know if I would have gone if the two of you had not insisted I go."

"Right, and what did most of your friends' parents do? Didn't they insist their boys stay in school to avoid the draft? Didn't most of your friends not go to Vietnam because they were smart enough to get into college and receive a college deferment from military service?"

"Yes," I replied.

"Do you see how much this country has changed? We were a country founded on the ideal of freedom, but now security is far more important than freedom. Security and freedom are not the same ideal. People who seek security are very, very different from those who seek freedom. And that difference, the difference in people, will also lead to the biggest stock-market crash in the history of the world. Millions of people are now putting money into their defined-contribution plans, into mutual funds, and other investments that they hope will ensure their security. Boy, are they in for a rude awakening in the future.

"That is why I am so concerned about ERISA. We are no longer the same people we were when the Boston Tea Party took place. As a people, we no longer fight for freedom. Instead, we are a people who now fight desperately for security. Millions of unwilling and financially unsophisticated people will be pushed into the stock market and, as you know, the stock market is not a place for people who are lovers of security. The stock market is a place for those who want their freedom. I am afraid that those who love freedom will win, and those who love security will lose. And when they lose, they will face the real world, unfortunately at an old age. That is my prediction."

"So freedom is not the same as security?" I asked, still not sure that there was a difference.

"Not only are they not the same, they are exactly the opposite. The more security you seek, the less freedom you have."

"Explain that to me," I said. "How can more security mean less freedom?"

"That job you turned down may have given you a lot of security, but wasn't it at the price of your freedom? Did it not hinder what you could earn, when and where you worked, and even when you took a vacation?"

"Yes, job security would have limited my freedom. For many people, their job security even tells them what time they can eat lunch," I added. "But don't most people want security more than freedom?"

"Exactly," said rich dad. "That is their choice. But always remember that the more you have of one, the less you have of the other. In fact, the more security you have, the more trapped you become. Just look at the people in the world who have the most security. They're called prison inmates. They have a house, food, free time, and exercise yard. They have maximum security, but they have no freedom." Rich dad paused for a while, letting the idea of maximum security settle in. He then said, "Look at people who depend primarily on Social Security. They have a little financial security but at the cost of their freedom, the freedom of lifestyle. People who depend upon Social Security are some of the poorest people in America and with the least freedom."

"So you want me to choose between security and freedom. Freedom takes courage and strength, and if you lack courage and strength, you lose your freedom," I said. "So freedom is not free."

"No way," said rich dad. "Do you remember coming home from Vietnam and having people spit on you and call you 'baby-killer'?"

"Well people spit *at* me, but no one spit *on* me. But I do understand what you mean. We fought for the right for them to have the freedom to do that, even though we did not like it."

"That is why the song goes, 'Land of the free and home of the brave.' Freedom takes courage, and it takes bravery. You are in the middle of facing that test of courage and bravery inside of you right now. If your courage wins even when you have nothing, you will find a freedom few people ever know. Even if they live in the land of the free, they are not free. The need for security robs them of their freedom."

We were soon on the sidewalk, and rich dad waited for the valet to bring his car. "Want a ride?" he asked.

"No thanks," I said with a very big smile. The warrior character in me was feeling pretty good, even though I still had no money and did not want a job. I wanted to face the real world with nothing for as long as I could and let the stronger person inside of me get stronger. I wanted freedom from the tyranny of needing a job. The talk with rich dad had given me a greater insight into what it took to live in his world, the real world he had to face when he was 13. "I kind of like the real world, and I want to make it as real as possible," I said to rich dad with a smile, as the valet brought him his car. "I want to face the real world today rather than tomorrow." Rich dad smiled, waved, and drove off with the valets envying his car.

During this period of facing the real world with nothing, I had the free time to reflect back on my life and recall some very important lessons I had forgotten. One cool morning while I sat on Waikiki Beach watching the waves, my mind drifted back a few years to a day when my Marine Corps squadron was preparing to go into battle. Early, before sunrise, our commanding officer stood before all the pilots flying that day and said, "Remember that the lives of our men are an integral part of this mission. Great leaders and great pilots bring their men home alive. If you take care of your men, your men will take care of you."

On another day during this period of having nothing and facing the real world, my mind drifted back over 25 years, back to Sunday school and hearing my teacher ask the question, "Are we not our brothers' keepers?" It seemed that I had forgotten that lesson also.

So 1979 was a turning point for me. I realized that in my desperation to become rich, I had forgotten many lessons from my youth. Now in my thirties, not only was I not rich, I had become someone I was not proud to be. It was time to make some changes.

So while the truth hurt, the benefit is that I learned some priceless lessons, not only about myself, but also about the future. It was time to change my future.

The Rich Don't Work for Money

About six months into my experiment, the person who had taken over the remains of the nylon-and-Velcro wallet business called. He said, "This business is a bigger mess than I had expected. Will you come back and give me a hand?"

I thought about it for a moment and agreed and went back to the business as his partner. Our agreement was that if I did not improve the business, I would not be paid. In other words, I was true to rich dad's number-one rule, the number-one rule from my *Rich Dad Poor Dad* book: The rich don't work for money. I was now a partner with equity, building a business. If the business did not become profitable, I would not get paid.

By this time, I had several other business ventures that were profitable. One of my business ventures was a joint venture with a local radio station doing promotions and product sales. The venture would eventually become one of the most successful radio retail merchandising promotions in the history of U.S. radio. I was able to move into my own place and afford a car again. But most importantly, I began to repay the investors who had trusted me and loaned me money. Many refused to take the money, since they had already written the losses off. Instead, they asked me to call them for my next business venture.

In 1981, I merged the growing nylon-and-Velcro wallet company with my success in rock-and-roll radio. The rock band, Pink Floyd, called and my nylon-and-Velcro wallet company began building licensed logo products for the band. Bands and performers such as Van Halen, Boy George, Judas Priest, the Police, and Duran Duran asked us to manufacture similar products for them. Soon the wreckage of the first company transformed to become a bigger and stronger company. In 1982, MTV hit in a big way and we were off to the stars again. This time I was a lot less foolish, had more business savvy, had better advisors, and I was more honest and far less afraid of failing again and facing the real world. This time I knew that if I failed, I could stand up again—and stand up taller and faster.

I know the real world can still knock me down. I am wise enough to realize that markets go up and markets go down. I also know that mutual funds are not safe. Even though I know a massive stock-market crash could potentially wipe people out, I am not afraid of it. I have already gone through the embarrassment of losing everything. I have enjoyed the process of getting it back and more. Today, having already faced the real world with nothing, I know I will learn even more if I am knocked down again. I know I will bounce back even faster, and I am preparing daily for the biggest stock-market crash in history.

Unfortunately, my real dad never recovered, and the older he got, the less able he was to take on the harshness of the real world. In 1982, he was 63 years old. At that age, there were no more job offers for him, except jobs as a security guard or at a hamburger joint. He lived in the glory of his past successes, which allowed him to call himself a consultant. But if not for his teacher's pension, Social Security, and Medicare, the real world would have crushed him. The kids helped him a little, but he often rejected that financial help because he was too proud. He had been well prepared and well educated for the world of government education, but outside that world, that sanctuary, he found he was not prepared at all for the real world—a world millions of my generation will soon face, prepared or not.

Personally, I have no plans to follow my poor dad's plan. I am not counting on lifelong job security, my retirement plan, mutual funds, stocks, Social Security, Medicare, and other forms of government charity to keep me alive in the future. But unfortunately, millions of my peers are following in their parents' footsteps, some only now beginning to realize that there is a difference between a DB pension plan and a DC pension plan.

Most are hoping and praying the stock market will always go up and that mutual funds and a diversified portfolio will save them from the real world. I am afraid such simple, unsophisticated investor strategies will not work for most people. A major stock-market crash will wipe out most mutual funds. As we have seen, the stock market is not a place for people who seek security. The stock market is a place for those who seek freedom. Unfortunately, many people who seek security do not know the difference.

ERISA may have been signed into law with good intentions. The problem is that the act and subsequent amendments to the act have flaws. But the flaws are nothing compared to the panic that will occur when the people who spent their lives seeking security find out the real-world stock market can take that security away.

The point of this book is to give you some ideas on how to be prepared and do well, regardless if the real-world stock market goes up or the real-world market comes crashing down. The point is to be prepared for whatever happens in the real world outside the sanctuaries of home, school, and business. Just as Noah built an ark in the desert, it may be time for you to begin building an ark in your mind while you have the time to build it.

Chapter Four

THE NIGHTMARE BEGINS

The front page of the "Money" section of the November 30, 2001, issue of *USA TODAY* had a large color photograph of a 58-year-old man. His hair is gray, his arms are crossed, he appears intelligent and distinguished-looking. Although he could pass as the CEO of a large corporation, he isn't. Instead he is a loyal employee of Enron, a company where the CEO and other top executives may have personally made millions of dollars, but the company is now bankrupt.

The reason this man, and not the CEO, is on the cover is because this loyal employee's 401(k) has been devastated due to the stock-market crash, a down economy, and the downfall of the company he spent a lifetime working for. At one time, his company's stock was worth nearly $100 per share. This loyal employee felt rich and bought more and more shares of the company he worked for and put those shares into his retirement plan. On November 30, 2001, that same company's stock was worth less than 35 cents per share and falling. At one time, his 401(k) was worth $317,000. Today he estimates its worth to be about $100,000. It is beginning to dawn on him that he may never be able to retire. He is nearly out of his most important asset—time. Some 25 years after the original passage of ERISA, rich dad's prophecy is starting to come true.

The December 2, 2001, edition of the *Miami Herald* ran a headline calling for government reform in 401(k) retirement plans. The journalist who wrote the piece argued that we have laws requiring people to wear seat belts in cars, but we don't have laws requiring investors to invest wisely. I say, why not tell our school systems that?

Soon thereafter, every newspaper, and television and radio station was shouting words of outrage. "How could the government let this happen?" one local broadcaster insisted over the radio. "Why didn't the accounting firm of Arthur Andersen warn the shareholders?" "Employees who are ready for retirement can now never retire." "How can the senior management of Enron run off with hundreds of millions of dollars and leave the employees with nothing?" Other stations went on to compare Enron to a disaster like the attack on the World Trade Center on September 11, 2001. I finally heard a voice of reason say on television, "While Enron is an extreme case, it is not an isolated case. What about all the millions of employees who have lost billions of dollars in their retirement plans? What about the employees working for hundreds of other companies who may not have lost everything, but have lost years of retirement savings in the stock market? How do they feel now, knowing that their dreams of retirement may never come true? Do they feel more trust in the stock market today or less trust? The lack of confidence among investors is growing and is the bigger problem. There is more to this problem than simply Enron and questionable accounting."

In response, a few stations had financial planners repeat the standard company line of, "This problem would not have happened if the employees had diversified." Another famous mutual-fund manager came on and said, "We have always advised our clients to diversify. Why didn't the management of Enron advise their employees to diversify their portfolios? If they had diversified, they would not have the problems they are having today."

If rich dad were asked, he too would agree that Enron was an extreme case—extreme because of the magnitude of greed and apparent corruption. But he would also know that it is not an isolated case. In the last few years, not only did Enron employees take sizable losses, but so did employees of Ford, Cisco, Coca-Cola, Xerox, Lucent, Maytag, Polaroid, Rite Aid, United Airlines, and on and on. If rich dad were asked to comment on the plight of the Enron employees and all employees who have money in the stock market, he might say,

"The problem is not the lack of diversification. The problem is a lack of financial education and financial sophistication. Those are flaws that simple diversification alone cannot solve."

Just as we were coming to grips with the tragedy and pain of the 2001 attack on the World Trade Center and the Pentagon, news of Enron and the questionable accounting of Arthur Andersen burst into the headlines. Even the war in Afghanistan had taken a back seat to Enron, at one time reportedly the seventh-largest company in America, and today the biggest bankruptcy in U.S. history—so far.

During all this media sensationalism, the public often misses the more important points because the real problems are not front-page news. During this meltdown period of Enron, one of the many flaws in pension reform was brought to light in that same December 2, 2001, edition of the *Miami Herald*. To me, more important than the Enron fiasco is the simple question that this retiree asks of a certified financial planner who regularly contributes to the paper.

Question

I am 70 years old and retired, hoping that my IRA would sustain me when the time came. Since I have to begin withdrawing next year, I would appreciate your advice.

I was advised several years ago to invest my IRA in mutual funds. For a while it was great, but along with so many other people, I have lost a great deal in the last two years. Should I take my losses and reinvest in a secure savings program, even though the interest rates are low?

Answer

If ever there was a time to stick with the plan, it's now. The ups and downs of the market are to be expected, and if you've been an investor for more than a few years, you've ridden a few waves yourself—mostly up markets, just no down markets this long and nasty. I feel your pain, but two-percent CDs and no growth aren't going to cut it.

Check your mutual funds and make sure they're solid and leaning more to the conservative growth and growth income funds. Aggressive funds tend to be more volatile. Instruct your custodian to send you your required minimum distribution monthly by selling shares of your funds. This is called a systematic withdrawal and it works like a charm.

Did you pick up one of the flaws in the law? Did you notice the statement by the 70-year-old retiree who wrote, "Since I *have* to begin withdrawing next year, I would appreciate your advice."? Did you notice the response from the financial planner? "Instruct your custodian to send you your *required* minimum distribution *monthly by selling* shares of your funds."

More Sellers Than Buyers

As I said, while most of the world was sipping their coffee and reading about Enron and thinking Enron's problems were not their problems, this retiree's simple question points out how Enron is everyone's problem. One of the flaws that rich dad noticed 20 years earlier was the requirement that the retiree must begin withdrawing from the market by selling shares monthly at age seventy and a half. Now that may not sound like a big deal, but as most of us know, it's the little things that count.

In other words, as the years go on, more and more people will, by law, be required to withdraw by selling shares, while younger workers are required to buy shares. Now, it does not take a rocket scientist to see the flaw in this plan—a flaw that will get bigger and bigger as more and more people get older. In other words, how does the price of a stock go up when more people are selling than buying?

The question is more important simply because of the numbers of people involved. While the ripple effect of the Enron disaster will affect hundreds of thousands of people in one way or another, this 70-year-old retiree's question will affect tens of millions of people, maybe hundreds of millions, in one way or another, just because of its ripple effect.

Speaking of large ripple effects, Japan, once a financial powerhouse, a nation of hardworking people who are diligent savers, is on the brink of financial ruin. Is it the fault of the Japanese people or the fault of their country's leaders? In other words, if America, the richest country in the world, falters and Japan, the second largest economy in the world, goes down, the ripples may soon turn to tidal waves, waves big enough to cause the need for an ark in the desert.

When the December 2, 2001, issue of the *Miami Herald* ran, the retiree's question had little impact simply because only a relatively few people were over 70 in the year 2001 and less than half had DC pension plans. Most still had DB pensions, which operate via different rules. Also, many of those born before 1946 had good-paying jobs, made money on their home when they sold it to a baby boomer, and many actually had savings. So the question this retiree asked was shoved to a back page, yet it is a most important question to be asking.

The question is: *What happens when millions of baby boomers are required to begin withdrawing money from the stock market?* Will the stock market still go up by 10 percent, 20 percent, or 30 percent each year as it did in the 1990s? If you were born after 1946 and have a DC pension plan filled with stocks, bonds, and mutual funds, for your sake, I hope the market keeps going up and never stops. But history is against that fantasy.

Because there are so few people over 70 with DC plans, this flaw has had very little effect on the market. But by the year 2016, when the first of the 75 million baby boomers begin to turn 70 years of age, many of them will have DC pension plans. Each year, more and more will be added to that list. When rich dad made his prophecy, he was not using a crystal ball or tea leaves to look at the future. He was using the change in the law, time, market experience, and the fact that people do get older. In other words, he was not guessing. He was just using facts, history, and realities.

Supply and Demand

The price of stocks or mutual funds or bonds or anything, for that matter, goes up as long as there are more buyers than sellers. Between 1990 and the year 2000, the stock market boomed because there were so many 30 to 50-year-old baby boomers entering the stock market, saving for their retirement in their DC pension plans, so there was a stock-market boom. There was a similar boom in the 1970s when baby boomers left home, left college, and began buying their first home. If you are old enough to remember those years, you may remember the mania over real estate—a mania that was also followed by a panic and a bust when interest rates went over 20 percent. Interest rates were raised in order to slow down inflation, which was caused partially because 75 million baby boomers had entered the job market and now had money to burn. In other words, 75 million people buying anything will cause a boom. The reverse is also true—75 million people selling anything will cause a bust. It is the basic law of economics, the law of supply and demand.

Within the next few years, but most certainly by 2016 if they haven't already figured it out, people will begin to understand that stock markets do not always go up by 20 percent per year as they did in the 1990s. Unfortunately, millions of employees will not exit their 401(k) or IRA plans or may only exit after it is too late. Millions of baby boomers may not sell early, even though they know the market is crashing, because of government-imposed tax penalties for early withdrawal. So instead of withdrawing, they will stay in the market—diversifying, moving money from one mutual fund to another, looking for the next hyped safe sanctuary. Most people already realize that they are in financial trouble, but still do not realize the full impact of the many flaws of the law. When this realization hits critical mass, a panic will occur as people fight desperately to save their retirement and their lives. Unfortunately, all the diversification in the world will not save them from a crash of that magnitude.

Warren Buffett, reportedly America's richest and smartest investor, has this to say about diversification:

Diversification is a protection against ignorance.
It makes very little sense for those who know what they're doing.

Warren Buffett is not saying to not diversify. He has repeatedly said that he does not diversify, but he is not advising you or anyone else to not diversify. He is simply saying that diversification is protection against ignorance. In other words, if you don't want to diversify, get educated. If you're not financially educated and have no plans on becoming financially educated, then diversify, diversify, diversify.

Rich dad, being more blunt, would have said, "If you're financially ignorant, diversify." He did say to me way back in 1979, "One of the many flaws is that the law has failed to advise people to get financially educated. President Ford and Congress changed the law, but failed to tell the educational system to provide the proper financial education— the financial literacy required for people who have DC pension plans. Instead, the politicians have left the job of financial education to the Wall Street people."

On a more sarcastic note, rich dad later said, "Asking Wall Street to provide financial education is the same as asking a fox to raise your chickens. If the fox is smart, the fox will be patient and raise very fat chickens. The fox works hard to gain the chickens' trust, so he cares for them by providing slick brochures, branch offices, and good-looking salespeople who have been trained to sound like investors. The salespeople are all trained to use the same intelligent-sounding financial jargon disguised as advice, such as, 'Invest for the long term, have a plan, choose a family of funds, sector funds, small cap growth funds, tax free municipal bonds, 20 percent in cash, REITs, Roth IRAs, rollovers, tech stocks, blue chips, the new economy, and of course, diversify, diversify, diversify.'"

As rich dad pointed out to me, "Pension reform will change the vocabulary we use, but most people will not have a clue what the new words mean." Meanwhile, the fox smiles and knows the chickens are happy. They feel safe in their new sanctuary. They have a safe secure job and they have their money safely entrusted to financially astute people. Then they see the stock market go up and up in the 1990s, and they feel even more intelligent and well advised. They know their financial planner is looking after them, will make them rich, and protect them from the harsh, cruel world outside the chicken coop.

But in March of 2000, the world began to change. The tech bubble burst, and the stock market began to deflate. TV commentators began to say, "The recovery will come in the next quarter," but the next quarter came and went. The TV commentators again said, "The recovery will come in the next quarter." Financial planners began to say, "Be patient. Invest for the long term. Diversify." The chickens began to feel a little more secure. They knew they were doing the financially intelligent thing. They were in it for the long term, they were diversified, and they knew the recovery was right around the corner.

September 11th dropped the market, but the market bounced right back. Again the chickens felt more confident as the market began to climb. Then Enron hit and suddenly many very fat chickens from all over America began to cluck loudly from the sanctuary of their securely wired chicken coops. Although they clucked and cackled loudly, the foxes again said, "Be patient. Invest for the long term. Diversify." One of the reasons the biggest stock-market crash in the history of the world did not take place right after the Enron collapse is because the foxes aren't ready for their chicken dinner yet. They know that these chickens have a few more years to get a little fatter. They know that by law, the chickens will have to keep coming to the stock market, buying more mutual funds, and diversifying. The problem is, some of the chickens are getting nervous and are beginning to ask questions—questions such as the one the 70-year-old retiree in Miami asked. He got the standard financial-planner-disguised-as-investor preprogrammed sales answer: "Don't worry, be happy, buy more, and diversify."

Now I want to restate that the advice of, "Invest for the long term, be patient, and diversify," is solid advice for those who have limited financial education and investment experience. The point I want to reinforce is the idea that you as an individual have three basic choices.

1. Do nothing.

2. Follow the same old financial planning advice to diversify.

3. Get financially educated.

The choice is yours. Obviously, I recommend long-term financial education. Today, many other people are joining the chorus.

In February of 2002, Alan Greenspan, the head of the Federal Reserve Bank, was concerned about the loss of confidence in the stock market and in the accounting profession, so he went before the nation and spoke about the need for financial literacy to be taught to our school kids. He knew that if people lose confidence in the stock market, capitalism as we know it is in trouble. Without investor money, the economy begins to implode. Due to that concern, he addressed Congress and said that this country needs to financially educate its children. The following is from an Associated Press article:

> *Schools should teach basic financial concepts better in elementary and secondary schools. A good foundation in math, Greenspan said, would improve financial literacy and "help prevent younger people from making poor financial decisions that can take years to overcome. "It has been my experience that competency in mathematics, both in numerical manipulation and in understanding its conceptual foundations, enhances a person's ability to handle the more ambiguous and qualitative relationships that dominate our day-to-day financial decision-making," he said.*

Immediately after the live telecast of his speech to Congress, the financial news television station on which I was watching Mr. Greenspan's speech asked the head of a large and famous mutual fund to comment on Greenspan's remarks. Immediately, this famous mutual-fund manager said, "I agree with Alan Greenspan. I agree we need to teach financial literacy, and financial literacy means to diversify, diversify, diversify."

"Thank you for your wonderful words of advice," said the TV host to the famous mutual-fund CEO. "If we are going to teach our kids financial literacy, we must teach them to diversify."

If rich dad were alive, he would say, "Alan Greenspan did not say 'diversify.' Alan Greenspan called for the need for financial literacy to be taught in our schools. Greenspan stated that for our nation to make progress and evolve, financial education is essential for a first-world nation to remain a first-world power." Rich dad might have also said, "Financial literacy does not mean diversify. The definitions are not even close. Saying that financial literacy means diversification is just another example of the fox teaching the chickens."

Now all of us who are in business want customers to buy our products or services forever. The same is true with mutual-fund managers and owners of financial television stations. You do not have to be a genius to see that the primary advertisers of this financial news TV station are mutual funds. So naturally they would have a mutual-fund manager comment on Alan Greenspan's call for financial literacy rather than Warren Buffett, a man who does not advertise with that TV station simply because he does not have to. Warren Buffett's own mutual fund, Berkshire Hathaway, is possibly the most expensive fund in America simply because it is so well managed and successful. His fund is so successful and expensive that he has been known to tell his investors *not* to invest in it because he believes the price of his fund is too expensive. If he is telling people to not invest in his fund, he obviously does not need to advertise on any financial news television station, which is why he probably was not asked to comment. The station invites someone who pays them ad revenues, a paying customer, and naturally that mutual-fund manager will say what is best for his mutual fund.

If rich dad were alive, he would probably say this: "A mutual-fund manager advising you to diversify is like a used-car salesman saying, 'Don't buy just one car. Buy many cars. You never know when the car you are driving may break down and you may not get to work. So instead of risking buying just one car, diversify that risk. Buy six cars and pay me for them every month for 40 years until you stop working and retire.'"

I ask you, what businessperson would not want millions of customers like that? The reason most of us do not buy the line of needing to diversify to six cars to protect us from car trouble is because most of us are better educated than that. But when it comes to financial vehicles, vehicles such as stocks, bonds, and mutual funds, most people are clueless as to the differences between different financial vehicles. That is why rich dad saw the lack of financial education as one of the major flaws in pension reform.

Because of this reform, one of the fastest growing professions is a group known as financial planners. Schoolteachers, housewives, ex-real estate agents, insurance salespeople, retirees, plumbers, and firefighters are taking a three-day to three-week to six-month course, and suddenly they are qualified to advise you on the security of your financial future.

The problem with the financial planning industry, as rich dad noted, is that not all financial planners are equal. While many financial planners are well educated and dedicated professionals, many planners lack the proper training and financial education to be dishing out financial advice that will affect a person's financial future and financial security.

The profession of financial planning is very confusing because of this huge variance of expertise, not to mention varying methods of compensation. When your financial planner gets paid to sell you something, do you really feel comfortable that it is the right buy for you? So let the buyer beware. Just because someone says they are a financial planner does not mean they know anything about financial planning, much less investing. It is this lack of professional training that rich dad saw as one of the very big flaws in pension reform because millions of people are now taking financial advice from people who are often poorer and less educated than they are.

The May 5, 2002, business section of the *Washington Post* discussed this very issue in an article titled, "When Hiring a Planner, Know the Bottom Line," with the subtitle, "Financial Planners Proliferating in Largely Unregulated Market."

In it, the following observations were made:

Experience points to a growing issue in financial planning, where many different types of professionals now offer services in a largely unregulated marketplace. And even more players will presumably be attracted to the planning field as the big boomer generation continues its inexorable march to retirement and beyond...

Full-fledged financial planners come in several versions—CFPs, 39,500 strong, being one. CFP certification entails testing, continuing education and course work. CFPs charge fees (as an hourly rate, a flat rate, or percentage of assets under management), commission, or a combination of the two.

Another group's members charge only on a fee basis... the 16-year-old National Association of Personal Financial Advisors (NAPFA)...

This growth in the financial planning field is in response to a demand for investment education and advice. To repeat because it is important to repeat: *One of the biggest flaws in pension reform is that it failed to tell the educational system that financial education is no longer an option. It is now mandatory.*

This flaw truly shocked rich dad. To him, Congress not requiring the schools to teach basic financial literacy after the law was changed bordered on criminal negligence, a crime far more serious than the crimes allegedly committed in the Enron scandal. When Congress passed that law and left the job of financial education up to the people who work in the financial markets, rich dad smelled a very big rat— not a fox, a rat. When that law was passed, rich dad realized that many people in Congress knew exactly what they were doing. Many of our leaders knew that they had just made it mandatory for millions of workers to turn trillions of their hard-earned dollars over to those who run the financial markets.

Let me be clear again. Rich dad was not against investing money in the stock market or against investing becoming more or less mandatory. Rich dad was angry at men like my real dad, the schoolteacher, who had absolutely no idea what was going on in Congress. Rich dad was against the sleight-of-hand and the lack of formal financial education. To him, leaving financial education up to those who profit from financial ignorance was criminal.

There are now thousands of professional financial planners, stockbrokers, real estate agents, insurance agents, accountants, and attorneys all handing out investment advice for money. Rich dad's concern was that most of these people are not investors. They do not live off their income from their investments, which a true investor does. Rich dad constantly reminded his son and me that the majority of people dishing out investment advice are salespeople working for commissions, salary, or a fee. It is these salespeople who do the financial education for the financial institutions and, obviously, most will say what the institution tells them to say and promote, or they lose their job. Then we wonder why we have millions of people who grow more and more worried about their future financial security. They grow insecure because, instead of receiving unbiased financial education, they receive a sales pitch disguised as financial education from a salesperson. As rich dad often said, "The reason salespeople are often called brokers is because they are often broker than you are."

Warren Buffett has this to say about financial advice from Wall Street:

Wall Street is the only place that people ride to in a Rolls-Royce
to get advice from those who take the subway.

Again, I must clarify something. I love the salespeople who sell me financial services and investments. Some of them are my best friends. Some of these salespeople have made me very rich, which means I like them even more. In other words, I need them as much as they need me. I pay my commissions because I want the people who sell me investments to prosper. If they prosper, they bring me more deals, and they often bring me the best investments first. Investors who hate paying commissions always get the worst investments—as they should because they are cheap. In fact, I have friends who will tip their waiter 20 percent for a burger and fries and then refuse to pay the commission on an investment that could make them rich. Talk about being wired up with a poor person's financial value system. You tip those who make you poor and hesitate to tip those who can make you rich. I have several friends like that. The point is, as an investor, you may want to become better educated and find advisors you can trust. If you are not educated, then one financial salesperson is just as good as another.

Again quoting Warren Buffett, "The market, like the Lord, helps those who help themselves."

In other words, if you want to do well in the future, do not leave your financial education up to someone else.

Two Flaws

In closing, let's review the two flaws in pension reform. The first is that the law requires participants to begin selling once they hit seventy and a half years of age. Within the next few years, we will see the panic begin. When the first of 75 million—83 million if you count immigrants—of the baby-boom generation reach the age of 70, simply put, more and more money will begin to come out rather than go in. While the year 2016 is bandied around as when this occurs in a major way, beware that the financial impact may begin much earlier. You do not need advanced math to figure out that it's tough to keep prices going higher when, each year, more and more people are selling.

The second flaw rich dad saw was that financial education was left up to those who make more money if the investor is less educated. Hence, financial education today is really a sales pitch.

In the next chapter, I will go into the third flaw in the system, and again that flaw was glaringly obvious in the letter from the 70-year-old retiree who wrote the newspaper asking for advice. As I said, while most people were sipping their coffee reading about Enron and Arthur Andersen, glad that they were not affected by the scandal, many of these people were missing the important facts hidden in the back pages of the newspaper—flaws in a system that will affect them today and tomorrow.

Chapter Five

WHAT ARE YOUR FINANCIAL ASSUMPTIONS?

Professional negotiators know that one of the most important watchwords in any negotiation is the word *assume*. When I was just beginning my business career and was actually negotiating for real money, rich dad would always remind me to watch my assumptions, as well as tune into the other person's assumptions. To rich dad, the word *assumption* was not a word to be taken lightly. He often would accentuate the word *assume* in this way: "ass-u-me." In business today, this punctuation tells a fairly common story of warning. If you have not yet heard what ass-u-me means, then ask around. I am certain someone close to you knows exactly what ass-u-me means.

Dr. R. Buckminster Fuller, one of America's most accomplished citizens who had many patents in his name, had this to say about the word *assume*: "You cannot question an assumption you do not know you have made." As one of his students, it took me a while to begin to understand how profound that statement was.

In business and investing, I have noticed many people lose and lose badly because they did not know they had made certain assumptions. In other words, it was their unconscious assumptions that cost them dearly—assumptions they did not even realize they had. For example, an attorney friend of mine told me of a couple who lost everything because they bought their dream piece of land and assumed it was clean. Three years from retirement and after holding the land for 15 years, they found out the land was once used as a toxic waste site, and the previous owners were long gone. The couple was sued by the federal government and ordered to pay for its cleanup, at a cost of millions of dollars. Naturally they fought the lawsuit in court and even won a few concessions, but the legal battle cost them everything they had saved. My attorney friend said, "The couple later said, 'When we looked at this beautiful piece of wooded land, we just assumed it had never been used for anything or by anyone.'"

When I lived in San Diego, I read about a local couple who decided to take the family to Disneyland. Due to conflicting work schedules, the husband and wife agreed to travel separately in two cars. When the couple met at the hotel, neither parent had brought the children. They had both assumed the other would be driving with the kids. Since it was an assumption they did not know they had made, they never bothered to ask if the other was going to bring the children. That is why Dr. Fuller emphasized the need to ask ourselves what assumptions we have made that we do not know we have made.

In business today, I often ask my attorney and my accountant to check the contracts. I never used to do this, but today I realize I need to have other eyes look over my agreements to check for anything I may have missed. I often ask them to question my assumptions or lack of assumptions in the process. I have learned a lot about myself by questioning my assumptions, especially those assumptions I do not know I have made.

I have found that many legal fights are not over the main points of the contract, but often over simple assumptions no one realized were made. Recently I was in a disagreement with a holiday lighting company that put up some holiday lights on my property. The owners, a couple, came over in early December to give me a quote for putting the lights up, and then put them up a few days later. Once the lights were up, I paid the bill in full. We shook hands and I was very happy with the great job they did, a far better job than I could ever do.

After the holidays, I called to ask them to take the lights down. The owner replied, "We said we would put them up. We never said we would take them down." Because I did not have a written agreement, the discussion became a heated disagreement on what was said and who said what. Finally, I hired someone else to take the lights down. Needless to say, I will not use that company again, even though they did do a good job of putting the lights up. I assumed that any company that put lights up would also take lights down, but obviously I made an assumption I did not know I had made. You can be certain that with the next company I hire, I will have a written contract stating that the price includes taking the lights down as well as putting them up. That is another case of ass-u-me.

As you can see from these examples, assumptions are very important in many different facets of life, but rich dad was especially cautious of assumptions when it came to money, business, and investing. He said, "More money has been lost, more friendships have been destroyed, more people have been hurt, more accidents have happened, and more people have gone to court because someone failed to question their assumptions." So the question is How does the word *assume* apply to retirement, the coming stock-market crash, and the advice people are receiving?

To answer that question, all we need to do is go back to the question asked by the 70-year-old retiree in the December 2, 2001, issue of the *Miami Herald*. The retiree was seeking advice, but was the advice wise?

> *Check your mutual funds, and make sure they're solid and leaning more to the conservative growth and growth income funds. Aggressive funds tend to be more volatile. Instruct your custodian to send you your required minimum distribution monthly by selling shares of your funds. This is called a systematic withdrawal, and it works like a charm.*

So here are some test questions:
- From the financial-planner's answer, how many different assumptions can you pick up?

- How many assumptions can you *not* pick up?

- How can the assumptions be right, and how can the assumptions be wrong?

- What happens if this retiree follows the financial planner's advice, but the advice is based upon faulty assumptions?

- What assumptions need to be questioned?

- What assumptions has the financial planner made in handing out this advice?

- What other questions does the financial planner need to ask before handing out any financial advice?

Before I give you my answers, I would suggest you sit around with some of your friends and have a discussion on the number of assumptions found in this financial-planner's answer. Just take the planner's answer, read it out loud, or give everyone a copy of it. Then ask your group to find as many assumptions as possible. I think you will find the process enlightening, educational, and possibly frightening. It may even inspire you to ask yourself about your own personal financial assumptions. All you have to do is question the assumptions found in the answer, and you might greatly improve your financial IQ.

The first assumption I would question would be: "If ever there was a time to stick with the plan, it's now." Obviously, the planner assumes this retiree has a plan or knows what the plan is. While many people do have plans, most are ignorant of the laws behind the plan.

I find this response interesting: "I feel your pain, but two-percent CDs and no growth aren't going to cut it." The financial planner assumes this retiree knows nothing about investing and is most likely thinking about putting money in two-percent CDs, which the retiree never said he was considering. I suspect that the reason the planner mentioned the option of two-percent CDs is because that is all the planner is familiar with. For all he knows, this 70-year-old retiree could be the best hedge-fund trader in the world, capable of taking his retirement and gaining a 100-percent leveraged return every 30 days in the futures markets. I realize this is doubtful, but my point is that the planner assumes this person knows nothing, even less than the planner.

If I were the planner, I would ask, "What is your investment experience? Do you have a portfolio of assets outside your retirement plan? Have you invested in other assets and done well? What investments do you feel comfortable and confident investing in?" In other words, I would first ask questions before handing out advice based upon the common financial-planner assumption that this retiree knows nothing about investing.

After assuming the retiree knows nothing, the planner then swings the advice around to this statement: "Check your mutual funds and make sure they're solid and leaning more to the conservative growth and growth income funds." The planner first assumed this retiree knows nothing. Then he assumes this retiree is savvy enough to know how to check out mutual funds to make sure they're solid.

The question I raise is: How does *anyone* know which mutual funds are solid? I sure don't. Besides, a mutual fund may be good one year and bad the next year. If you check the facts, many of the mutual funds people thought were solid turned out to be disasters during the last downturn. In 1999, there was one famous and well-promoted fund that was the darling of many financial advisors. It was considered a solid mutual fund and still is. But by 2001, this fund family had lost nearly 60 percent of its value. It will take years for this fund to return to its 1999 level.

The facts are that, today, there are more mutual funds than there are public companies whose shares the mutual funds buy. If this retiree could tell which of the approximately 12,000 mutual funds was the most solid and what's the next winner, then maybe he should come out of retirement and make a fortune advising the millions of people who are today wondering which mutual funds are solid. I find it absurd that this planner first assumes this retiree knows nothing about investing, and in the next sentence assumes this retiree is far more financially sophisticated than most people in the market.

There are many more assumptions and contradictions I could get into from this financial planner's advice. My point is this: I do not know how anyone can offer any kind of financial advice knowing so little about the special conditions of the person seeking answers. Yet the facts are, millions upon millions of people are being given what rich dad would call "white-bread financial advice." He called it that because it is financial advice for the masses. It is financial advice that follows a formula repeated by tens of thousands of financial advisors who are simply repeating sales pitches they are taught to say by the company selling the financial products.

Rich dad also called it "fast-food financial planning." When you look at the health problems of millions of people today, many are suffering because they are eating fast food that tastes good, is extensively advertised, well packaged, and easy to buy. Rich dad's concern was that the Western world would not only have a health problem caused by too much fast junk food, but also a wealth problem caused by too much fast junk investments.

He said, "Any food or investment that is too easy to buy, overly advertised, wrapped in convenient attractive packages with sales offices and salespeople on every corner, is probably not good for you." Rich dad went on to say, "Just as some of the best-tasting, healthiest, and best-value food I have found has been in tiny, out-of-the-way restaurants, some of the best investments I have found have been in tiny, obscure places run by true artists and gifted geniuses." He would remind his son and me, "Great food and great investments are found in similar places in every part of the world. The trouble is, bad food and bad investments can also be found in such places. If you want to find great food and great investments, you first have to know what great food and great investments are. Just because something is convenient, looks good, sounds good, is affordable, and everyone else is buying it, does not mean it is good for you."

Obviously, I could go on finding and challenging more of the assumptions found in the financial-planner's answer. That is not the point of this chapter. And in defense of the financial planner, the people in that profession have a massive job with millions of people to serve. Many times, all they can do is give fast, quick, prepackaged words of advice. I have several friends who are financial planners, and they often say, "If a person does not have at least $250,000 in cash to invest, I cannot afford to spend much time with them." In other words, if you don't have much money, most financial planners cannot afford the time to give you much advice. They too need to earn money so they can feed their family and invest for *their* retirement.

The primary assumption that I challenge in the newspaper article is the statement: "This is called a systematic withdrawal, and it works like a charm." The reason I challenge this assumption is because it is the underlying assumption of much of the financial-planning industry, so I am not going after the financial planner, but rather I am questioning the assumption of the industry. Much of the financial-planning industry runs on the assumption that the stock market always goes up. So when this financial planner said that "it works like a charm," a more accurate statement would be that "it works like a charm as long as the stock market goes up, if you have chosen the right funds, and if you have enough money in your portfolio." To me, that would have been a more truthful and accurate answer.

Any professional investor who has taken the time to study the history of markets knows that all markets go up and all markets go down. A true professional investor would never bet their future on the assumption that markets only go up, yet that is what millions of people are doing.

In *Rich Dad's Guide to Investing*, book number three of the Rich Dad series, I included charts of different market booms and busts. The following is the chart of the 1929 stock-market crash on Wall Street. Applying the assumption of the financial-planner's statement: "This is called a systematic withdrawal, and it works like a charm," to the actual numbers following the 1929 crash, this is what working like a charm would look like.

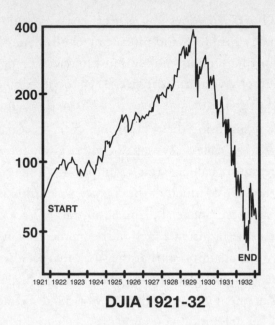

DJIA 1921-32

Let's say you follow the "systematic withdrawal" advice and you take out eight percent of the balance of your account per year, leaving the rest to grow "so you'll never be poor"—another assumption of the financial-planning industry. Let's say that at age 65, you have $1,000,000 (one million dollars), and you stay invested in the S&P 500 Index—a group of large, stable companies. The market behaves exactly like the market did in 1929.

The following is what would have happened to your DC retirement nest egg, adjusted for inflation, in the years following the 1929 crash:

Year End	Value Change	Ending Value	Cash to Live On
1929	just retired	$1,000,000	$80,000
1930	($461,840)	$487,719	$39,017

The 1930 numbers reflect a loss of $461,840 (parentheses around a number in accounting means it is a loss, not a gain), which means the remaining balance in the account is $487,719, down from the starting 1929 value of $1,000,000. This person has $39,017 (8 percent of $487,719) to live on in 1931.

Year End	Value Change	Ending Value	Cash to Live On
1931	($294,797)	$169,976	$13,598
1932	($10,946)	$162,166	$12,973
1933	$63,407	$211,441	$16,915
1934	($3,307)	$187,389	$14,991
1935	$98,267	$262,941	$21,035
1936	$145,144	$382,564	$30,607
1937	($291,789)	$58,391	$4,671
1938	$25,678	$81,632	$6,531
1939	($601)	$74,884	$5,991
1940	($13,503)	$54,826	$4,386
1941	($10,592)	$36,334	$3,242
1942	$10,864	$40,530	$2,935
1943	$18,644	$54,205	$4,336
1944	$23,887	$72,196	$5,776
1945	$70,339	$133,795	$10,704
1946	($39,389)	$70,858	$5,669

Summarizing these numbers, if a baby boomer with a DC plan has $1,000,000 at age 65, and the market follows the exact path the market followed after 1929, this baby boomer will lose over 90 percent of the $1,000,000 by age 82. Instead of living on $80,000 annually, by age 82 this baby boomer would be trying to live on $5,669 per year, which would be tough to do.

When the financial planner said, "This is called a systematic withdrawal, and it works like a charm," it will only work like a charm if the assumptions hold true (meaning that the market keeps going up).

But what if the assumptions do not hold true? What if the market does not respond according to predetermined assumptions? Then what would you say to that retiree 10 or 20 years from now?

Many of the financial-planning formulas assume that things will work out, based on the assumption that the market generally continues to go up. For the sake of millions of people, I hope these assumptions hold true.

Yet most professional investors know that in the real world, markets move in three basic directions.

1. Markets move up, which is called a bull market.

2. Markets move down, which is called a bear market.

3. Markets move sideways, which is called a channeling market.

The problem with most retirement portfolios is that they are based upon the assumption that markets ultimately move up in the long run. That is why they always say, "Invest for the long term." To compensate for market volatility—that is, the up, down, and sideways movements of markets—financial planners advise diversification as the solution. Again, this could work if the investor does invest for the long term and the investor does not happen to retire just at a market peak, leading to a market crash. If that happens, as you can see by the tables, all assumptions are off.

You may notice from the first table above that the market was very high in 1936, even higher than the 1929 peak. Yet, if the retiree had followed the law and continued to withdraw each month, the retiree would have had far less money with which to take advantage of the boom in 1936. This points out an unintended flaw in the law. The flaw is that the retiree has no downside protection and has only limited upside potential, because of systematic withdrawals, when the market does move up. As a professional investor, that scenario is far too risky to the downside and far too limiting to the upside.

Since markets move in three different directions and most portfolios are filled with investments that do well only in up markets, that means that most portfolios of average investors will only do well in one out of three market directions. Rich dad once told me, "Most of us have heard of Russian roulette. That is where a person takes a revolver with six chambers and puts one bullet in one of the chambers. They then spin the cylinder, put the gun to their head, and pull the trigger, hoping that the hammer lands on one of the five empty chambers. In other words, the odds are five to one in their favor. With most retirement plans loaded with mutual funds, a person is spinning a cylinder with only three chambers, and two out of three chambers are loaded." In other words, your chances of losing are two out of three. Talk about risky!

The truth is, diversification will not necessarily protect you from a flawed system with unlimited downside risk and limited upside potential. That means your retirement plan may not deliver what you need to live on if things do not go as planned, or assumed.

While it is true that the market did eventually rally and come back up after 1929, the facts are that the market was, for all practical purposes, down for nearly 25 years. While that may be a short period of time in the overall history of the markets, bear in mind that when the market plunged from 1929 to 1932, it wiped out 80 percent of most people's portfolios. Losing 80 percent of everything you spent a lifetime saving would have made those two years into two very long years. So even if the averages state that the markets tend to go up, living through years of successive down markets and watching your portfolio slowly diminish might cause you a few sleepless nights, even if you know that markets eventually do go back up again—as most people assume.

More Flaws

Before concluding this chapter on assumptions, I think it important to review some of the flaws already stated, as well as new flaws not yet covered—flaws caused by assumptions that are not usually questioned. The following are some of the more apparent flaws that rich dad saw.

1. **The law has a mandatory withdrawal mechanism.**
    This flaw will cause major problems around the year 2016
    when it is estimated that more than two million baby boomers
    will turn 70 years of age in America. In 2017, the number of
    people turning 70 years of age jumps to almost three million.
    The number continues to increase each year. In one year there
    is a jump of nearly 30 percent. That may give you an idea of
    the effect this baby-boom generation will have on DC pension
    plans and the stock market. As stated earlier, it's tough for a
    market to keep going up if people are required by law to sell
    what they own. It's like trying to fill a bathtub while more and
    more holes are punched in the tub. Pretty soon people do not
    want to fill the tub.

    When people ask why there is a mandatory withdrawal, the
    answer is simple—taxes. Since the money in a DC plan is
    contributed tax free and grows tax free, the question was:
    When will the government get its share? When will the money
    be taxed? So the government provided the answer: at 70.5
    years of age.

2. **The law failed to require the education system to provide
    the proper financial education.**
    A high financial IQ is mandatory for anyone who is serious
    about investing. When ERISA was passed, no one told the
    schools to start teaching financial literacy, and financial literacy
    is the basis of a person's financial IQ. Most people think
    investing is risky, when it does not have to be, simply because
    they have never been trained in the basics of financial matters.
    As rich dad said, "Anything is risky, even crossing the street, if
    no one has ever taught you how to do it."

3. **No one is questioning the assumptions.**
    The assumptions of the law are based on just that—
    assumptions, not facts. What happens if a retiree finds out
    at age 65 that the assumptions his financial planner used

40 years earlier were wrong? Does the retiree have any recourse? Advisors are simply handing out financial advice, and people are buying investments without asking many questions.

4. **There are too many mutual-fund companies.**
    Today, there are more mutual-fund companies than publicly listed companies, which makes it hard to figure out which funds are good and which funds are bad. That also means chances are good that the average investor may choose the wrong funds that do not provide the gains required for a financially secure retirement.

5. **The cost of retirement keeps going up.**
    Having more and more mutual funds chasing only a few real stocks from real companies causes the price of these companies' stock to be overinflated, which means the cost of retirement keeps going up.

6. **A DC plan does not protect you after retirement.**
    The stock market may crash after the person retires, wiping out the retiree's nest egg and financial security. Out of a job and out of time, it would be tough to rebuild that nest egg if the funds were lost. That is what happened to many of the Enron employees. They had all their eggs in one basket, Enron, which is why diversify, diversify, diversify is an essential strategy for anyone who has a limited financial education. The problem with diversification is that it is still a risky and poor choice.

7. **Many employees are not contributing to their retirement plans.**
    I have seen figures that range from 50 percent to 20 percent to 10 percent or less of all baby boomers have enough money set aside for retirement. That means an extra financial burden for the generation that follows the baby boomers—specifically, your kids.

One of the reasons workers are not contributing to their DC pension plans is because their taxes are high, the cost of living is high, the cost of raising and educating children keeps going up, and many workers simply do not realize that time— investing for the long term—is essential for the plan to work. If workers do not begin setting money aside early, the next flaw in the system takes priority.

8. **A DC plan may not work for older workers.**
   If a person is 45 years of age or older when they begin setting money aside for retirement, a DC pension plan may not work. There is simply not enough time for the plan to work. That means if a person begins setting money aside at 45 or older and has little to invest, or they lose their retirement and must start over again, the DC strategy may not work.

An article in the *Washington Post*, "401(k) Catch-Up Won't Be an Easy Game," includes the following observation:

Suppose that a person retires at 65 with a $600,000 nest egg and decides he needs $3,000 a month to live on and wants to maintain that level of buying power (meaning he will withdraw increasing amounts to keep up with inflation). If he lives 20 years to age 85, he has about a 3-in-10 chance of running out of money, according to calculators devised by T. Rowe Price.

Many of the baby-boom generation are only today finding out what they should have found out 25 years ago. And the truth is, many of them will have nowhere near $600,000 put away for retirement. It seems that millions of baby boomers are out of time because DC plans are not get-rich-quick plans. If a person is out of time, all the diversification in the world will only make their financial problems worse. Diversification is a defensive investment strategy. If you are out of time, a defensive strategy won't delay the inevitable.

9. **Too many non-investors are handing out investment advice.**
Many investment advisors educating the public are not really investors. They are salespeople. On top of that, many financial advisors do not really know if their advice will stand the test of time through the ups and downs of financial markets. Many investment advisors do not really know if the person they are advising will be able to survive on the advice and products they are selling. Most investment advisors are required to only sell their company's financial products, which limits their objectivity. On top of that, most advisors only know one category of investments such as paper assets, or real estate, or businesses. Very few have a well-rounded education and are qualified to talk on the synergy of these different asset classes. As Warren Buffett says, "Never ask the barber if you need a haircut."

10. **Can you afford to stay alive after you retire?**
As more and more baby boomers begin to retire, we will see the real test of the assumptions of a DC plan. While this act focuses on retirement, I wonder if a DC plan will provide for something more important than retirement, and that is health care. The question I ask is: "After retirement, will a retiree be able to afford health care for as long as they live?" A person can scale down and live frugally after retirement, but the price of health care is only going up. In the year 2000, the cost of health care and prescription drugs reportedly jumped by 17 percent. In other words, while the rest of the economy was deflating, the cost of health care was inflating. My concern is that, in the near future, whether a person lives or dies will be a matter of whether they can afford medical care or not. My concern is that millions of people will not have enough money inside their DC pension plans to afford that medical care.

What about Medicare and other forms of socialized medicine? Well, if the statistics are correct, American socialized medicine may already be bankrupt. If socialized medicine is to be a national right, then taxes will go through the roof. And if taxes go up, businesses will leave the country, aggravating an already overtaxed population.

If a person wants to plan for retirement in a DC pension plan, they must start early and put a lot of money away—enough money to not only afford retirement living, but also medical survival. In the coming years, many retirees may need to liquidate their portfolios to pay for medical care to extend their lives. My question is: When that financial planner said to the 70-year-old retiree, "This is called a systematic withdrawal, and it works like a charm," was the cost of this retiree's long-term health care factored into that answer? In other words, what were the assumptions behind the financial advisor's answer? Did the assumptions include health care?

In just a few years, not only will the market be hit by millions of baby boomers beginning their systematic withdrawals, the market will also be hit by millions of baby boomers needing money for medical expenses. Using a hypothetical crystal ball, let's say a 75-year-old retiree with a DC plan with $500,000 in assets in his portfolio has limited medical insurance and suddenly needs $150,000 for life-saving cancer surgery. Do you think this retiree will choose to save money and not have the surgery, or will he sell $150,000 worth of mutual funds to cover those expenses? My guess is that there will soon be millions of retirees selling large portions of their portfolios and not following the plan of systematic withdrawal in order to cover medical expenses. If that happens, what happens to the stock market? Will it continue to go up?

Many financial advisors are handing out financial advice that no one can yet prove will work. But sometime in the near future, we will find out if the assumptions of pension reform were right. Soon we will also find out if the assumptions that the financial-planning industry uses can withstand the financial tests that real life after retirement will present—assumptions based upon the idea that the stock market, on average, always goes up.

Are the Assumptions Valid?

Some people have referred to ERISA as a modified Ponzi scheme. Ponzi was a con man who had people give him money on the promise of high returns. He would then find a new group of people and promise them the same thing. He would take the money from the second group and give it to the people in the first group. The first group would tell all their friends, and then their friends became the third group, which gave high returns to the second group. The whole Ponzi scheme might have worked if someone had not figured out what Ponzi was doing. So instead of being the name of a hero, the name Ponzi today is infamous. When someone says that someone was caught in a Ponzi scheme, that means someone or a group of people were gullible enough to believe in what they knew was too good to be true.

I suspect that many of us have a part of us that wants to believe in things that are too good to be true. We like believing in magic, fairy godmothers, the Easter Bunny, and good spirits looking over us. That is why, when a financial advisor says, "This is called a systematic withdrawal, and it works like a charm," people believe it because they want to believe it, even though deep down they know it may not be true. Ponzi knew this about people, and that is why there will always be new Ponzi schemes, even though Ponzi is long gone.

I am not saying that ERISA is a Ponzi scheme, but I am saying that people do like believing in the idea that things will work like a charm. And things will work like a charm as long as the assumptions come true. If they don't come true, then the word *assume* turns into ass-u-me.

On a Positive Note

In theory, rich dad thought ERISA was built on some excellent ideals and values. The problem was the theory part of it. As we all know, there is often a very wide gap between theory and reality.

Upon researching the act, rich dad discovered that one of its ideals was to give the worker a piece of the action. Up to that point, a worker with a DB pension plan may have had financial security after retirement, but the worker had no real asset base to pass on to his or her heirs. For example, if a worker retired at 65 and died at 75, his benefits often ceased and the investment assets remained with the company. By utilizing a DC pension plan, if a worker passed away at age 75 and there was still something left in his portfolio, then the remaining assets in the retirement plan would be passed on to the family.

My poor dad had a DB pension plan so he had very little to pass on to his kids. He had a small government teacher's pension which provided him some degree of financial security each month, but when he died, he really had nothing to pass on. In other words, a DB pension plan is not a plan you pass on to your heirs.

On the other hand, if my dad had a DC pension plan, his kids would have inherited the remaining assets in his portfolio, if there were any—minus, of course, death taxes. In theory, a DC pension plan has some great benefits that the DB pension plan did not.

So a very positive point of DC pension plans was that it was an attempt to help spread the tremendous wealth of America and the world into the hands of the workers. In theory, the DC pension plan would give every worker a small piece of wealth since there is plenty of wealth to go around.

But of course, that is a great idea only in theory. The reality is, 90 percent of the wealth is held by only 10 percent of the people, and there is a reason for that. That reason will be further explained in the next chapter, a chapter about the biggest flaw of all that will trigger the biggest stock-market crash in history, the same flaw that causes the wealth of the world to remain with only 10 percent of the people.

The good news is that if you understand the next flaw and can overcome it, you have a better chance of becoming part of that 10 percent who controls 90 percent of the wealth.

Chapter Six

JUST BECAUSE YOU INVEST DOES NOT MEAN YOU ARE AN INVESTOR

Of all the flaws of pension reform, rich dad felt the biggest flaw of all was that it forced people who were not investors to invest. To rich dad, the assumption that a change in the law would suddenly turn people into overnight expert investors was an oversight of epic proportions. He said, "How can you take someone who has been programmed from birth to be a job-seeking employee to suddenly become a risk-taking investor? A security-seeking person is not the same person as a risk-taking investor." To rich dad, this assumption was the biggest flaw of all and would ultimately lead to the biggest stock-market crash in history.

Those of you who have read *Rich Dad's CASHFLOW Quadrant*, book number two in the Rich Dad series of books, are very familiar with the following diagram of the CASHFLOW Quadrant®.

For those not familiar with the CASHFLOW Quadrant or who have not read the book, I will briefly explain what the four letters stand for.

E   stands for employee.

S   stands for self-employed, specialist, or small business owner.

B   stands for big business owner.

I   stands for investor.

These are the four ways you earn money, or the four types of people. Each quadrant represents a different way of thinking about money and financial security.

Rich dad said, "The biggest flaw with ERISA is that the law assumes that people on the left side of the CASHFLOW Quadrant can easily switch to becoming people on the right side. People in each quadrant are different—very, very different. It's absurd to assume that someone in the E quadrant can become an investor in the I quadrant just because a law mandates the change. You can change laws with the stroke of a pen, but you cannot change people with the stroke of a pen."

Simply put, ERISA and subsequent amendments to ERISA mandated the following:

ERISA required employees to become investors.

They required millions of employees to become professional investors and, as we have seen, did so without developing an educational system to support this small but monumental change.

Our public school system trains people primarily for the E or S quadrants, which is why most people are either E's or S's. My poor dad, the head of education, constantly said, "Go to school and get good grades so you can get a safe, secure job." In other words, my poor dad was advising me to find safe sanctuary in the E quadrant. My mom, knowing that I wanted to become rich, often said, "I know you want to become rich, so go to medical school and become a doctor." She was advising me to find sanctuary in the S or self-employed quadrant. My response to her was, "There is only one problem with that idea, Mom. I'd have to be smart to be a doctor, and you know what my grades are." The S quadrant could stand for the smart quadrant since that is where professionals like doctors, lawyers, accountants, and engineers often reside, although any profession or intelligence level could reside in any of the four quadrants. S can also stand for specialists, people with some unique trade or skill, and it also stands for the millions of small independent business owners.

My rich dad trained his son and me to be people who operate in the B and I quadrants. For those of you who read my previous books, you may recall that rich dad had his son and me do almost every job possible inside his businesses. He was training us to know how many different types of jobs it takes to keep a business running. He also played *Monopoly*® with us by the hour, teaching us to think like investors. One of the primary reasons I have had a normal job for only four years is simply because rich dad trained me to operate on the right side of the CASHFLOW Quadrant, not the left.

When I was still a boy, rich dad said, "People gravitate to the different quadrants because people are different. A person who seeks the E quadrant wants security. That is why most people in the E quadrant, regardless if they are the president or the janitor of the company, will often say the same thing, which is, 'I'm looking for a safe, secure job, a steady paycheck, and excellent benefits.' Safety and security are paramount to people in the E quadrant. The world of the I quadrant, the investor quadrant, is not a world perceived as a world of safety and security. It can be, but not without proper training."

Again, there is a vast difference between the words *security* and *freedom*. Rich dad pointed out that people in the E and S quadrants often want security—security from a job for people in the E quadrant, and security of doing it on your own and not depending upon other people for those in the S quadrant.

People in the B and I quadrants want freedom, so they focus on assets that work for them. I can hear the howls of protest from the people in the S quadrant, generally people who want to do their own thing. But before you protest, consider that while most people in the S quadrant are free to be doing their own thing, the problem is *they* still have to be doing it, even if they love doing it. A person who is truly in the B or I quadrants is free to do nothing and still get paid, and that is the difference in freedoms. (For those who have not read *Rich Dad's CASHFLOW Quadrant*, you may want to because the book goes into far more detail about the core differences between the different people in the different quadrants. It is a very important book for anyone serious about making changes in their life, rather than simply going from job to job in the E quadrant or working hard all your life in the S quadrant.)

The other day, I was talking to a young man at an investment conference who told me he was an investor. I asked him what he invested in. His reply was, "I have a company 401(k) plan that has a well-diversified portfolio of large cap, small cap, a few sector funds, and of course a bond fund."

As I nodded my head, I silently said to myself, "Wall Street has done a good job educating this lifelong customer." Not wanting to burst his bubble, I asked, "How much income do you receive a month from your investments?"

"Income?" he replied. "Why, none. I don't have any income. Each month I send a portion of my income through a payroll deduction to these mutual-fund companies."

"And when do you expect to receive some income from these investments?" I asked.

"Oh, I'm 27 now. I plan on letting my money grow tax free until I retire, hopefully by age 60. Then I'll switch my portfolio to a self-directed account and live off my investments. You see, I'm investing for the long term."

"Congratulations," I said, shaking his hand. "Keep on investing,"

The point is, this young man may be *investing*, but I would not call him an *investor*—at least not from the definition rich dad used when referring to the CASHFLOW Quadrant. According to rich dad, investors receive money from their investments on a regular basis. Until you begin receiving money, you may be investing, but you are not an investor. To prove to rich dad that I was an investor, I had to prove to him that money was flowing *in*, and had stopped flowing *out*. Recently, millions of DC-plan investors found out that the money they have been investing flowed out of their pockets and then flowed out of their DC plans. That is why there are so many upset investors today. They may be investing, but they are not investors.

When it comes to investing, many people are excellent at having money flow out, but only a few are excellent at having money flow in—and having money flow in is what makes you a good investor. When it comes to investing, most people have money flowing out and almost nothing flowing back in. After ERISA was passed, millions of people began investing, but we do not yet know if they will become investors. Only time will tell how many make the transition from the E, S, or B quadrant to the I quadrant once their working days are over.

In the movie *Jerry Maguire*, there is a classic line that goes, "Show me the money." My friends who are hard-core investors consider that line sacred. They know investing money does not necessarily mean the investment will return the money. For my circle of friends, an investment is not real until the invested money comes back. Once the money comes back, that investment should have more money flowing in. Right now, for millions of people with DC pension plans, money is flowing out, and millions are wondering if it will ever flow back in. Many have called their brokers and asked them to "show me the money."

The other night, my wife and I were at a party and the hostess asked my wife what she did for a living. Kim simply said, "I invest in real estate." The hostess's eyes lit up and said, "So do I. My husband and I started with a small house and sold it when it went up in value. We have done this three times and now look at our home. We kept investing in real estate and now we live in this lovely home."

I know that in her mind, our friend thinks she is a real investor, and technically she is. Yet in our circle of friends, she would not be called a real estate investor. She would be called a homeowner who got lucky. Although she does have a lovely home, there is a tremendous difference between a real estate investor who owns a home that *costs* them $5,000 a month and a real estate investor who *earns* $5,000 a month in net income. By our investment group's definition, a real estate investor has income coming in every month from rental homes, commercial property, warehouses, office buildings, and so forth. In other words, regardless if we work or not, we can show the money coming in.

The Biggest Flaw of All

So why did rich dad feel that forcing people from the E quadrant into the I quadrant was the biggest flaw of all? The answer again is because they have completely different personalities.

People in the E and S quadrants work for money.

People in the B and I quadrants work to build or acquire assets.

This may seem like a small difference on paper, but after a person retires, the differences are substantial. As a professional investor with years of training, learning to "show the money" on a monthly basis from my investments is not the easiest thing to do, but that is what ERISA has asked everybody to do. Once a person with a DC plan retires, they will be shoved out of the safe sanctuary of their job. For many, they will have to face the real world for the first time in their lives—the real world rich dad faced at 13, that I faced at 32, that my dad faced at 53, and that the Enron employee on the front page of *USA TODAY* faced at 58.

Meeting the Real World

In the good old days, once an employee retired, there may have been a retirement party, a gold watch, and a DB pension plan to watch over them for the rest of their lives. In other words, they could retire and count on the check being in the mail. That is all they had to do.

Also in the good old days, if the retiree had worked for a generous company or the company had a strong union, they might have received a COLA, a Cost-Of-Living Adjustment. As inflation went up, so did their defined-benefit payments. Some also had medical plans for as long as the retiree lived. The retiree could go to the doctor, and the company would show the doctor the money.

DB pension plans became very, very expensive as more people retired and lived longer through improved health care. These large liabilities are some of the real reasons why ERISA was legislated. Employees with DB and medical plans were simply too expensive in a world of increasing global competition.

In today's world, once employees retire, there may still be a retirement party and a gold watch, but they may very likely find themselves on their own. Some may keep their money with the company's pension plan, while others may elect to roll it over into an IRA, an individual retirement account. Still others will sell their financial assets for cash and put the money in the bank.

The following are the three real reasons why rich dad saw the coming of the biggest stock-market crash in history.

1. *There will be a market sell-off caused by baby boomers converting to cash.*

   Rich dad said, "E's and S's work all their lives for money, not for financial assets. Most E's and S's do not trust the stock market. Once they leave the company, all the fear and insecurity that have always been there—the fear and insecurity that caused them to be an E or S all their lives—will only increase. Once they leave, they will cling to what they know and trust, and that is cash—not stocks or mutual funds."

According to *Business Week* magazine, in 1990 there was $712 billion in 401(k)s and similar plans, with only 45 percent in stocks. Ten years later, that amount had swelled to $2.5 trillion, with 72 percent in stocks or similar equities. In other words, as the money from retirement funds came in, a market boom was underway. As the boom increased, so-called investors became more confident and began taking their cash and buying equities with it, simply because they could get a much higher return from equities. As the boom progressed, many so-called investors entered the party late and began taking money out of their savings and putting it into the market, primarily into mutual funds, swelling that asset class to $4 trillion. About that same time, reports came out that the family savings rate of America had dropped to less than 1 percent. A mania was on, and people who should never have been in the market were now in the market.

Many people who were investing in their DC pension plans saw their plans increase in value. Immediately they believed that they were now real investors and began taking their savings and putting it all into the market. Most of these people came from the E and S quadrants. People who should have remained savers suddenly starting investing, but they were not investors.

Rich dad believed that the biggest stock-market crash in history will be caused when millions of people begin to sell financial assets they do not understand and do not trust. Rich dad said, "People in the E quadrant love security. If they feel their security is being threatened, they will not hold on to their financial assets. If they feel insecure, there will not be any "systematic withdrawal," as the pension reform calls for. Instead, there will be a wholesale panic caused by baby boomers converting financial assets back to cash for their savings accounts—as quickly as possible."

At first, I did not understand what rich dad was getting at. Now that I am older, I am more aware of that subtle difference. Today, I am very aware of that difference whenever I hear people say, "I am saving for my retirement," or "I am saving for my child's education." Rarely do I hear people say, "I am *investing* for my retirement," or "I am *investing* for my child's education." As rich dad said, "Savers and investors are not the same people. Savers feel secure with money, not with mutual funds. When push comes to shove, they will sell. And when millions of them begin to sell, the market will crash. There will be no systematic withdrawal."

Japan has teetered on the brink of a banking and financial disaster for many years now. At the same time, Japan's banks are bursting with money because most Japanese are employees and savers. In fact, Japan has the highest savings rate in the world. Because the banks are so flush with money, the interest rate paid on those savings is nearly zero percent. Even though the banks pay the Japanese nothing for their savings, the money sits in the banks. Why? Because employees and savers would rather have money earning nothing than take a risk. I predict that in a few years U.S. banks will also be flush with money. If banks are filled with money, it's going to be tough for them to pay 10-percent interest to savers on that money. As I write, the U.S. banks are paying 2-percent interest on savings. Two percent is not a very good return on your investment.

So the primary reason for the coming crash is that most people today do not naturally feel secure with mutual funds and stocks. Once they begin to retire, millions of baby boomers will cash in their stocks and mutual funds and return to what they have spent their lives working for—cash. As rich dad said, "You can change the law, but you cannot change people."

2. *The cost of living and medical expenses will go up.*
   As stated earlier, with many DB pension plans, there was a cost-of-living adjustment. With a DC pension plan, after retirement, when the cost of living goes up and medical expenses go up, the retiree will sell their assets to pay for these life expenses. Again, this will blow the systematic-withdrawal theory out the window. These slight differences between a DB plan and a DC plan will also add to the coming market crash. People have to have money, not mutual funds, to live on, so the mutual funds will be sold for cash.

3. *The number of fools will increase.*
   Quoting Warren Buffett, "The fact that people will be full of greed, fear, or folly is predictable. The sequence is not predictable."

Most of us know that any market is run on greed and fear. The reason the market went up in the 1990s was because of greed, and the reason it will go down is because of fear. In the near future, one more reason people will turn their retirement account into cash is because of folly.

I will give you an example of investment folly. During the 1990s, I met many rich employees who thought they became rich because they were investors, but in reality, they were lucky employees. One person I met was an employee of Intel. In 1997, just as the market was climbing, he cashed in his options for nearly $35 million. He thought for sure he was an investor, rather than just a lucky employee. He was soon out investing in investments only reserved for what the Securities and Exchange Commission classifies as an *accredited investor*. By definition, an accredited investor is a person with over $1 million net worth. Now, how that qualifies a person to be an accredited investor is beyond me, but those are the rules. I have a better way for a person to prove they are an accredited investor, but the SEC has not called to ask me for my opinion.

In any event, this ex-Intel investor with his millions of dollars let the money go to his head, and he began investing in anything that moved. He bought private placements and partnerships in companies. He bought companies outright and had his sons and daughters run them. And he bought doodads that only truly rich people buy—doodads such as a private jet, a yacht, and two large homes. On top of that, he met a woman younger than his daughter and then divorced his wife, who received a sizable sum of money. Rich dad often said, "A fool and his money are one big party." And let me tell you, this guy could throw a party.

Today, he is bankrupt. How do I know? I know because he came asking me for a job. He needs a job because his second ex-wife got the rest of the money. He is only one of dozens of such people I met during the roaring 1990s. They were employees who got lucky and thought they were investors, but found out they were fools who threw big parties. Nothing wrong with big parties. Just make sure you can afford to throw another one.

This example of investment folly is found with sports stars, movie stars, rock stars, lottery winners, people who suddenly inherit a large sum of money, and anyone else who is fooled into believing that investing money and becoming an investor are the same thing. A few years from now, as some of the luckier baby boomers begin retiring with large sums of money in their DC pension plans, you will begin reading about fools being swindled out of their retirement money. Many will be swindled because they did not make the distinction between investing money and becoming an investor.

In conclusion, the biggest flaw of all, according to rich dad, was that although people invest, most do not become investors. He said, "This small and seemingly trivial point has the potential to bring down the stock market." So rich dad's prophecy was that sometime in the near future, millions of people will slowly wake up and realize they were encouraged to buy something (a DC plan) they really did not want and could not sell unless they were willing to pay a huge tax penalty for early withdrawal. On top of that, many are encouraged to invest in products they do not really value, do not understand, and think they paid too much for. He said, "At that point, savers will begin converting their investments back to what they have worked all their lives for. And what they worked for was cash—not stocks, bonds, or mutual funds. The market crash will take place because people were encouraged under law to invest, but they never learned to become investors. Remember, investors love assets. Savers love *cash*. That is why you hear so many people say, 'Safe as money in the bank.'"

Rich dad once explained to me that his definition of *financial mania* is "an irrational conversion of cash to financial assets such as stocks, bonds, real estate, and mutual funds." Over the centuries, there have been many manias. One of the more famous (or infamous) is the tulip-bulb mania in Holland from 1634 to 1637. The tulip-bulb mania was caused when the Dutch fell madly in love with this new flower imported from China. Soon they began to create new varieties, and it was not long before a mania was on. Certain tulip bulbs were commanding more than a hundred times their weight in gold. Suddenly the mania was over and a panic began, the panic to convert their bulbs back to cash. Today, the tulip-bulb mania sounds as ridiculous as the dotcom mania of just a few years ago.

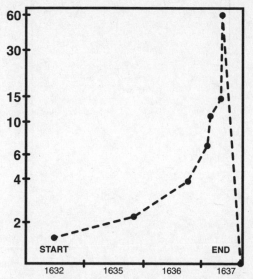

Gouda Tulip Bulb Mania 1634-1637
Based on historical estimates

Rich dad's definition of a *financial panic* is "an irrational conversion of financial assets back to cash." In other words, people suddenly wake up and realize that what they bought is not worth what they paid, and they want their money back. It's often called "buyer's remorse." When millions of people who invested in mutual funds and other financial assets experience buyer's remorse and demand their money back, a panic will occur. That panic will lead to a crash—the biggest crash in the history of the world. As rich dad said, "Just because you invest does not mean you're an investor."

Chapter Seven

EVERYONE NEEDS TO BECOME AN INVESTOR

"Don't they realize how important investing is?" I asked rich dad. We were walking out of a hotel ballroom where rich dad had held a meeting for his key management team and his top employees, about 125 people.

"We shall see," said rich dad. "I've done my best to convince them, but I can only push so hard. This 401(k) plan we've implemented is a benefit, but many of the workers aren't contributing to the plan. Some only contribute a little. Even some in the management team have stopped contributing. I don't know what they expect to live on once they retire."

The year was 1988. I was passing through Hawaii on my way to the Far East, and rich dad asked me if I wanted to attend this meeting. The 1987 stock-market crash had frightened many of them, and they had stopped contributing to their DC retirement plan.

"I called in the representative from the fund management company to explain to the workers once again how their 401(k) plan works. The potential fiduciary liability prevented this investment advisor from giving specific investment advice. She only presented the information, but did not advise the person what to buy. So she explained the plan but did not go into much detail. That did not make the employees feel too secure since they have no idea what to invest in. Why does the law prevent the people who run the plan from giving the employees a little bit more specific advice?"

"I did not know that," I said. "All these years, I never understood why the advisors just presented the plan but not much advice. Today I learned it was because of the potential fiduciary liability. The representative did say you were a generous employer because you were willing to match the employee's contribution dollar for dollar."

"Many employers do not match any funds at all, and some only match 50 cents on the dollar. Even though I am willing to be generous, there are still only a few employees contributing on a regular basis," said rich dad.

"Even if they don't get much investment advice, don't the employees realize that every dollar you contribute is like receiving tax-free money?" I asked. "All they have to do is put in a dollar that is also tax free."

"They hear the words," said rich dad. "I've been saying the same thing for years, but nothing seems to change. I even told them that a person who is contributing to the plan is making more money than those who are not. Even that failed to change things. Then after the stock-market crash, some of those who used to contribute stopped contributing. That is why I asked the representative from the fund company to stop by and speak to them. I hope it does some good."

We continued our conversation all the way back to his office, which was just down the street from the hotel where the meeting was held. Again I asked the question, "Don't they realize how important investing is?"

"I believe they do," rich dad replied.

"So why don't they invest?" I asked.

With that question, rich dad sat down at his desk and began to write the following words on his yellow legal tablet:

RICH

MIDDLE CLASS

POOR

Looking up at me, he said, "Every one of us invests in one way or another. We simply invest in different things and in different ways." He then wrote the following after each class:

RICH

Good financial education

Build businesses

Large real estate investments

Private-equity funds

Hedge funds

Personal money manager

Private placements

Limited partnerships

MIDDLE-CLASS

Good education

High-paying job

Profession

Home

Savings

Retirement plan

Mutual funds

Small real estate investments

POOR

Large family

Government support programs

"These are the different investments the different classes invest in," said rich dad. "The poor often have large families, trusting that their kids will take care of them in their old age. They also count on government programs such as Social Security, welfare, and Medicare."

"The poor invest in kids?" I responded incredulously.

Rich dad nodded. "That is a broad generalization, but you will find some truth in that statement. They may not say it, but they expect their kids to support them when they stop working."

"And the middle class invests in a good education so they can get a high-paying job," I said, reading from rich dad's tablet. "To them, that is an investment?"

"Sure," smiled rich dad. "Isn't it true in your family? Isn't it important to your mom and dad that you have a college degree, and possibly a profession such as doctor, lawyer, or a job title such as vice president or general manager?"

I agreed. "Education is very important in our family. My mom really wanted me to become a doctor, and my dad always thought I should go to law school."

Rich dad chuckled. "And don't they insist you buy a home and have a retirement plan? In fact, didn't you tell me that your dad wanted you to stay in the Marine Corps because it had a great retirement plan with benefits?"

Again I nodded. "But don't the poor want the same things, at least in their work?"

"They may dream of a high-paying job, but dreams are dreams and reality is reality. If you notice, most of my lower-paid employees move from job to job simply because it's easy to move from job to job, as long as you do not expect high pay. So they may dream of finding a great high-paying job, but in reality, without a good education or some technical skills, a high-paying job is out of the question."

"So they spend most of their money just surviving, keeping their kids clothed and fed. That is what they invest in."

Rich dad nodded, tapping his pencil on the investment of the poor.

"Now my college-educated managers are different," he said, shifting his pencil to the investments of the middle class. "As employees, they tend to stay longer because they know that if they leave, they have to start all over again, often at the bottom of the ladder. That is why they like job titles and seniority. It also takes longer to find a job if you expect higher pay. So they invest more time in a good education, high pay, job security, promotions, and titles. That is what is important to the middle class. As I said, people invest, but they invest in different ways. People invest time and money only into what they think is important."

"So the rich build businesses and invest in larger pieces of real estate," I said. "Or they invest in private-equity funds or hedge funds, while the middle class has mutual funds."

Rich dad went on, "Or the rich invest in syndications, partnerships, or they have personal fund managers who do it for them. They invest in investments reserved only for the rich."

"But isn't a college education important to everyone?" I asked.

"Yes, it is," said rich dad. "In fact, if you look at all three classes and their investments, all three classes of investments are important, even to the rich."

"You mean the rich need large families?" I asked.

"Not necessarily large, but family is important to all of us, regardless of which class. And government support is also important for the rich. If the government did not support the poor with welfare programs, there would be beggars in the streets and burglars in the homes of the rich. So the rich invest in government support through their taxes or charitable donations."

Rich dad went on to explain that if I wanted to be rich, I needed to invest in all three classes. In other words, if I wanted to be rich, I had to invest far more than the other two classes of people. He said, "If you want to be rich, I strongly recommend you invest in what the poor invest in, the middle class invest in, and what the rich invest in. Do not—I repeat, do not try to skip over any of the first two investments. If you want to be rich, you must invest more, not less, than the first two groups."

He continued by pointing out to me the importance of family, home, and a retirement plan. He said, "Many people try to get rich without those pillars of support, and that is very risky. Pointing to family he said, "Family is very important to me. That is why I invest a lot of time and money in my family. I need them for emotional support, just as you need Kim for emotional support. I have met many people who ignore their families. They sacrifice time with family for time at work. Or even worse, people cheat on their families. You and I have met people who cheat on their husband or wife thinking that a little affair doesn't matter, but it does. A strong family is important to me, and I trust it is to you."

The discussion of family made sense to me. Before rich dad left the discussion of family, I added, "Because you are rich, you have more time with your family. My dad was often gone for days on business trips. He said he needed to travel if he wanted to get his pay raise and promotion so he could put food on the table and buy a bigger house."

"I know," said rich dad. "Many people ignore their families for a pay raise, promotion, and trying to look rich by buying a big house. As I said, people invest in what they think is important. But in my mind, that is not investing. That is financial and family suicide. How many parents today have no time for their kids? Where would you be today if I had not spent so much time with you teaching you about business and investing? Your father did not have the time. He was too busy working hard to make big house payments."

As rich dad spoke, it began to sink in why he always talked about a plan. Rich dad said there were investment plans to be safe, comfortable, and rich. He was a stickler for developing a plan and following it. He had a plan to become rich because he wanted the free time to spend with his kids.

My poor dad's plan was to continually go back to school so he could be promoted and receive higher pay. Although he did his best to be at home with the kids, the reality was that he was often on the road while rich dad was at home, letting his employees run his businesses and investments. I now realized how important all three levels of investment were. Suddenly, it struck me that I had many friends who only wanted to get rich and did not invest in the first two classes of investments. So I asked, "But what about people who invest in the investments of the rich but do not have the first two levels. What happens to them?"

"Some make it," said rich dad, "but very few do. I meet so many people investing in the investments of the rich before investing in the first two steps. I meet people who invest in wild business schemes with lofty tales of making billions of dollars, but most of those people lose their money because they fall victim to the con men, crooks, and dreamers of the business world. Most who try to win big without a strong foundation wind up losers."

Nodding, I could only laugh at myself, saying, "I've met many of those people along the way. In fact, I was one of those people when I was just starting out."

Rich dad grinned and said, "I know. You sure had some wild stories about how you were going to strike it rich. The problem is, you did strike it rich with your first business. The trouble was that you got lucky, but you did not have the skills to maintain your luck. That is when you and the three clowns who were your partners went broke. You had the business, the rich level of investment, but you boys forgot about the importance of the first two levels, the middle-class and poor levels. That is why, when your business struck it rich, instead of you and your partners becoming rich, you became clowns and lost it all."

"So now I have all three levels," I said. "Hopefully, I have the skills and the maturity to develop all three levels."

"I hope so too," said rich dad quietly. "But don't worry. Investing on all three levels is a full-time job, and you will have your challenges in the future, just as my employees will have their challenges in the future."

"So the lesson of the day is that as individuals, we tend to only invest in what we think is important," I added. "Many of your employees know investing is important to them, but investing is not yet important enough. They have other things they invest in that are more important, and that is where their time and money goes."

"Exactly," said rich dad. "Look at the differences between your dad and me. Your dad says his house is his biggest investment. To him, his home is far more important than his stock portfolio or industrial real estate, which I invest in. That is why his college degrees and job title are more important to him than going to school to learn to invest. I invest time and money in what I think is important, and he invests time and money in what he thinks is important. The problem is, now that he has lost his job and most of his savings, he is finding out how unimportant what he thought was important really is in the real world. He is finding out that his big house is not really an asset, and he found out that his college degrees and work experience did not help him in the real business world or in the investment markets. The real world is very different than the world of education or the world of government. What he invested in will not pay off in the real world."

You Can Train a Monkey to Save Money

In my previous books I wrote about the three different types of education.

1. Academic education

2. Professional education

3. Financial education

My poor dad was well educated in the first two. My rich dad was very well educated in the third—financial education. When ERISA was passed, rich dad quickly realized that the law failed to make universal financial education essential. In 1988, he also found out that some financial advisors were by law limited in what kind of advice they could offer. The result is that most people will do what they always do. They will not make the transition from the E or S quadrant to the I quadrant when they retire.

Again taking his legal pad, rich dad pointed to his comparison between the rich and what the middle class thought was important. Pointing to the word *save*, he said, "How much financial intelligence does it take to save money?"

"I don't know," I replied. "I never really thought about it."

"Well, in my opinion, it takes no financial intelligence at all. I could train a monkey to save money," he chuckled. "Many people think they're so smart for saving money. All one has to do is walk up to the bank teller, and if you're really incompetent, the teller will fill out the deposit slip for you. What is so hard about that? Saving money may be smart, but it doesn't require much financial intelligence."

"You could train a monkey to save money?"

"I'm sure I could," smiled rich dad. "Look, I'm just making a point about how little financial intelligence most people have. If most people have trouble saving money, how much chance do they have with more sophisticated investments? Look at your dad. He is a highly educated man, but he couldn't make a simple ice cream stand profitable. He was a saver, but he was not an investor, much less a businessman. He had no business investing in that venture."

"He felt he got cheated, but the facts were that he could not read a financial statement or the prospectus on the franchise," I said. "I asked him to have you look at the business and the numbers, but his pride wouldn't allow that to happen. He said that you did not have a college degree so he would never ask you for any advice."

Rich dad shook his head. "It takes financial education to invest in these investments, financial education your dad does not have even though he has a college degree," he said, pointing to the investments of the rich.

RICH

Good financial education

Build businesses

Large real estate investments

Private-equity funds

Hedge funds

Personal money manager

Private placements

Limited partnerships

Then, pointing to the column of the middle class, he said, "It takes very little financial education to invest in any of the investments this group invests in. As I said, I could train a monkey to save money. After that, I would train it to buy mutual funds. In fact, every year someone has a contest where a monkey throws darts at a list of stocks to see if the monkey can beat the pros who pick stocks—and the monkey often wins."

MIDDLE CLASS

Good education

High-paying job

Profession

Home

Savings

Retirement plan

Mutual funds

Small real estate investments

"So the reason the middle class does not get rich is because of the lack of financial education?" I asked.

"Well, some do get rich," said rich dad. "But without a sound financial education, it takes a lot of hard work to make a lot of money, and it also takes a lot more money to stay rich. Also, the lower your financial IQ, the more at risk you put your money. That is why the middle class focuses on saving money while the rich focus on investing money. That is why the middle class often puts so much money into their home instead of investment real estate. The difference is financial education. If they had a better financial education, they would understand why owning a home and saving money are really risky, and why investing in investment real estate is more intelligent."

"So after I rebuild my business, then I can begin investing in the investments of the rich," I said, pointing to the top line of what the rich invest in.

"You can do what you want. Today I am only pointing out to you that people only invest in what they think is important. Many of my employees do not think their pension plan is important. They have other things to do with their money, things they think are more important," said rich dad. "If you want to invest in the investments of the rich, I'm recommending you continue to invest in your financial education. If you have a high financial IQ, what seems risky to most people will be safe to you. And what seems safe to the poor and the middle class will seem risky to you. It's all a matter of what you think is important. That is what you will ultimately invest in. I leave that decision to you."

A large market crash only frightens people with a limited financial education. A large market crash is the best time to get rich for those with a strong financial education. As rich dad often said, "If you have a strong financial education, you are not worried about markets going up or down. You're just happy they are going up and down."

Chapter Eight

THE CAUSE
OF THE PROBLEM

ERISA will not be the cause of the coming stock-market crash. ERISA, Enron, and the coming giant crash are really only symptoms of a much deeper problem. This chapter is about the problems behind the problem and how we can begin once and for all to solve them. In this chapter, we get to the real reason behind rich dad's prophecy.

Social Security and Medicare are taking on water. The Clinton administration's fiscal 2000 budget report stated, "Government trust funds do not consist of real economic assets that can be used in the future to fund benefits." In other words, the government is finally admitting that there really is no Social Security trust fund. It is a figment of our imagination. Is Social Security merely a modified Ponzi scheme?

In America today, every employee looks at their pay stub and they see 7.65 percent of their pay, matched by the employer's 7.65 percent, for a total of 15.3 percent, going to Social Security and Medicare. Every employee is hoping that after retirement, they will be on the receiving end. They can be if there are enough employees still at the front door turning in their money. The problem is, because people are living longer, there are more and more retired people waiting at the back door. Is this a scheme that works only as long as there are more people at the front door than the back door?

For decades, the federal government has borrowed and spent the Social Security surplus—the difference between Social Security's tax revenues and outlays. The government replaces the money it borrows with IOUs in the form of U.S. Treasury bonds. In recent years, many critics began to say that the Social Security system is a shell game, that there is nothing in the trust fund. In return, government bureaucrats criticize the critics, denying that there is a problem. In the year 2000, the Clinton administration came clean and published the statement fundamentally saying that there really is no trust fund. It marked *the first time* that the government finally acknowledged there is a problem. Does the problem sound similar to the problems with Enron?

The Social Security system worked fine when it began in the mid-1950s when there were 42 workers for every one Social Security recipient. In the year 2000, the number was 3.4 workers per one recipient. By 2016, according to the commission's report, Social Security will collect less money in tax revenues than it pays out. In other words, there will be too many people at the back door.

If you remember from an earlier chapter, 2016 is the same year that the first of the baby-boom generation turns 70—a jump of 700,000 people turning 70 in that year alone. The number of people over 70 years of age will continue to increase with each subsequent year. That is what I call a perfect storm brewing.

In 1979, I did not fully understand why rich dad was so concerned about the future. I wondered why a rich man would have such a doom-and-gloom prophecy. I wondered why he would care. Although I did not fully understand his logic, I trusted him enough to continue building my ark. That is why I did not take the sales-manager's job, or any other job, even though the pay and benefits were great. Instead of taking the job, I decided to stand and face the real world early in life, rather than face the real world later in life. By 1994, Kim and I were financially free. We had built an ark that kept us afloat. Our ark did well when the stock market went up in the late 1990s, and the ark kept us afloat even as the market crashed in March of 2000. In fact, we made even more money as the market crashed. Today, because of my own personal experiences on what it takes to build a personal ark, I better understand why rich dad was so concerned about the future—a future he knew his son and I would see.

Pushing the Problem Forward

Rich dad saw that the real cause for concern was that the issue of personal financial survival after retirement was being pushed forward. That is why he repeatedly said, "ERISA is the problem my generation is passing on to your generation."

One of the more important lessons rich dad taught his son and me was the difference between a businessperson and a government bureaucrat. Rich dad said, "A businessperson is a person who solves financial problems. If they do not solve their financial problems, they are out of business. If a government bureaucrat cannot solve a problem, a bureaucrat can afford to push the problem forward."

Rich dad was not being critical of government. He was just being observant. He said, "Governments solve many problems for the good of society. It is the government that uses our tax dollars to provide military defense, fight fires, provide police protection, build roads, provide schools, and provide welfare for the needy. But there are problems that government cannot solve and when those problems are pushed forward, they often become bigger and bigger problems. This problem of financial survival once a person's working years are over is a monster of a problem that is growing bigger. The problem constantly grows bigger because too many people expect the government to solve what is really a personal financial problem."

Rich dad was worried that people were never taught how to build their own ark. Over the years, they have been taught to depend on a company and the government to provide that ark for them. As the problem became too complex to solve, laws were passed to pass the expense of retirement on to the next generation. In other words, Social Security and ERISA pass the expense of the care of one generation on to future generations.

Then in 1996, a new DC investment plan entered the market. It is the Roth IRA, named after the senator who championed it. The Roth IRA is a newer DC plan designed only for the middle class. If you are rich, you are not allowed to have one.

Soon after the Roth IRA came out, my tax advisor called me. She was very concerned about this new DC plan, which allows its owner to receive tax-free payouts after retirement for funds taxed before entering the plan. The Roth IRA was once again pushing the problem forward, this time from the baby-boom generation to future generations.

The Roth IRA was primarily created to collect more taxes. She said, "If you notice, there was a surplus of money in the budget soon after the Roth IRA was passed. I suspect the Clinton administration passed this law because they needed more taxes and wanted to create the illusion that they were doing a good job. The problem is, when the baby boomers begin to retire, it is their kids who will have to pay those taxes to make up for the future budget shortfalls." In other words, the problem has been passed forward again.

Almost immediately, the Roth IRA was the darling of the middle class. They loved the idea of paying taxes now but being allowed to pull out the gains tax free in the future. Because the market was going up in 1996, many people saw this Roth IRA as a gift from heaven. Money, greed, a rising market, and the new Roth IRA were all these people needed. Money began pouring into these new IRAs and directly into an already overheated stock market. The market took off like a rocket ship.

One of the ways the government made more money was that many people stopped contributing to their 401(k) DC plans and shifted money to their new Roth IRA. That meant the taxman collected more money from the middle class, since only after-tax dollars are allowed to go into a Roth IRA.

The traditional 401(k) DC plan allows the employee and employer to put untaxed dollars into the plan. That means the taxman gets no revenue from those dollars. The taxman then has to wait until the employee retires before the government can begin collecting taxes.

With the Roth IRA, many people stopped contributing to their company's 401(k) plan and put the money instead into this new Roth IRA. When this happened, the government got paid today but not tomorrow. The problem is tomorrow. In the future, there will be fewer taxes to be collected. Again, this will be a major problem down the road.

But the Roth IRA did one more thing. It inspired many people without a retirement plan to open one. Not only were there many new people entering the market via their new Roth IRAs, money was also flowing out of savings accounts and some people were even borrowing money to invest. With so much money pouring into the market, the market continued its climb. People began to say, "This time it's different. It's the new economy." By 1998 millions of non-investors who got lucky in the market the year before and who now thought they were investors suddenly began an investing frenzy just because of fear and greed.

People even quit their jobs to become investment advisors. Little old retired ladies formed investment clubs, wrote books, and began handing out investment advice. Unfortunately, it was later disclosed that the little old ladies really hadn't done as well as they thought they had with their investments. Nevertheless, they did inspire others to form investment clubs all across the country, which I think is a very good idea. Investment expos sprung up and they were packed with thousands of people who had been bitten by the bug. By 1999 shoeshine boys and taxi drivers were handing out hot stock tips, and the stock market went straight on up to all-new highs. Between 1996 and 2000, many people who had no business investing began pouring money they could not afford to lose into the market. A mania was on. Greed and fear had become one, 25 years after the passage of ERISA. The foxes were grinning as they watched the chickens cluck with excitement. The foxes knew it was time to take a little of their winnings off the table—not all, just a little. The foxes know there is still one more run to go.

In March of 2000, the party came to an end, but of course, many people did not want to believe it. Yet slowly but surely, the reality of the real world sank in. The opening paragraph of the lead story from the February 25, 2002, *Business Week* says it all:

> *It's 2 a.m., and Jim Tucci is staring wide-eyed at the ceiling— another sleepless night. Instead of counting sheep, he's anxiously tallying up how much he has lost in the stock market. Half of his $400,000 nest egg, he figures, has evaporated in just two years. Forget the retirement property on the Gulf coast. Forget the long-planned trip to Italy with his wife. Tucci, a 60-year-old sales manager at a voice recording company in Boston, admits he blew a wad on speculative tech stock during the Internet bubble. But a year ago, he dove for safety in blue-chip stocks like IBM, Merrill Lynch, General Motors, and Delta Airlines. Now 40 percent of that is gone. Tucci feels suckered. "I'm paralyzed. I can't sell because I'd take such a big loss. I'm sure as heck not going to buy anything. And even if I were, whom would I listen to for advice? No one seems to give off a whiff of honesty about any of this stuff. These days, I just pray a lot."*

The article goes on:

> *Some 100 million investors, about half of all adult Americans, can relate to that. They're the new Investor Class that has emerged over the past decade. Predominantly middle-class, suburban baby boomers, they bought into the idea that stocks could make them richer. They exulted during the long bull market of the 1990s. But they've lost $5 trillion, or 30% of their stock wealth since the spring of 2000 when the dotcom implosion launched the second-worst bear market since World War II. It wasn't Monopoly® money. It was money earmarked for retirement, for college tuition, for medical bills.*

The Problem Gets Bigger

The concern with pushing problems forward, rather than solving them, is that the problem only gets worse. When the Enron scandal broke, millions of people got their first glimpse at how big, and personally devastating, this problem can be, especially for older workers who have had their 401(k) wiped out, who know that Social Security and Medicare are going broke, and who know their kids are not much better off than they are. Instead of retirement being a dream, the retirement becomes a nightmare.

Rich dad explained to me how this problem came to be. "When America became a world power back in the early 1900s, millions of farm hands began to move off the farm and into the city for higher-paying jobs in the new factories. Soon our factories were booming, but a new problem was created—the problem of what to do with older workers."

"That's why the Social Security Act was passed during the Depression," I said, remembering that Social Security began in the 1930s. "I'll bet it made a lot of older workers happy."

"It did," rich dad agreed, "and it still does today. But when World War II broke out, the factories picked up and the boom in America continued, even after the war ended. Because a boom was on, many unions began demanding that their workers receive a pension after retiring. In order to keep the union leaders happy, corporate management agreed, and DB pension plans began to grow."

"But the problem of how a person survives once they are no longer able to work persists," I said.

"That is correct," said rich dad. "That is the problem behind the problem. How does a person survive once they are no longer able to work? That is the problem that led to Social Security, DB pension plans, and ERISA."

"That's the problem that needs to be solved," I said.

Rich dad just nodded his head and said, "The World War I generation solved its problem by passing on its expenses via government legislation to the World War II generation. The World War II generation passed its expenses on to your generation with pension reform."

"So the government passes the problem on rather than solve it," I said, "and that is the basis of your prophecy."

Rich dad looked at me silently and solemnly. He could tell I was beginning to understand why the problem will get worse.

I sat quietly for a while, letting the idea sink in. As I sat there, I began to recall speeches by famous politicians saying words that made people happy, making promises that would keep them hopeful. Snapping out of my silence, I said, "So that is why you say there will be a giant stock-market crash. The problem is not the stock market. The problem is that the original problem has been passed on rather than solved, and someday soon, the problem will become too big. It's all going to come tumbling down like a house of cards."

"That's correct," said rich dad. "We now have too many people who have come to expect the government to solve their problems. And politicians, in their desire to win votes, will promise to solve those problems. But of course, we know that a politician will do and say anything to remain popular, be liked, and get reelected. I don't blame them. If they told people the truth, they would be thrown out of office. So the problem grows, the government gets bigger, and the taxes have to get higher."

The Rise and Fall of the Roman Empire

All through my years growing up with rich dad, he encouraged me to study the history of the rise and fall of great empires. One of the empires he had me study was the Roman Empire. During one of these study sessions, rich dad said, "The Roman Empire had great technology for conquering and taxing people so they were able to create a vast empire. Their difficulties began as people moved off the conquered lands and into cities such as Rome. As the city of Rome grew, the leaders became concerned that the urban mobs would revolt if they had no jobs, shelter, or food. So the Romans fed the people and created great distractions such as the Colosseum to entertain the masses. Soon Rome became a great city of people who expected to be entertained and fed."

"So Rome became a welfare state?" I asked.

"More than a welfare state," said rich dad. "It became a large government bureaucracy. Instead of solving problems, they created more problems. It was also a very litigious state. There were more lawsuits per capita than even in America today, because more and more people wanted to blame someone else for their problems, rather than solve their own problems. As a result, the problems only increased. The more problems they created, the more bureaucrats were needed. As the problem got bigger, so did the government."

"So how did they afford it all and keep control?" I asked.

"Well, for one thing, they had a strong army. As I said, they knew how to conquer. Conquering people was their technology. In order to pay for this form of mob control, the Romans increased taxes on the working class throughout the empire. Soon the taxes got so high that workers began leaving the land and moving to the cities because life on the land made no sense. All their work was taxed, so why not move to where food and entertainment were inexpensive, or even free?"

"So the problem got worse, not better," I said.

"Well, it was one of the many problems that was getting worse," said rich dad. "As I said, the workers were leaving the land. That meant food production as well as tax collection was beginning to decline as more and more workers moved into the cities."

"So how did they solve that problem?" I asked.

"The same way any military-based conquering nation solves its problems. Rome passed a law making it illegal for a worker to leave the land. In other words, the workers were now bound to the land. If the worker left, the law allowed the government to punish the relatives."

"And that did not solve the problem?" I asked.

"No, and because the Romans could not solve their problems, the great Roman Empire began its decline," said rich dad. In closing, he said, "If we do not solve our problems, the same thing will happen to America."

In 2001, a new president took office in America. Just before he took office, there was a stock-market crash which led to a recession. At the time, we had a surplus in the budget so, to solve the problem, the Bush administration immediately cut taxes and the Federal Reserve repeatedly reduced interest rates in hopes of spurring the economy.

The Next Argentina?

Many Americans hate being compared to Japan. Many economic scholars in America say that what is going on in Japan will not go on in America. I tend to agree. If anything, Argentina is a better example of what might happen to America in the future. Only a few years ago, Argentina was a rich industrial powerhouse with a fantastic standard of living. It was a rich land, a favorite place for many Europeans. In many ways, it was more European than South American. But in just a few years, this very rich country became a poor, debt-ridden, bankrupt nation with a weak currency. Money left, and so did the rich. Taxes became high, and the currency collapsed. Corruption was everywhere. There was a real potential for anarchy to erupt.

Could that happen to America in a few years? Most Americans think not. Unfortunately, too many Americans have come to expect that government will solve their problems. I am afraid that, rather than solve the problems, an older America will vote for more government and higher taxes. With Social Security the most popular act ever passed, I am afraid that those who depend upon Social Security (soon to be a major voting bloc) will vote once again that the younger workers take care of them. If that happens, taxes will skyrocket. While it took hundreds of years for the Roman Empire to finally collapse, with today's speed of money transfers, the great American Empire could fall pretty fast.

Rich dad noted that one of the reasons the Roman Empire fell was because the Romans never evolved from a basic technology of conquering and taxing. If they had evolved, their empire might have gone on for centuries.

Unfortunately, great empires seem to forget that they need to evolve. Spain was also a great nation that grew by taking and not creating. So it too fell from greatness after attaining great power and great wealth. It fell from power because it did not evolve.

Hopefully, this won't happen to America if Americans are willing to face the problem honestly and allow people and business to solve the problem once and for all. In his speech in February 2002,

Alan Greenspan, then chairman of the Federal Reserve, called for the need for financial literacy. He too spoke of the need to evolve. He said it was important that all our children learn financial literacy in our schools if we are to evolve as a civilization and continue to be a world power.

Rich dad would agree wholeheartedly with Alan Greenspan. In fact, in many ways they sound alike. Rich dad often said, "The government tries to solve the problem of poor people by giving them money. Giving poor people money only creates more poor people." He also often said, "If we don't improve our children's financial education, they will not be able to solve the financial problems we have passed forward. If we do not solve these problems, the American Empire will come to an end. It's up to your generation to solve the problem before this happens."

We have a number of years to solve the problem, so I recommend we begin solving it rather than pushing the problem forward. The problem is too big to be pushed forward anymore. This book is meant to be a call to action. The baby boomers still have time to solve this problem if we will address the problem honestly and truthfully.

Rich dad was very optimistic about America. He said, "Although America is a military power, it does not use its military power to take. America uses its military to protect its lines of commerce as well as keep order in the world. America is also a business power, and a business power has the ability to create rather than take." He would say, "It's time to use our business power to create solutions to this very big problem of how a person survives once their working days are over. If we as a nation solve this problem, America can evolve into an even greater world power."

If we do not solve this problem, we contribute to the approaching perfect storm of our financial lives.

Chapter Nine

THE PERFECT STORM

I saw a great movie, *The Perfect Storm* starring George Clooney, which was based on a true story of a series of very severe weather patterns, all coming together at the same time. In other words, it was a story about what would happen if everything went wrong in the weather at once. In many ways, the year 2000 marked the beginning of the coming "perfect financial storm."

The year 2000 has been held as a significant time throughout history. Over 400 years ago, Nostradamus predicted that in 1998 the third Antichrist would appear. Many believe Osama Bin Laden could fit the description and time. You may also remember the terror around the computer millennium bug that would bring the world to a halt. I have heard people say that the year 2000 was to be the end of the world, and in some ways it has been—at least the world we used to know.

I have written about the significance of the change between the DB pension plan and the DC pension plan. The DB pension plan is an Industrial-Age pension plan and the DC pension plan is an Information-Age pension plan. Many of us are beginning to realize that the rules between the Industrial Age and the Information Age have changed. For example, in the Industrial Age, there was job security and company loyalty. In the Information Age, there is less and less of each. In the Industrial Age, the older you got, the more valuable you became. In the Information Age, the opposite is often true, especially in the field of technology. These changes at the end of the Industrial Age and the beginning of the Information Age are adding to the coming of the perfect financial storm.

Sailors all over the world repeat this saying: "Red skies at night, sailor's delight. Red skies in the morning, sailors take warning." Just as Noah had the vision to build an ark, students at the U.S. Merchant Marine Academy—the school from which I received my bachelor's degree, a school that trains ship's officers for the ships of commerce (such as tankers, freighters, passenger liners, tugs, ferries, and barges)—were taught to always be vigilant for signs of approaching changes in weather, changes out of sight and over the horizon. It is training that has served me well in my business career.

My concern is that many people are not able to see the coming changes, simply because they cannot see the differences between the Industrial Age and the Information Age. Just as most people do not know the differences between a DB pension plan and a DC pension plan, most people are not paying attention to changes that are coming, but are not yet here.

Before any storm such as a hurricane hits, people on the beach begin to notice a change in the wind, the water, and the mood. Such a period of time is upon us now. Millions of us are aware of this change, but most of us are not certain exactly which direction the storm will head, how strong it will be, and exactly where it will come ashore. Nevertheless, if we were on the shore, most of us would know that we need to do something different.

The following changes will help fuel the perfect storm. I am watching these changes with concern, wonder, and excitement.

Change #1: Millions will be left destitute in old age.

The World War II generation had secure jobs, secure retirements, and medical care in old age. Beginning with the baby boomers, that all changed. Although we are feeling the mood change and the shift in the wind today, I forecast that the full force of this storm will hit around 2025, some 50 years after the act was put into law. By 2025 we will have millions of baby boomers entering their eighties who will be out of money, nearly out of time, and needing the most medical care of their lives. Without government programs such as

Social Security and Medicare, which will probably be financially bankrupt, an aged and poor population will be a financial challenge for the generations following the baby boomers.

Change #2: Medical care will get even more expensive.

In the year 2000, while the stock market and mutual fund values were crashing down, the cost of medical care was going up by 17 percent. When you add to this the fact that many medical professionals are leaving the industry at a time when more and more baby boomers will need their services, we have another storm brewing.

Change #3: Terrorism will increase.

On September 11, 2001, Kim and I were just checking into our hotel in Rome, Italy. The bellman put our bags on the floor, grabbed hold of the remote control, turned the television on, and suddenly dropped the remote control on the floor. Kim and I turned to see pictures we have all seen over and over again, pictures of airliners flying into the World Trade Center. Since the audio was in Italian, we could not understand what the commentator was saying, but the bellman did. He just stood there speechless. Finally switching to an English station, we realized that an event that had been predicted for years was taking place.

The reason I say that this event was predicted is because there is a book entitled *The Great Reckoning* by James Dale Davidson and Lord William Rees-Mogg that I recommend people read. It is about the coming depression in America. The first edition was published in 1993, written well before the first World Trade Center attack. In this book there are many predictions, many of which have come true, although not at the exact times they were predicted to come true. I have read their earlier books on the future, and many of their earlier predictions have come true as well.

In *The Great Reckoning*, Davidson and Rees-Mogg predicted that terrorism will increase because terrorism is cheap. You do not need multitrillion-dollar armed forces to be a terrorist. Columbine High School, the anthrax letters, urban gangs, tribal war lords, drug lords in South America, and of course Bin Laden have proven that concept. Terrorism is on the rise all over the world, and because terrorism feeds on people's fear, the media broadcasts it over and over again. Terrorism is effective even if nothing happens. Just the fear of terrorism can be as effective as the act itself. Every time I hear a political leader warn that the threat of terrorism is high, the terrorists have won. They win because they have a politician doing their work for them. As Davidson and Rees-Mogg state, terrorism is cheap, really cheap, and it will only spread. Even if we destroy Bin Laden and his network, we will not destroy the cause of terrorism.

A month after the September 11 event, a U.S. television host was interviewing a terrorism specialist from Israel. The American host was intimating that we were now safe because we were bombing Afghanistan. The terrorism specialist replied, "It's only beginning for America."

The TV host then said, "But you haven't had a hijacking in years in Israel. We are following your procedures to stop hijacking."

"Yes, it is true that we have stopped hijacking, but we have not stopped terrorism. Today, we have terrorists bombing shopping centers, nightclubs, and anyplace else that people gather." The specialist went on to say that the new tactic of terrorists was to steal an army uniform and equipment, walk into a crowded shopping center pretending to be there to protect the shoppers, gain their trust, and then begin shooting them. The terrorism specialist ended by saying, "That tactic has effectively made all of our soldiers and police potential terrorists in the minds of our people. Today, we trust no one. Today, we feel safe nowhere. The same will happen in America." As airline passengers, we are constantly searched, frisked, and patted down. I remember when only crooks were treated that way. Today, every time we fly, we are all treated as suspected terrorists instead of law-abiding passengers.

In other words, the terrorists have won because today we are all treated as terrorists.

In 1920, a truck packed with explosives was parked in front of the New York City Stock Exchange and the J. P. Morgan bank. When the truck exploded, many were killed and injured. If you go to New York City, you can still see the scars on those buildings. The people responsible for that truck bomb were never apprehended. It was not the first attack on capitalism, and it was not the last.

Increased terrorism will mean that many businesses such as shopping centers, restaurants, churches, and office buildings will be adversely affected just as any business associated with the airlines has been affected. Since terrorism is cheap, any whacko can be an effective terrorist. You do not need to be from a foreign land to be a terrorist. The problem with terrorism is that terrorism's greatest effect is simply the idea of terrorism. Ideas in the Information Age spread faster and farther than at any other time in history. In other words, although terrorism has been around forever, in the Information Age, terrorism will be more effective.

Change #4: Japan, currently the world's second largest economy, is on the brink of financial collapse and depression. Many of us remember when, just a few years ago, Japan's economy was the shining star of the world. Americans by the hundreds of thousands began studying the Japanese way of doing business. Suddenly, almost overnight, everything changed.

Can the same thing happen here in America? Many Americans bristle at the idea. Other Americans are not too sure. Regardless, we can all learn some lessons from Japan's sudden fall as a global economic powerhouse. Some of the lessons are:

- Japan's counterpart to our baby-boom generation hit retirement age in the late 1980s. America's baby boomers will become aged in 2010. What effect will an aging American population have on our economy? Will it be similar to Japan's?

- Japan's aged population has maintained control of the country. The question to America is: In 2010, who will control the United States? Will the aging baby boomers still run the country as they did in Japan? If aging baby boomers still run the country, there will be laws passed to increase taxes to take care of their needs after retirement. If taxes are raised on the younger generation, the economy of America will probably go down faster. Businesses move to countries where the tax laws are favorable to businesses, not to old people.

- Japan is an old economic culture resistant to change. It has been said that an indigenous person is someone whose family has been on the island for over 500 years. One of Japan's problems is that its people have been on the island, more or less isolated, for thousands of years so its cultural roots take longer to change.

  Except for the Native Americans, most Americans do not qualify as indigenous people. That means we do not have the thousands of years of cultural traditions to contend with, as the Japanese do. Nevertheless, even though most of us are not indigenous people, we can learn from the lessons of being slow to change and slow to adapt to a changing world. The people being left behind financially are often the people who are stuck in old ways of thinking and doing things, so we can learn a lot, both good and bad, from indigenous people and their cultures.

- The Japanese are a tightknit group, well educated, hardworking, religious, and with a very high savings rate. Yet, even with those virtues, the country is still heading for a depression. Why?

As a fourth-generation Japanese-American familiar with both cultures, I can offer one difference we can all learn from. In the Japanese culture, there is a high need to save face. Shame is disgrace. Shame combined with failure is reason for hara-kiri or suicide. In other words, in the Japanese culture, death is more desirable than disgrace.

America is different. After the 1986 Tax Reform Act in America, literally trillions of dollars of American real estate became worthless. The 1986 act changed the rules and removed some of the phony tax incentives that had bloated the values of real estate. A stock market, real estate market, and savings-and-loan (banking) crash followed. Rather than hang on to overvalued and overleveraged real estate, the federal government stepped in and bankrupted the savings-and-loan industry.

A federal agency known as the Resolution Trust Corporation, the RTC, was formed, and it bundled trillions of dollars of real estate and sold it for pennies on the dollar. In other words, the U.S. government realized that the country was in trouble because several mistakes had been made, and it tried to clean house as quickly as possible. Japan has not done that. For years, their banks have hung on to real estate they loaned too much money for, refusing to admit they made a mistake, continuing to save face, and hoping that the price of real estate in their portfolios will increase in value.

In other words, they hung on instead of cleaning house. In their attempt to save face, the Japanese banks, its politicians, and people have become a worldwide disgrace. The need to save face has destroyed an economy of well-educated, hardworking people—everything everyone in the world should all strive to be. If America does not learn from this lesson, it too could follow in Japan's footsteps.

I have written about the difference between savers and investors as well as the difference between people in the E quadrant and people in the I quadrant. One of the biggest differences between E's and I's is that a professional investor knows to cut their losses quickly. Professional investors are not afraid to quickly admit they made a mistake. Professional investors are not into saving face. They are into saving money. When they make a bad investment, they cut and run, even if they lose some money. I have seen so many non-investors buy an investment and hold on to it all the way down to the bottom. That is what happened to many Enron employees. What is a good trait as an employee—loyalty and tenacity—is a bad trait in the investor quadrant. A true investor has very little loyalty to any investment. If the investment turns and begins to go bad, they cut their losses and go looking for a good investment. I have seen many average investors do exactly what the Japanese have been doing. They refuse to admit they made a mistake and hang on until all the money is gone.

Over the years, I have heard the following words from many loser investors who refuse to admit they made a mistake. I have used these words myself. As the stock price is going down, I hear them say, "This is only a minor correction. I know it will come back up. After all, the market on average always goes up." And after their stock hits rock bottom, they say, "You don't lose as long as you don't sell. I'll hold on till the stock price comes back up and then I'll sell." In other words, "As soon as the stock begins to win, I'm going to sell it. As long as it is a loser, I will hang on to it." After the stock is dead and has been down for months, I hear them say, "I'm investing for the long term." When I hear people of any nationality saying those words, I am reminded of my Japanese heritage—a heritage that puts a high importance on being smart, being right, and saving face. Funny, that sounds sort of like my American heritage also.

If you want to be a professional investor, you need to learn from the American example of cutting losses quickly rather than following the Japanese example of death being preferable to disgrace. Losing money is not a disgrace. Losing money and becoming a loser is primarily an issue of arrogance and ignorance—and arrogance and ignorance are abundantly available to people everywhere.

Always remember what my rich dad taught me about the difference between winners and losers. He said, "Losers cut their winners and hang on to their losers. Winners cut their losers and hang on to their winners." To rich dad, that was one of his golden rules of life. Now that I am older, I know how valuable that rule has been for me, especially when I violated it. I have also seen so many people violate that golden rule by hanging on to losing jobs, losing businesses, losing marriages, losing friends, losing investments, and losing ideas— just to avoid admitting they may not be right or they made a mistake. In America, we don't usually call it "saving face." In America, we call it "looking good and going nowhere."

Change #5: China will become the world's largest economy.
While Japan is on the brink of falling from the number-two
spot in the world economy, China is set to become number one.
America is contracting financially, while at the same time China
is booming. It is estimated that sometime around the year 2020,
China is expected to pass the United States as the economic
powerhouse of the world. As reported in the May 6, 2002,
Business Week, China has 21 percent of the world's population.
It has an almost unlimited supply of human capital, and now as it
opens its borders through joining the World Trade Organization,
its economic impact is just beginning to be seen.

All of these factors are leading up to a perfect financial storm. Just
when the U.S. baby boomers enter old age, China's boom will be
in full force. China's rise to power, along with the expansion of the
World Wide Web and all the new technology it will spawn, will
definitely cause the future to be different than today. One thing is
for certain, the gap between the haves and have-nots in America and
the world will definitely widen. Those who move with these global
changes will become richer than ever before. Those who do not
change will be left even further behind financially and professionally.

Back in 1271, a young man named Marco Polo traveled to China
to find a large nation booming with industry and trade. Europe at
that time was just at the brink of entering into the world of business.
Sure enough, when Marco Polo returned from China, Europe
passed China as the world economic power. In 1492, Christopher
Columbus sailed west looking for a shorter route to Asia, and the
world changed forever after that. Spain soon became the world
financial power in the 1500s by plundering the gold from South
America. The financial power then shifted to Europe—from France,
Holland, and then to England. From the 1600s to the 1900s,
America was considered a Third World nation, a very risky place to
invest. But in 1920, right after the end of World War I, the financial
power shifted to the United States. Now, after all these years, China's
era of dominance is about to return. With a massive labor force, low
labor prices, and great technology, who knows what will happen?

I found it interesting in 2001, just as we began retaliation bombing in Afghanistan, that President Bush was not in the White House or the country. Where was he? Was he cheering our troops on in Afghanistan? No. He was in China with business leaders such as Bill Gates of Microsoft and Carly Fiorina of Hewlett-Packard talking about trade, not war. If I were in my thirties and thinking about climbing the corporate ladder, I would be worried. Why? Because as the saying goes, "Whatever can be made in America will now be made in China." So much for a nice secure job in middle management or on the assembly line.

Every time I travel to China, I can still hear Ross Perot say: "That loud sucking sound from south of the border will be jobs…" He was referring to Americans losing their jobs to Mexico after NAFTA, the North American Free Trade Agreement. In a few years the sucking sound will get louder, but it will not be coming from Mexico. Rather, it will be coming from China and other countries as technology spreads to countries with lower labor costs, bright younger minds, and a hunger to get rich and enjoy the good life we have enjoyed.

In 1805, William Playfair wrote: "The general conclusion is that wealth and power have never been long permanent in any place... and that they travel over the face of the earth, something like a caravan of merchants. On their arrival everything is found green and fresh; while they remain, all is bustle and abundance; and when gone, all is left trampled down, barren, and bare."

We have all heard stories that, by the third generation, the fortune of a family is gone. The family fortune is gone because the third generation has not appreciated the hard work of the previous generations to gain and preserve the wealth. So instead of reinvesting and rebuilding true wealth, the third generation is spoiled and expects life to be rich and easy. Why should they study hard or work hard? After all, Mom, Dad, Grandma, and Grandpa worked hard and now have money. They'll give the kids anything they want. The kids expect life to be easy. They expect simply to go to school, get a high-paying job, nice house, nice car, put money in the stock market, the stock price goes up, and they become rich. Is that what we have come to expect? If a generation is approximately 25 years in length, then America is on its third and fourth generations after 1920. Has the baby-boom generation, the third generation after 1920, squandered our wealth? Or have wealth and power simply decided that it is time to move on?

Change #6: The world population will continue to age.
Many of us have heard the theory of an asteroid that collided with earth millions of years ago and wiped out the great dinosaurs. If Japan's economic reforms do not work and work quickly, Japan could be the financial asteroid that collides with the world's economic system and wipes out many financial dinosaurs.

Here's what might happen. As we have seen, the Japanese by nature are frugal, savers, and hardworking. If their economy goes down, the Japanese people will cut down on consumption, work harder, and attempt to export their way out of their financial problems. That will mean that they will cut prices drastically on everything they make, which will mean the world will also have to cut prices in order to compete. That means lower wages for most people worldwide.

Even if Japan does not go bankrupt, its economy faces the same problem that America, France, and Germany face—the problem of a large aging population followed by a smaller younger generation. How these three economic giants deal with this challenge will also have great impact upon our economic future.

Looking at the population of workers and retirees as assets and liabilities, the picture looks like this:

Japan, France, Germany and USA Today

BALANCE SHEET

Assets	Liabilities
Many workers	Few retirees

Japan, France, Germany and USA Tomorrow

BALANCE SHEET

Assets	Liabilities
Few workers	Many retirees

In the Industrial Age, there were more workers than retirees. In the Information Age, retirees are living longer and the rules of how we as a society care for our elders will need to be addressed.

China faces a similar but different problem. China's challenge is the law of one child per family. This is their problem in the near future:

China Prior to Birth Restrictions

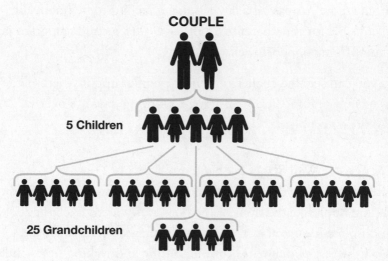

China with Birth Restrictions

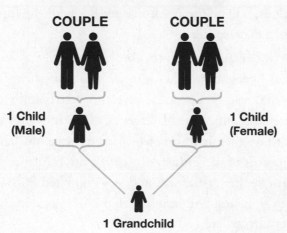

In a few years, that one grandchild may have to support two parents and four grandparents. If you extend this government-enforced policy one more generation, you will have a single great-grandchild responsible for two parents, four grandparents, and eight great-grandparents. Talk about a strain on the budget.

A similar challenge is going on in Singapore. The birth rates there are so low that the government is offering cash incentives for couples to have more children. On top of that, the government of Singapore has passed a law requiring a child to be financially responsible for their parents. In other words, a child can go to jail if they do not support their parents.

As you can see, the challenge of how people support themselves financially and medically once their working days are over is a worldwide problem.

Change #7: Wall Street is obsolete.
After dominating the world economic scene, the idea of a physical trading floor, like the floor of the New York Stock Exchange, is an obsolete idea. Today, we have stock markets in cyberspace. With the rest of the world coming online and waking up to the idea of buying and selling stocks, millions of online traders, with their portable computers and real-time quotes coming from the markets, will be the stock-market floors of the future, stock markets in cyberspace.

In many ways, that makes stockbrokers actually an icon of the Industrial Age, and it makes mutual funds big slow dirigibles—airships that fast, independent investors watch and whose every move they can anticipate. That means investors who use traditional brokers to do their investing for them in large mutual funds are also dinosaurs of the Industrial Age. In the Information Age, faster, more nimble, better-trained, and less-regulated individual investors will win the richest and fastest global 24/7 game in the world. In fact, they already are.

The February 25, 2002, cover of *Business Week* ran the headline, "The Betrayed Investor." On the cover under the headline, the magazine wrote, "In the 1990s, a new class of investors became a powerful economic and political force. Now many feel misled by Wall Street, corporations, accountants, and the government." The magazine article said that investors slapped a record 341 class-action lawsuits on brokers—lawsuits that cost brokerage houses as much as $14 billion. They charged the brokers "with everything from issuing misleading prospectuses to taking kickbacks for IPO allocations. Individual complaints for bad advice soared as well." Instead of titling the cover, "The Betrayed Investor," a more accurate statement would be, "The Obsolete Investor." That whole system of buying and selling stocks and other securities through a traditional broker and brokerage house is a dinosaur, a Tyrannosaurus rex of the Industrial Age. If you have a laptop with a connection to the World Wide Web, you can beat the Street and the slower investors from anywhere in the world. The stock markets of today are in cyberspace, and so are the *real* investors.

Change #8: Big corporations are losing the public trust and failing.

The May 6, 2002, issue of *Business Week*'s cover story was, "The Crisis in Corporate Governance: Excessive Pay. Weak Leadership. Corrupt Analysts. Complacent Boards. Questionable Accounting—How to Fix the System." In the article were the following observations:

> *The latest wave of skepticism may have started with Enron Corp.'s ugly demise, but with each revelation of corporate excess or wrongdoing, the goodwill built up by business during the boom of the last decade has eroded a little more, giving way to widespread suspicion and mistrust. An unrelenting barrage of headlines that tell of Securities & Exchange Commission investigations, indictments, guilty*

pleas, government settlements, financial re-statements, and fines has only lent greater credence to the belief that the system in inherently unfair...

In many ways, Enron and its dealings with Arthur Andersen are an anomaly, a perfect storm [italics added] where greed, lax oversight, and outright fraud combined to unravel two of the nation's largest companies. But a certain moral laxity has come to pervade even the bluest of the blue chips...

At risk is the very integrity of capitalism.

(As a side note, the *Business Week* quotation in Change #8 was added in the final draft of this book, well after I had titled this chapter, "The Perfect Storm." I find it interesting that the *Business Week* writers chose the same term in their article. Maybe we should pay attention!)

Life Outside the Chicken Coop

In 1974, when I had to make the decision to follow in my poor dad's footsteps or my rich dad's footsteps, rich dad gave me this bit of advice that helped me in my decision-making process. He said, "When your dad advises you to go back to school to get your master's degree so you can find a better, more secure job, he is talking about security within the chicken coop. Most people think that your dad's advice is good advice, since most people seek security inside the chicken coop. Most people want a secure job, a steady paycheck, great benefits, and a secure retirement. That is life inside the chicken coop. My advice is for life outside the chicken coop. So you need to choose between the two. When I was 13 years old, I was forced to face life outside of the coop, and I have stayed outside all my life. That is the choice you face today. You need to choose between a life inside the coop or a life outside the coop—and believe me, they are not the same."

In 1974 I chose to prepare for life outside the coop. In 1979, I had to rechoose again. As you know I had nothing—no money, no job, no roof over my head. When I was interviewing for that high-paying sales-manager's job, the lure of the coop was very tempting. One of the things that gave me the courage to stand up and turn down the job was rich dad's simple story of the chicken coop.

Although it took me another 15 years to feel comfortable surviving outside the coop, I would say the process was worth it. Today when I hear of people losing their jobs, their retirement savings, their homes, and their hopes for the future, I cannot help but reflect back on rich dad's simple story of the coop. I know that the world outside the coop looks frightening for many people. Jobs seem scarce, money seems scarce, and opportunities seem to be dwindling. But I assure you, life outside the coop is strong, optimistic, vibrant, and filled with more opportunity than ever before. My friends and I read tales of doom and gloom, yet in our world, there is more money available, more opportunity, and more excitement than ever before. In my opinion, it is simply a matter of seeing the world from inside the chicken coop, or from outside of it. It is also a matter of whom you listen to. Do you take advice from people who are also in the coop, or do you listen to people outside the coop—people who are saying, "It's great out here"?

Obviously, in 1974, I chose to learn about life outside the chicken coop. After my decision, rich dad said to me, "Life outside the chicken coop is filled with liars, cheats, whores, cowards, crooks, idiots, losers, and con men. It is also filled with saints, warriors, noble people, winners, and geniuses." He then said, "If you choose to live your life outside the chicken coop, you must learn to do business with all of them, simply because you will not know who they really are until after you have done business with them." In other words, in every one of my deals outside the chicken coop, everyone puts forth the face of saints, warriors, noble people, and geniuses. Some time into the deal, regardless if things go bad or good, you find out if the people you were dealing with are liars, cheats, whores, cowards, crooks, idiots, and con men—or if they really were the saints, warriors, noble people, and geniuses they appeared to be when you first met them.

Rich dad explained to me that many people leaving school and searching for a secure job with a big company or the government are searching for a place where they are protected from the real world. When they invest, they often search for similar investments that protect them from the real world. That is why mutual funds became the investment vehicle of choice over the last few years. My friend, Rolf Parta—a former bank-product manager with his MBA and CPA—says, "People like mutual funds because they believe mutual funds are sanitized. Many new investors feel safe with mutual funds because they think their fund manager has the power to wipe off the germs from the real world and deliver them a safe, secure investment."

After the Enron scandal and the demise of so many blue-chip companies, many investors are waking up to the reality that life *inside* the chicken coop is beginning to look a lot like life *outside* the coop. The problem is, most are not prepared for that outside life. That is why we are cruising for a very large stock-market crash.

Business Week's article, "The Betrayed Investor," is about an investor who is still in the market and still hoping that the government can tighten things up to protect them. Instead of learning to become professional investors, I predict that most of these betrayed but smarter investors will stay in the market. Just before retirement, they will sell their mutual funds and cling to what they know and trust the most—cash. When that happens, the biggest stock-market crash in the history of the world will be on, and those outside the chicken coop will find life more exciting than ever before. Unfortunately, those still inside the chicken coop will find life frightening—very, very, frightening.

Many have designated the year 2000 as the year that the world shifted from the Industrial Age to the Information Age. This shift is the cause of much of the volatility in the markets and also in our lives. As the winds of the perfect storm pick up, there are those inside the chicken coop who are sitting tight at their job or dusting off their resumes looking for a new "secure" coop, yet they are afraid of opening their retirement-account statements. Many others may find themselves outside the chicken coop involuntarily through layoffs or unemployment, frightened and without the financial education to survive. While the sounds of the howling winds scare many people, as the winds pick up, there are others *outside* the coop who are having hurricane parties.

In the next section of this book, I will explain how to prepare for the years to come, regardless if you plan to live inside the chicken coop or outside the coop.

SECTION TWO
BUILDING THE ARK

Rich dad said, "Everyone has the ability to build a financial ark to survive and flourish in the future. But you must invest time in your financial education to build an ark with a solid foundation."

This section of the book is for people who want to build their own arks rather than expect someone else, or their government, to provide one for them.

Chapter Ten
HOW DO YOU BUILD AN ARK?

Many people already know they need to build their own ark. The need to build an ark and build it quickly is not news to them. But the question remains, "How do you build an ark?" The answer is, "It depends upon whom you ask." For example, if you ask a:

1.   **Politician**

Many politicians today are saying that the way to save Social Security is to allow younger workers to invest two to four percent of their Social Security-taxed money into personal investment accounts and then reduce the benefits promised to them by the Social Security Administration.

I don't know about you, but that solution sounds vaguely familiar. To me, it has a ring similar to defined contribution plans. Once again we are forcing people to become investors without the necessary financial education to help them.

Not only does it sound familiar but, if this law passes, it will mean that Social Security will begin to run negative before 2016 because less money will be coming in to pay for the older retirees. The politicians who are proposing this today in 2002 know they will be out of office long before this happens. Again, the problem is pushed forward.

2. **Union leader**

   Union leaders would recommend you find a job with a company that has a strong, well-organized union with a well-funded pension plan and benefits.

   My poor dad, as head of the Hawaii State Teachers Association, was a strong advocate of this idea. If you like this idea, get a job with the government.

3. **Schoolteacher**

   A schoolteacher would probably recommend staying in school to get as high an advanced degree as possible. In fact, get several of them. Then go find a safe, secure job with benefits.

   Our institutions of higher learning are filled with students who are in school because the job market is tight. Only a few years ago, during the dotcom mania, students were leaving school early in search of jobs with start-up companies offering stock options. Many of them are back in school now or are looking for jobs.

4. **Professional person**

   There are many people who recommend going to school so you can learn a profession such as doctor, lawyer, plumber, accountant, electrician, or chef. People who believe in this course of action often say, "Get a skill or trade you can always fall back on."

   In other words, in this era of job insecurity, be sure you can work on your own. This group includes the millions of small business owners, often called mom-and-pop businesses.

5. **Financial planner**

   We know what these people say. This group always recommends that you start early, invest for the long term, stick with the plan, and diversify, diversify, diversify.

While this is great advice for the average investor, it is what the financial planners don't tell the average investor that concerns me. Also, if you are a baby boomer over 45 years of age, this advice may not work.

6. **Religious person**
They recommend attending church regularly and praying twice a day. They know God will save them and provide for them.

I am not knocking the power of prayer, but I believe this is an entitlement mentality. I believe that God wants people to take control of their own lives and provide for themselves and their families.

7. **Stockbroker**
Many recommend picking individual stocks over mutual funds, but they are happy to sell you mutual funds also.

8. **Real estate agent**
Most real estate agents support the idea that your home is your biggest investment and your most important asset, even though in most cases a home is a liability.

9. **Poor person**
Many of this group believe that the rich and the government should help care for the less fortunate.

10. **Hardworking person**
They believe in working until the day they cannot work any longer, saying, "I never plan on retiring."

11. **Animal lover**
Since this group loves animals, they would recommend buying a monkey. They would recommend training the monkey to first save money, then diversify with mutual funds, and after that, teach it to throw darts at a mutual funds dartboard.

12. **Gambler**
Wait till you feel lucky, and then go to Las Vegas. But even if you do not feel lucky, always stop to buy a lottery ticket on your way home.

13. **Gold digger**
Find a rich person and do whatever it takes to marry them.

14. **Optimist**
What, me worry? In their mindset, the stock market always goes up.

15. **Pessimist**
Build a fallout shelter, hoard food, water, gold, guns, and cash.

16. **Dreamer**
The dreamer would suggest believing in magic and creative visualization. They have crystals, aromatherapy candles, and wind chimes to keep away the evil spirits.

17. **Banker**
Bankers always recommend that you save, save, save. After you save some money, they call to inform you that they also sell mutual funds, stocks, insurance, annuities, and other financial-planning products.

Today, even CPAs, tax preparers, and attorneys are getting into the act. Many professionals, such as accountants, also have a financial-planning service in the next room from where they do your taxes. All that separates them is a thin corporate wall and business license. It's hard to tell who's doing what in the financial world. They all have some advice on how to build your ark.

18. **Rich dad**
Take control of your own financial ark and buy or build assets that generate cash flow. Include real estate, businesses, and paper assets. As soon as your income from your assets (money working for you) exceeds your expenses, you are financially free.

All 18 categories exist. Some have more merit than others. The real question is: Which of the 18 sounds best to you? Rather than getting into which of the 18 possible answers works best, I think it's important to say that there are many ways to build an ark. As Warren Buffett said, "There is more than one way to get to financial heaven."

The point is, find a way that works best for you. We are all different. We have different strengths and different weaknesses. How I built my ark was very different from the way rich dad built his ark, although we often used similar asset classes to do the job of building an ark. Rich dad used businesses and real estate, and I too used businesses and real estate. The difference is, we built very different businesses and invested in very different types of real estate. So a very important point in building an ark is to find the way that works best for you.

Years ago, rich dad said to me, "If you want to find true financial security or even become financially rich, you must play your own game. Don't play someone else's game." After ERISA passed into law, rich dad felt that millions of people would be forced to play Wall Street's game. Rich dad said, "The problem with playing Wall Street's game is that Wall Street is in control, and you aren't. Find your own game, become good at it, and then take control of your life."

Building Your Ark

The first thing I recommend is deciding how big an ark you want to build. Obviously, the poor person's ark would be a small and leaky boat. If all you desire is a poor person's ark, you really do not have to do that much. Social Security remains the most popular government program in the history of the United States. Personally, I would not want to depend upon my family to care for me, nor do I want to be dependent upon the government or charities for support.

The middle-class ark was a good ark for the World War II generation. All the middle class had to do prior to 1950 was go to school, get a job, work hard, buy a house, save money, and retire. This plan may still work if you get a job with the government or a well-unionized business. But ever since the shift from the DB to the DC pension plan, this new middle-class ark may not be strong enough to survive the rough seas ahead. If this DC pension plan is all you want for your ark, then rigorously follow traditional financial planning advice—have a plan, start early, work for years, and diversify. A middle-class ark can work, but there may be rough sailing the next few years.

If you want to have a rich ark, obviously you will need to dramatically commit to increasing your financial education. There is one thing a person who wants to become wealthy must understand. To build a rich ark, many of their traditional middle-class ideas and values will have to be expanded. For example, many people in the middle class think saving money, having a DC pension plan, and owning a home are the most intelligent financial decisions. While these are important to a person's overall financial well-being, the truth is that saving, DC pension plans, and a home are not cornerstones of a rich person's ark. The rich know that buying or building assets that generate passive income is the real foundation needed for a rich ark.

Why Savers Are Losers

Be careful about the word *save*. The act of saving worked well for the World War II generation, a generation that lived in an era of inflation. In fact, for the generation that lived before 1900, there was very little inflation and also no taxes. So saving worked even better for the *parents* of the World War II generation. But ever since 1950, savers have been losers simply because savings are taxed at a high rate, and inflation wipes out most of the gains. In early 2002, the interest rate paid on saving is about two percent. Many savers have been severely crippled because of this drop in interest. For example, only a few years ago, if a person had a million dollars in cash in the bank and the bank paid them five-percent interest, the saver then received $50,000 in interest income, before taxes. But when the rate hit two percent, that same million dollars paid them $20,000 in interest income before taxes. That means, in just a few years, savers took a 40-percent cut in pay, before taxes. The point is, advising people to save used to be good advice, and it still is good advice for the poor and the middle class. But for anyone wanting to build a rich ark, simply saving money in the old-fashioned way is bad advice.

Invest Your Time Before You Invest Your Money

Even though the interest rates today are approximately two percent and taxable, by shopping around and knowing what questions to ask, it is possible to find higher rates of interest, often tax free. For example, in February 2002, by having my stockbroker watch the market, Kim and I were able to find a tax-free government bond paying 7.75 percent. Since they are tax free, that is the equivalent of earning 12 percent taxable interest. Everyone else who has money in passbook savings is earning approximately two percent interest that is taxable.

Obviously, to receive a 7.75 percent tax-free rate, there is a little more risk, but very little. This is an example of how a person with a strong financial education could make more money with less money and less risk. For Kim and me, this is a very low-risk investment simply because we understand the investment and its risks. For a person without much financial education, a traditional bank passbook savings account paying a two-percent taxable interest rate would make more sense. Again, the point is that your investment in your financial education can pay a greater percentage return, even on something as simple as a savings account.

Without a financial education, it takes a lot more money to get rich and a lot more money to stay rich. The higher your financial IQ, the less money it takes to get rich. The lower your financial IQ, the more money it takes. As the saying goes, "If you think education is expensive, you should try ignorance."

In other words, don't invest in something you do not understand. Rich dad would say, "Before you invest in something, invest the time to understand it." Kim has personally invested nearly 15 years in this market, and I have a few more years in the business. That is where financial intelligence comes from. It comes from investing time in the real world. Financial intelligence does not come from handing your money over to a fund manager and hoping and praying they do a good job. You do not increase your financial intelligence investing in that way.

As stated earlier, many people invest, but they fail to become investors. Investing in your financial education may not pay off early in the process, but it does usually pay off later. What I am strongly recommending is that you invest in your financial education, especially if you want to build a rich ark. In fact, I would say your financial education is mandatory for building a rich ark and keeping it afloat once it's built.

Why the Middle Class Are Risky Investors

Rich dad said to me, "The middle class plays it risky financially, and that is why they are such risky investors." He went on to say, "The reason the middle class is taking a huge financial risk with a DC plan is because they invest a lot of money into the plan, but they invest very little time learning to invest. If you want to become rich, start out investing a lot of time before you begin investing a lot of money." So before you switch your savings account over, invest some time finding out about the investment.

Obviously, a 7.75-percent return is not a high rate of return, but it is an example of the difference between a financially educated investor and a middle-class investor. I used the example only to point out the cost of the lack of financial education. In reality, as a professional investor, I like a minimum of 40 percent cash-on-cash return from my investments, which is why I do not save money.

On many of our investments, Kim and I receive a return of infinity, which means we have no money making a lot of money. Our last real estate investment rental property yields a 45-percent return, cash-on-cash, most of it tax free. This 45 percent is actually received in two parts. We receive a cash-on-cash return of 15 percent, which means that our net rental income exceeds the amount of cash we invested each year by 15 percent. Then when you add the impact of depreciation, we have an additional tax savings, and therefore, additional cash return (cash we get to keep instead of paying the government) of 30 percent for this property. For us, this 45 percent return is an average return on investment. Yet when I mention that rate of return to some of my friends, they think I am exaggerating or lying to them. Again, it is the difference in one's financial education.

So a 7.75 percent tax-free interest return is interesting, but not particularly exciting. We use that rate simply to park excess money for periods of six months or more, while we work on putting the next investment together.

Saving money in a bank may sound intelligent to many people, but for me it is a waste of both time and money. The reason I began with the subject of savings is because so many of the middle class think that saving money is intelligent, but it is a financial drag for a rich person. Saving money makes no financial sense to a rich person.

Before going into building a rich ark, I want to bring up a few important points.

Point #1: If you plan on building a rich person's ark, saving money will eventually not make sense. Why? The answer is because the interest from savings is taxed at ordinary-income levels, the highest tax rate there is. For example, if you have a million dollars in savings, earning $20,000 from 2-percent taxable interest rate, and you earn more than $65,000 as a single person or $110,000 as a couple a year, that $20,000 will be taxed at approximately 30 percent, leaving you an effective return from your million dollars of about $14,000. That equates to an effective return of 1.4 percent before inflation. If you earn even more money and are in the 40-percent tax bracket, that 2-percent-interest-rate return drops to a 1.2-percent effective interest rate. Let me assure you that inflation is running at more than 1.2 percent, so a rich saver is a loser. The point is, if you are poor and at a lower tax bracket, the interest on your money is taxed at a lower rate. But if you are rich, your higher tax bracket causes that same interest rate to be taxed higher. So if you are rich, the more you save, the more you lose.

Point #2: If you plan on building a rich person's ark and you have a traditional DC plan, for example a 401(k), when you begin to withdraw money from your DC retirement plan, that income will be taxed at the highest levels. Again, the tax rates today are 30 percent for a single person earning over $65,000 a year. So for every $1,000 you receive in income from your 401(k) after retiring, that $1,000 will be reduced to $700 due to taxes. Again, a 401(k) or most other traditional retirement plans do not make tax sense if you plan on retiring rich.

One of the reasons Kim and I use real estate is because, with proper planning, we can reduce our taxes to zero percent from our real estate income. That is why the rich either made their money in real estate or hold their money in real estate. In other words, if you build a rich ark, income from real estate investments makes far more sense than income from a DC pension plan.

Point #3: Most people who aspire to higher income levels are not aware that, as their income grows, they will lose the benefits of their itemized deductions, including their home mortgage interest. A big house, the dream of the middle class, is not a write-off if you are rich. In America, if you earn less than approximately $137,300 in 2002, you are allowed by the tax code to write off some of your mortgage interest as a deduction from your taxes. But if you are rich, you lose that interest deduction. In fact, the higher your income, the less you may deduct, to the point where you are not able to deduct any of it.

The Main Point

The main point is that if you plan on building a big rich ark for retirement, you may have to let go of many of the traditional middle-class values and investments that the middle class think are important. In other words, there are some investments that work for the middle class—such as savings, DC pension plans, and interest deductions from your personal residence. But if you want to be rich and plan on building a rich ark, those middle-class money values will have to go.

The first step is to decide what size ark you want to build. If you want to build a poor person's ark or a middle-class ark, then stop here. The rest of this book is not for you. There are other books that will go into further detail on how to build those sizes of financial arks.

This chapter started with 18 different opinions on how to build an ark. Today almost everyone is handing out advice on ark-building. That is because you and I are not the only ones who know the perfect storm is coming. You and I are not the only ones who know the problem has been pushed forward for too long. So after you decide to build an ark, decide if you want a poor ark, a middle-class ark, or a rich ark to ride out the storm. As rich dad said to me years ago, "If you know the storm is coming, the size of the ark really does not matter. The first step is to simply make up your mind to build one. After you have made that decision, then decide on the kind of ark you want to build. Begin building it, build it as quickly as possible, and don't stop until it's built."

Build Your Ark

1. Do you need to build a financial ark for yourself and your family?

    Yes_____   No_____

2. How much time do you have to build your ark?

    Years before you turn 65

    Years before 2016

    (Take the lower number of years)

3. Do you believe you need to change your investing habits to build your ark?

    Yes_____   No_____

4. From which quadrant in the CASHFLOW Quadrant do you derive your income?

    E_____   S_____   B_____   I_____

5. Review the investment vehicles of the poor, middle class, and rich outlined in Chapter 7. Which investments do you want to start with?

    _____

6. If you want to become rich, are you willing to start investing time before you begin investing a lot of money?

    Yes_____   No_____

Chapter Eleven

TAKING CONTROL
OF THE ARK

"If you are going to build a rich ark," rich dad said, "you need to be in control of its construction, what is loaded in the cargo holds, and who is steering it." After the market crash of March 2000, millions of people came to feel less secure about their financial future. Why? Because they were not in control of their ark or its cargo, and many did not know who their skipper was.

Rich dad stated that *security* and *freedom* are not the same words. In fact, they are almost opposite from each other. Rich dad said, "The more security you gain, the more freedom you lose." He also said, "A person who seeks security often gives up control over parts of their lives. The more control you give up, the less freedom you have." Many people feel insecure about their financial future and retirement because they have given up most of the control over their financial future.

I wrote in *Rich Dad Poor Dad* that rich dad said the most important word in business is *cash flow*. In *Retire Young Retire Rich* (book number five in the Rich Dad series), I wrote that the second most important word is *leverage*,—the ability to do more and more with less and less. Although rich dad never directly said it, if there were a third most important word in his vocabulary, I believe it would be the word *control*. Here are a few observations about the word *control* as it relates to *cash flow*.

- One of the most important life skills to develop is to learn to gain *control* of your cash flow.

- When I saw the picture in *USA TODAY* of the 58-year-old Enron employee who had lost a significant amount of his retirement due to the fall of Enron, I saw a picture of a person who found out late in life that he had very little *control* over which way his cash was flowing.

- Most financial problems are caused by personal lack *of control* over cash flow.

- Kim and I were able to retire early in life because we took *control* over which direction our cash flowed.

One of the reasons so many millions feel less secure about their financial future is because they lack control of many aspects of their lives. Most people have very little control over a 401(k) defined-contribution plan, the ark of choice of the American middle class.

Rich dad was in control of his arks. He worked on design and cargoes, and knew his skippers well. The reason he had many skippers was because he had many arks. Obviously, if you decide to build a rich ark, one of the most important things to consider is whether you are willing to take back control of the entire ark or fleet of arks. If not, then stay with a defined-contribution plan, invest for the long term, diversify, pray a lot, and hope your skipper knows what to do.

By taking greater control over your entire ark, you may also slowly take back more and more control of your life and your freedom. Warren Buffett said, "I'm the luckiest guy in the world in terms of what I do for a living. No one can tell me to do things I don't believe in or things I think are stupid." In other words, he is in *control* of his arks—and he has a fleet of them.

Buffett controls, but is not into over-control. He buys companies with excellent management and treats them like owners of their businesses. In fact, many are allocated ownership positions. To this point, he says, "We wish to see the unit's managers become wealthy through ownership, not simply free-riding on the ownership of others. I think, in fact, that ownership can in time bring our best managers substantial wealth, perhaps in amounts well beyond what they now think possible."

The remark "not simple free-riding on the ownership of others" was made about a famous investment house, whose name shall remain anonymous. He felt this large investment firm did not care about the shareholders or their investments. The second half of this remark is about how he treats his managers. He lets them share in the profits of his arks.

He also hires the best people he can find to be skippers of his arks. He does that because he wants them to run the ark, not him. He says, "If they need my help to manage the enterprise, we're probably both in trouble."

Rich dad had the same style of ownership and management. That is why both men could manage many arks. It is a style of management that comes from the B and I quadrants, rather than the hands-on approach that many people from the E and S quadrants envision. It is the same style I am learning. I state this because many people say to me, "I don't have time to do my own investing. I'm just too busy." Many people from the E and S quadrants think they have to do everything, rather than learn to find smarter people to build, load, and sail their arks. So the word *control* does not necessarily mean you have to do it all by yourself. People from different quadrants control their arks in different ways. If you control in the style of the B and I quadrants, you can control many arks. If you control in the style of the E and S quadrants, you may only be able to control one ark—and you will be ark designer, ark builder, cargo loader, crew, and skipper. As I have said in other books and seminars, people from the E and S quadrants tend to have two theme songs running in their heads: "Nobody Does It Better" and "I Did It My Way." In my opinion, those are theme songs of people who tend to over-control.

Taking Control of Your Ark

Are you willing to take control of your ark? That is the question. If the answer is no, then the rest of this book may be too problematic—seeming to involve much too much time, effort, study, and money. For many people, it is much easier to work hard at their jobs and just hand their money over to someone they hope is better at managing arks than they are.

But if the answer is yes, then read on. Remember, being in control of an ark does not mean you have to do much. All you have to do is be willing to be in control. Warren Buffett is in control and lets other captains run the ships. You can do the same thing—if you want.

Learning About the Ark Business

From 1965 to 1969, I attended the U.S. Merchant Marine Academy in New York. For four years, that federal school trained young men, and now young women, to become ship's officers. Our training began with four weeks of rigorous physical and military indoctrination, which military academies are noted for. We got up early in the morning and ran till late at night. After our heads were shaved, we learned military discipline, how to wear a uniform, how to properly shoot a gun, exercise, and even proper etiquette at a dining table.

After the month of indoctrination, school began. We had to fulfill the academic requirements of a traditional college or university, which meant we had courses such as English, calculus, spherical trigonometry, thermodynamics, physics, literature, electronics, and the humanities. In addition to those traditional academic courses of study, we had to learn about life at sea, so we also had to learn Morse code, knot tying, wire rope splicing, semaphore, sailing, rowing, rescue at sea, astronomy, celestial navigation, weather, small-boat handling, large-ship steering, running an engine room, docking and undocking, handling a tugboat, business law, maritime law, cargo handling, naval architecture, oceanography, and other seagoing subjects.

On top of that, we spent a year at sea, taking a correspondence course while on merchant ships sailing the cargo lanes of the world, learning in the real world about what we had been learning in the classroom. My classmates and I literally went to every famous seaport throughout the world. To me, that was the best part of the program. Because of this year at sea, we had to finish a traditional four-year college curriculum in three years. It was a great well-rounded education. By the time my class graduated in 1969, we had lost over 50 percent of the class, but the rest of us were ready to take control of a ship as junior officers, ready to apprentice under the captain and other senior ship's officers. On graduation day, one of my instructors said, "Our training program is rigorous because we are training you to be more than captains of ships. We are training you to be captains of this industry." Many of my classmates did go on to become leaders in the shipping industry.

Rich dad put Mike and me through a similar program, starting when we were nine. He had us work in every aspect of his business from cleaning rooms and waiting on tables to working construction and doing office work.

I meet many people coming out of MBA programs today who have a great formal education, but very little real-world experience to back it up. For many of them, the only job they've held was working in a fast-food restaurant or clerking in a retail store. Then, upon graduation these young people are put into management positions, but lack real-world people skills.

Because they're smart, some are promoted before they ever gain those skills. Instead of knowing what it feels like to be the janitor, the warehouse foreman, or the receptionist, all they know are the people who are climbing the ladder with them.

Too many of these bright students end up as captains, but they don't understand the average worker, the real engine behind the business. When people lose touch with their workers, disasters like Enron and AIG happen. Did those so-called educated leaders recommend that their employees buy company shares while they themselves were selling? Perhaps it wasn't illegal to do so, but it was unethical. Sadly, this is a common practice in business and on Wall Street.

One thing both of my dads demanded was that I never lose touch with people at all levels of society. Rich dad said, "Never lose your humanity. Always remember that each member of your business is a human being with a family. Your job as the leader of the business is to do your best to protect their welfare and well-being." That is why rich dad had Mike and me work in all parts of his business. He wanted us to understand the workers in every area of the business.

A few years before he died, my poor dad said, "I have no doubt that someday you will be a rich man. Please never forget the home you come from and the values we hold. Always remember the people who have touched your life along the way. You may never see them again, but always remember them and be grateful for the gifts they have given you. And when you get to where you are going, have the humility to remember that rich or poor, friend or enemy, we are all human beings. Money does not make you superior to anyone. Please remember that you are a human being too." In my humble opinion, there are too many skippers of ships who have forgotten that they are responsible for human beings as well as for the ship and the ship's cargo.

Rich Dad's Lesson

At the start of this book, I related a story of how rich dad began our meetings by asking me to show him my current financial statements. That is how we started almost every meeting. As a child, he had me do very simple financials. As an adult, my financials became more adult-like. As I grew richer, my financials became more complex. Once I became financially free, my financials became even more sophisticated. As I grow older and hopefully wealthier, my financials will also grow in sophistication, and so must I. Getting into the habit of always having up-to-date personal financials is a learning process, a habit my rich dad stressed.

Needless to say, my poor dad never had a financial statement, much less a current up-to-date one. He knew how to fill out credit applications for such things as a home loan or a car, but he never made it a habit to have a bookkeeper do his monthly personal financial statements.

All through this book, I refer to financial greats such as Warren Buffett, America's richest investor; Alan Greenspan, chairman of the powerful Federal Reserve Board; and Paul O'Neill, the Secretary of the Treasury. They all say basically the same thing my rich dad told me. All of these financially smart men stress the importance of financial literacy and a financial statement. None of these men advised people to start with real estate, savings, a business, tax liens, stocks, day trading, options trading, or mutual funds—which is where most people start building their arks. That is why so many arks cannot stand rough seas.

So are you willing to take control of your ark? If the answer is still yes, then the next question is, "Are you willing to have current, up-to-date, audited, personal financial statements?" If the answer is no, then a DC pension plan such as personal savings, government retirement plans, a 401(k), and a home become very, very, very important.

If you are going to take control of your ark and maybe build a rich ark, you must make it a habit to have at least monthly income statements and balance sheets, the two documents that make up the basic financial statement. If you are to become richer and richer, regardless of the storms ahead, you must constantly work on improving your financial literacy. The best place to start your real-life education is with your own personal, up-to-date, real-life financial statement—even if it has nothing in it. I stress this point because I meet many people who read financial statements and annual reports of other companies, but they do not have financial statements on themselves. *The most important financial statement of all, if you are going to be in control of your ark, is your own personal financial statement.*

At the start of most meetings with rich dad, he asked to see my personal financial statement as well as my company's financial statement. Without those statements, he could not have helped me. He could have only guessed what my problems were and where they were.

In 1977, my financials looked pretty good because the business was just starting out and we had some investor money in the treasury. Rich dad helped me by making specific suggestions on what to do on my personal financial statement as well as the business's financial statements.

By 1978, the financial statements from my business were getting murky. By 1979, rich dad told me, "Your company has financial cancer." He thought the cancer would prove terminal, and it did. The company soon disappeared. Nevertheless, with his help and my constant reporting to him, my personal financial wounds healed and my fortune began to grow again. Even so, I did lose it all again, one more time. Again, by constantly checking in and handing over my financials, my rich dad was able to help me heal and grow.

Today, that process of making mistakes, learning, correcting, and reporting to rich dad with my financials has been the process that helped me evolve into a better ship's officer. Today, instead of fearing the storms brewing ahead, I look forward to them, knowing that it is by confronting life's challenges that we all become stronger.

In many ways, health and wealth are very similar. When we go to a doctor, the first thing he does is take a blood sample or X-rays. That is how the doctor can pinpoint exactly what is wrong and what needs to be corrected. The other day, my doctor reviewed my blood test and gave me some disturbing news. As much as I did not like the news, I was glad I received it early because it allowed me to make corrections early, before the problem became worse.

A financial statement with clean, clear numbers serves the same purpose as a blood test or X-ray. Regular updated financials give you a chance to find out the bad news early and take corrective action early. Unfortunately, because our school system has failed to educate people financially, millions of people will find out that they have financial cancer only after it is too late. That is what happened to the 58-year-old Enron employee in *USA TODAY*. He found out that his ship and the cargo were rotting and that the skippers had abandoned ship without telling the crew. The problem was, this worker found out a little late in life, but even now it's not too late. If that employee is willing to take control of his own ark, he may sail into a whole new world of financial wealth and financial well-being. All he has to do is look for professional bookkeepers, interview many, hire one, begin receiving monthly financial statements, review them monthly with a financial expert like a banker or accountant, and start making corrections. By facing his real-world finances with real-world financial documents, he enters a whole new real world of financial possibilities.

In the following chapters, I will explain the controls you need in order to gain greater control over the ark of your financial future. These controls are the basis of becoming a better captain of your own ark.

Build Your Ark

1. Are you willing to take control of your ark?

   Yes _____ No _____

2. Develop your own financial statement. Use the worksheet from the *CASHFLOW*® game to assist you. A sample is found in the next chapter and also at richdad.com.

3. Find a bookkeeper or accountant. Ask for references from successful people you know. Interview many, and select one.

4. Make an appointment with an accountant or bookkeeper to review your financial statements to make sure you have completed them properly.

5. Now you are ready to analyze where you are today and what changes you need to make in your investing habits.

Chapter Twelve

CONTROL #1: CONTROL OVER YOURSELF

The most important control of all is to take control over yourself and how you manage your money. If you can do that, you can build a rich ark and captain it wisely.

In 1996, I was in Peru looking for a gold mine to buy. Due to economic turmoil and terrorist attacks, many gold mines had been abandoned or left in the hands of poor management. High in the Andes Mountains at 15,000 feet, a banker showed me a mine he thought I could buy. Due to the altitude, the best I could do was take three steps, stop, catch my breath, and try to gain control from my dizziness.

Finally, down in the small, dark shaft of the mine, the banker, who owned the mine through foreclosure, pointed to a vein of quartz running through the rock. "Here," he said. "Look at how rich the vein is."

Stumbling over to the spot where he stood, I gazed at the spot his flashlight was hitting. "Wow," I said. "Look at all the gold." I could not believe the sparkling glitter of gold reflecting in the light.

"Sí, señor, I told you this was a good mine," smiled the banker.

Inching closer, I put my hand up to the milky green-and-white quartz vein and began touching the sparkling gold. "I can't believe how beautiful it is," I replied.

"Señor," said the banker, "what you are looking at is not gold. That is iron pyrites, or fool's gold. The gold I am looking at is in the quartz below the fool's gold. The real gold is in the dark part of the quartz vein. The gold is the part of the vein that does not shine."

Modern-Day Alchemist

When I was a little boy, rich dad often spoke of alchemy. Since I didn't know what alchemy was, I asked rich dad for an explanation. He said, "Years ago, many people were trying to turn different materials such as iron or coal into gold."

"Did anyone ever do it?" I asked.

"No," said rich dad. "No one has ever turned something into gold. Gold is just gold. But people have learned to create something even better than gold."

"What is better than gold?" I asked.

"Assets," said rich dad. "Today's modern alchemists turn money, resources, or ideas into wealth via assets."

"You mean assets they buy or build?" I asked.

Rich dad said, "That is correct. Today's modern alchemists can create assets out of thin air. They turn their ideas into assets, and those assets make them rich. A patent or trademark is an example of turning ideas into assets, or they turn trash into an asset, or they turn real estate into assets. That is modern-day alchemy."

As I rode down the twisting and bumpy road with the banker, staring out at the spectacular vistas high on the Peruvian Andes, I knew the banker knew he had a fool, not an alchemist, as a potential investor. If I could not tell the difference between veins of fool's gold and the vein of real gold, what chance did I have of turning that abandoned mine into an asset? Needless to say, I did not do a deal in Peru. I am just grateful that there are many ways to be an alchemist, other than mining for gold.

How Does a Banker Know the Difference Between a Fool and an Alchemist?

As rich dad was going over my personal and business financial statements in 1979, one of his comments is still appropriate today. He said, "The world is full of fools and alchemists. Fools turn cash to trash. Alchemists turn trash to cash. You and your partners are fools, not alchemists. You boys have taken a business and turned the cash into trash."

"But our banker said he would lend us more money," I replied. "We can't be doing that badly."

Rich dad chuckled and smiled, "First of all, bankers lend money to both fools and alchemists. Bankers do not really care, as long as you have the money to pay them back. Secondly, if you are a fool, you will pay higher rates of interest. The bigger the fool, the higher the interest rate. So your bankers love you boys. Your business makes a lot of money, and you boys are turning that cash into trash. These financials show that at one end of the business, you are alchemists, and at the other end, you boys are fools. Why wouldn't a banker lend money to you?

"The problem is that you boys are about to go broke. Instead of reinvesting the money from your business back into your business, I can see here in the liability column of your financial statement that you boys have invested in one Porsche, one Mercedes, and two Jaguars. Look at the interest rates you are paying on those cars. No wonder your banker loves you, and no wonder you're going broke. You boys must look good driving around in your flashy cars. I'm sure the women love you, but your financials tell me that you have financial cancer. Your financials tell me that you are fools, not alchemists. You seem to have forgotten everything I have taught you."

All That Glitters Is Not Gold

Rich dad then said something I recalled years later as I rode down from the mine way on top of the Peruvian Andes. Sitting in the bumpy four-wheel-drive vehicle, I could hear rich dad saying, "All that glitters is not gold. Fools are fooled by the glitter. That is why it is called fool's gold. Alchemists can find gold in the darkness."

Retirement Plans That Glitter

One of my routines is to turn on the financial news on two financial networks. I check the mood of the market in the morning, and then the mood of the market at the end of the day. I find it interesting to watch which mutual fund, stock, public company, or financial advisory service is doing the most advertising. In other words, which one is glittering?

Many people, low-income wage earners to high-income wage earners, are in financial trouble because too much of their money goes to buy things that glitter. We have all heard of poor kids spending $150 for a new pair of name-brand athletic shoes. On my inspection tours of apartment houses I am interested in buying, I always find name-brand, large-screen TV sets and video games in many of the apartments. I have friends who live in name-brand suburbs, drive European cars, and send their kids to private schools. In other words, when you look at their expense and liability columns, they are awash with glitter.

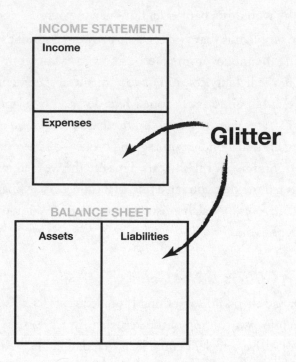

There is nothing wrong with name-brand glitter. I too love brand names such as Porsche, Ferrari, Armani, and Rolex. What good is life without a little glitter?

The problem is, too many people have asset columns overwhelmingly invested in glitter.

INCOME STATEMENT

Income
Expenses

BALANCE SHEET

Assets	Liabilities
Glitter	

When I hear someone say, "I buy only blue-chip stocks," I know this person buys stocks of companies that glitter. Or if I hear, "My broker is so-and-so," and this person is mentioning their name-brand brokerage firm as a form of name-dropping, I know this person has bought the glitter. I become a little suspicious of mutual-fund companies or stock-brokerage firms that advertise a lot. Those ads are expensive, costing millions of dollars. Someone has to pay for those ads, and that someone is obviously the investor. Warren Buffett's mutual fund, Berkshire Hathaway, doesn't advertise for investors and discourages people from investing in the fund. The point is, I do not see Berkshire Hathaway advertisements, but I do hear ordinary people talking about Berkshire Hathaway a lot. Maybe I hear about Berkshire Hathaway because it is run by an investor, rather than a large corporation.

Many professional investors look for gold only in the darkness. They do not follow glittering companies like Microsoft. Instead, they are looking for the next Microsoft. They are looking for the small start-up company that will grow into an international giant. They are not looking for a name-brand CEO with the silver hair, the Ivy-League degree, and the movie-star smile. Many are looking for an entrepreneur, laboring away in a basement or garage, working on the next product that will solve the next big problem facing humanity.

While playing *Monopoly*®, rich dad would remind me that many people also look for the glitter in real estate and want Boardwalk and Park Place, but the true wealth is from owning the other properties and loading them up with houses and hotels. It's not the glitter that counts. It's the cash flow. In fact, in a 2002 Harvard Business Review article entitled "Everything I Know About Business I Learned from *Monopoly*," Phil Orbanes says, "Casual players don't know this, but the 28 properties around the *Monopoly* board are not equally valuable in terms of ROI. Boardwalk and Park Place, which many regard as the most precious, actually are not. It turns out that the orange and red properties have the highest ROI and are the best properties to own."

When I look for real estate investments, I generally do not go to the new-home subdivisions where there are flags, helium balloons, large eye-catching signs, flashy model homes, and a sales trailer offering easy financing plans. I know these marketing ploys are to attract potential homeowners who are seeking emotional satisfaction. When I look for real estate, I am often looking in older neighborhoods at unattractive buildings, many with major problems. Often that is where the highest-yielding investments are, but not always. I have bought brand-new real estate in hot new areas that turned out to be a financial home run. I do know that sometimes things that glitter are gold. Again, it is financial education—being able to read financial statements, the deal, the trends, and the needs of the buyer and seller, that can turn glittery fool's gold into glittery real gold. That is financial alchemy.

The point is, millions of people, rich and poor, are in financial trouble because they are fools for the glitter. In just a few years, millions of aging people throughout the world will find out they are in financial trouble because their DC pension plans are invested in glitter, but not in gold.

This is the income statement and balance sheet from my *CASHFLOW* game's financial statement.

Income from Assets

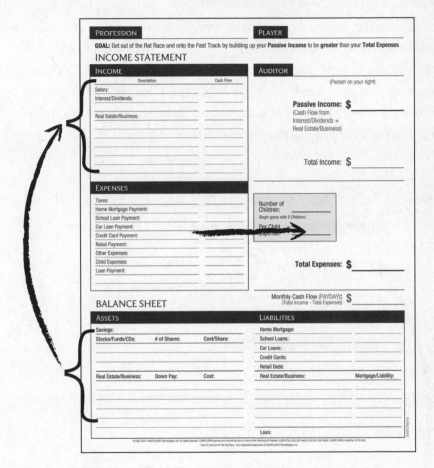

When bankers see income on the lines of the income statement that the arrow is pointing to, they know that this ark has a cargo of assets on board.

If there are no numbers there, they know this ark has no cargo on board and is sailing empty or, if there is cargo on board, this person has loaded their ark with fool's gold.

To find out if the ship is empty or loaded with fool's gold, the banker or ship's captain simply looks down at the balance sheet. If the balance sheet, which is the ark's cargo hold, shows the asset column is empty, they know the ship is empty. It could be the financial statement of a poor person or a young person just starting out.

If the balance sheet shows a cargo with a retirement plan, stocks, bonds, mutual funds, or real estate, but no cash-flow arrows to the income statement, the banker or the ship's captain becomes suspicious, suspecting that the cargo hold might have been filled with fool's gold. If the assets are name-brand assets, then you know this person loaded the cargo hold with fool's gold that merely glitters.

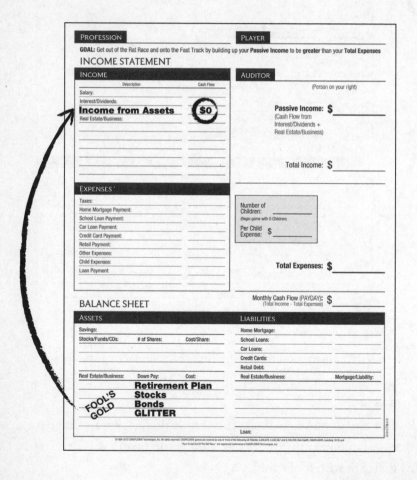

As a student at the U.S. Merchant Marine Academy, I was taught to watch the cargo holds closely. We were taught to be careful about what type of cargo was being loaded, how it was being loaded, where it was stored, if it was securely stored, and how and where it was to be unloaded. Cargo operations was a very big subject at the academy. It was a subject we studied in depth for four years.

One of the cargo-operations instructors was a retired sea captain with years of experience. His classes were very interesting because he told great stories as he explained the technical side of a rather boring subject. One of his stories was about a load of cargo that broke loose during a storm on the port side (left side) of the number-two cargo hold (the large cargo hold, second from the bow of the ship). He said, "Suddenly there was a large cracking sound, and the ship began to list (tilt) to starboard (the right side). The ship began to sail off course, and the helmsman (the seaman steering the ship) had to swing the wheel hard to port (turn the steering wheel to the left). Immediately the large waves began to come over the ship from the port side instead of hitting the ship on the bow. As the helmsman fought to get the bow of the ship headed back into the waves, there was another loud cracking sound. It was the cargo in the number-four hold (the biggest hold, just in front of the bridge of the ship) breaking loose. Instead of the ship correcting, the weight of the shifting cargo in hold number four made the list to starboard even worse. The monster waves were now hitting the ship broadside."

As the old sea captain spoke, the class was right there on board the ship with him. Since we were now seniors, we had all been to sea for a year. We knew what it was like to be out on the ocean on a large ship loaded with cargo. Many of us, myself included, had been through hurricanes, accidents, deaths, and other hazards and disasters associated with the industry. As the old captain spoke, I could feel the ship listing to starboard with the helmsman fighting to regain control over the forces of the cargo, the ship, the weather, and the ocean. We all knew that having your cargo break loose during a storm is a nightmare that few people live through.

The retired captain told us that the helmsman did eventually lose control of the ship. The ship's cargo continued to break loose, and the ship rolled rapidly to starboard and capsized when a large wave hit it. Luckily, the crew was picked up two days later by another passing freighter. The teacher's final words were, "Before you leave the harbor, make sure your cargo is tied down securely. All it takes is one hold to be tied down improperly, and the cargo that was supposed to make you rich could kill you."

When the next monster stock-market crash comes, many people will find out that their cargo holds are not securely tied down. Many of their assets will suddenly turn into liabilities, as many did in March of 2000. Many will not be able to handle the financial storm because, although millions of people have invested, they failed to become investors. When the financial crash comes, the real investors will be at the helm, working hard to keep the cash flowing from the asset column into the income column. Many of the people who invested but failed to become investors will find their little arks capsized, adrift at sea, hoping the government or some charitable organization rescues them.

Take Control of Your Financial Statement

The reason the financial statement is such an important financial tool is because it gives the banker or the captain of the ship a quick snapshot as to whether your cargo is gold or fool's gold. In book number four of the Rich Dad series, *Rich Kid Smart Kid*, the introduction to the book is entitled, "Why Your Banker Does Not Ask for Your Report Card." The reason the banker does not ask you for your report card or your grade-point average or what school you went to is because your academic success or professional success has little to do with your financial success As the crew of the good ship SS Enron found out, employees with PhDs, MBAs, CPAs, and JDs after their names were swimming right alongside employees who had not finished high school. Unfortunately, in just a few years, millions of highly educated people will also be swimming for their lives and hoping to be rescued.

If you are to be captain of your own ark, the number-one control is to take control of yourself, your financial statement, your cargo, how it is stored, and who is securing it. Your balance sheet is the cargo hold of your ark. In large financial storms, which do occur on a regular basis, people will find out that Porsches, Ferraris, Rolexes, their home, mutual funds, stocks, and real estate can suddenly shift in value from the port side (assets) to the starboard side (liabilities) in a flash. When that happens, and it will, people will find out how *worth less* their *net worth* really is.

So, the message is, if you love the glitter, you should not be captain of the ship. If you are to become captain, you must control the fool in you that tends to be attracted to the glitter rather than the gold. To be captain of your ship, take control of yourself. Take control of your income statement and your balance sheet. Always remember that your balance sheet is the cargo hold of your ark.

Know the Difference Between an Asset and a Liability

"If you want to be rich, you must know the difference between an asset and a liability," rich dad repeatedly said to his son and me. The reason he spent so much time on our financial education is because, without a solid financial education, a person cannot tell the difference between an asset and a liability. One of the fundamentals of building a rich ark is to know the difference between an asset and a liability.

A Book on Accounting

In January of 2002, I was asked to give a talk to a small group of very prominent business people in Phoenix, Arizona. After my talk, a senior vice president of a large regional bank asked, "I understand your book *Rich Dad Poor Dad* has sold more than 11 million copies worldwide in over 35 languages. Is that true?"

Nodding, I said, "Yes, and the numbers keep increasing. *Rich Dad Poor Dad* has been on bestseller lists like the *New York Times* and the *Wall Street Journal* for years. Have you read the book?"

"No, I haven't," he replied pleasantly. "Tell me what it's about."

"It's a book on accounting," I said with a smile.

"What?" stammered the banker. "How can a book on accounting be a worldwide bestseller? That makes no sense. I have an accounting degree. Accounting could never be the subject of a bestseller."

I spent the next few minutes telling him the story of my poor dad and my rich dad. I explained how my poor dad was an advocate of word literacy and my rich dad was an advocate of financial literacy. After explaining the story behind the book, I then asked the banker, "How many of your customers are financially illiterate?"

The banker shook his head, smiled, and said, "Some of my clients are very financially literate. Many of the richest clients are well versed financially. But most of my clients have no idea what a financial statement is, much less anything about accounting. Many of them make a lot of money, but they have no idea what to do with their money. It's good for me since most of them keep their money in savings. So yes, you are correct. Most of the people I meet are not financially literate."

Those of you who have read *Rich Dad Poor Dad* know how important the basics of accounting, the income statement and balance sheet, were to my rich dad. Rich dad often said, "Without both the income statement and balance sheet, you really cannot tell the difference between an asset and a liability." In *Rich Dad Poor Dad*, the part of the book that caused such a roar of protest was the idea that your home is not an asset. In most cases, a person's home is a liability. Some people put the book down after that point and refuse to read further. My rich dad never said not to buy a home. In fact, he encouraged home ownership. His main point was that we need to know the difference between an asset and a liability. Rich dad's point was that many people struggle financially simply because they purchase liabilities they think are assets.

"So how can a book on accounting be so popular?" asked the banker.

Smiling, I said, "Well, it's more than a book on accounting. It's also a book on personal accountability."

"Personal accountability?" replied the banker. "Why personal accountability?"

"First of all, understanding accounting gives me control over my finances and my future. I can run my own businesses and I don't need someone else to do my investing for me," I said. "Secondly, personal accountability means I do not let people lie to me."

"Lie to you?" said the banker. "What do you mean by that?"

"Well, look at this Enron case."

"Oh," smiled the banker. "I understand."

How Do You Tell Gold from Fool's Gold?

Warren Buffett, America's richest investor, believes that understanding accounting is a form of self-defense. He said:

> *When managers want to get across the facts of a business to you, it can be done within the rules of accounting. Unfortunately, when they want to play games, at least in some industries, it can also be done within the rules of accounting. If you can't recognize the differences, you shouldn't be in the equity-picking business.*

When the Enron affair broke, one of the questions asked was, "What is pro-forma accounting?" which was one of the methods of accounting Enron was using when the roof caved in. Rich dad would say, "Pro-forma accounting is an accounting report that should begin with the words, 'Once upon a time...' or, "In a perfect world...' or, "If everything goes as planned...'"

In 1999, at the height of the stock-market boom, I was invited to a school to talk about the importance of teaching young people financial literacy. A teacher raised his hand and proudly said, "We do teach financial literacy in our school. We're teaching kids how to pick stocks."

"Do you first teach them to read the annual reports and financial statements?" I asked.

"No. I just have them read the reports from the market analysts. If the analyst gives the stock a *buy* recommendation, we buy. When they recommend a *sell*, we sell."

Not wanting to be obnoxious, I simply smiled and nodded my head saying, "How are they doing?"

He beamed and said, "The average portfolio is up over 20 percent."

I smiled and thanked him for teaching. I did not say anything after the word *teaching*. I did not want to say what I feared he was teaching those kids to be.

Just before the Enron scandal broke, 16 out of 17 market analysts were giving Enron a *buy* recommendation.

When Warren Buffett says, "If you can't recognize the differences, you shouldn't be in the equity-picking business," he means, "If you are not financially literate, you shouldn't be picking stocks." Rich dad would say, "Picking stocks without first knowing how to read a company's financial statements is gambling, not stock-picking." In rich dad's mind, ERISA forced millions of people to become gamblers, not investors—gambling with their future financial security. Instead of filling their retirement arks up with gold, they spent a lifetime being fooled and filled their arks with fool's gold. So the problem of a worldwide lack of financial literacy is a problem far beyond just the Enron and the Arthur Andersen scandal.

Rich Dad Poor Dad is a book about accounting, but it is also a book about accountability. As accounting questions continue to surface with companies such as Enron, WorldCom, and Xerox, it is obvious that the basics of financial accountability, not just accounting, are being overlooked.

Enron used "off balance sheet" accounting to account for liabilities. In other words, its financial statement did not correctly show all liabilities. This would be similar to a person who doesn't want to list all of his credit-card debt on his personal financial statement. It's not only bad accounting. It's a lack of accountability.

With the financial collapse of WorldCom, we have to consider rich dad's definition of assets versus that of the conventional banker's definition. Rich dad told us that an asset puts money in your pocket. When an expense is capitalized (moved to an asset) and then amortized or depreciated over time (gradually expensed), it increases assets and decreases expenses. But remember that rich dad told us that an asset has to put money in your pocket. Changing an expense into an asset doesn't put more money in your pocket.

Should savvy analysts have discovered the shortcomings of WorldCom's accounting? It stands to be the largest accounting fraud in history at close to $4 billion, and new allegations of additional irregularities are arising every day. A careful study of the statement of cash flows should have revealed this alarming exercise of re-classifying expenses to assets. The net impact was to increase revenue (by decreasing expenses) and increase assets—all while the cash was flowing out of the company!

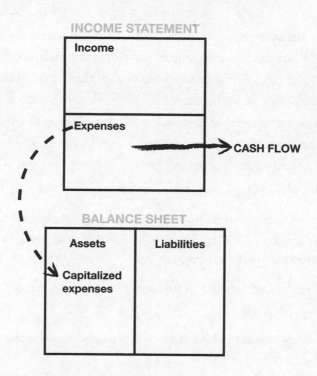

Many analysts and accountants place too much reliance on the accrual form of accounting, which is reflected in the income statement and balance sheet. This is where WorldCom was overstating its revenues and assets. Warren Buffett, in his 2001 Annual Report for Berkshire Hathaway, stated: "When companies or investment professionals use terms such as 'EBITDA' and 'pro forma,' they want you to unthinkingly accept concepts that are dangerously flawed. (In golf, my score is frequently below par on a pro forma basis: I have firm plans to 'restructure' my putting stroke and therefore only count the swings I take before reaching the green)." Later in the same report, he continued with: "Those who believe that EBITDA is in any way equivalent to true earnings are welcome to pick up the tab."

In fact, the creation of the statement of cash flows is usually one of the last statements put together for the financial statements. It seems the accountants start with two known amounts, beginning cash and ending cash, and the rest is a jigsaw puzzle until the difference is explained. Could more time analyzing the statement of cash flows have prevented many of the accounting irregularities in corporate America today?

Is a company a good investment? The answer is shown by reviewing all parts of all of the financial statements—the balance sheet, the income statement, and especially the statement of cash flows. Look for which way the cash flows for an investment. Does it flow in, or does it flow out? Look for clues that can give evidence of the board's accountability. Cash flow is a good place to start, but no one line item can ever give the answer regarding a company's viability.

Bear in mind what Alan Greenspan has said:

- *Many studies have pointed to a critical need to improve financial literacy, the lack of which leaves millions of Americans vulnerable to unscrupulous business practices.*

- *An informed borrower is simply less vulnerable to fraud and abuse.*

- *Schools should teach basic financial concepts better in elementary and secondary schools.*

- *Improved financial literacy would help prevent younger people from making poor financial decisions that can take years to overcome.*

As I watched Greenspan on TV delivering this speech, what I was most impressed with was his emphasis on the need for the American civilization to evolve. Given the financial complexities we all face today, financial literacy is important for that evolution.

At the same Senate Banking Committee meeting, Treasury Secretary Paul O'Neill said, "People need to be able to read, write, and speak basic concepts in order to make informed investment decisions." He continued, "Financial literacy is more important now with the decline in the number of companies offering defined-benefit pension plans and the growth in pension plans in which workers make their own investing decisions." In the year 2002, these prominent men sound very much like my rich dad did a couple of decades ago. At least they share the same concerns.

Understanding Assets vs. Liabilities

In *Rich Dad Poor Dad*, I wrote that my rich dad taught me to become financially literate starting at the age of nine. I believe one of the reasons for the success of the book is because it really never gets above a nine-year-old child's level of understanding.

For those who have not read the book, I will explain some its core points. For those who have read the book, I will add a few more important bits of information.

Years ago, rich dad drew this simple diagram of an income and expense statement. It is also known as a profit and loss statement, or P&L.

INCOME STATEMENT

Income
Expenses

Rich dad taught me that this accounting form is called a balance sheet, simply because your assets are supposed to balance your liabilities. He said, "This is where the confusion in accounting begins for most people."

BALANCE SHEET

Assets	Liabilities

My poor dad sincerely believed our house was an asset. My rich dad would say, "If your dad were financially literate, he would know that his house is not an asset. It is a liability."

Rich dad explained to me that the reason so many people call their home an asset is simply because a home is listed under the asset column. That means that even accountants and bankers call your home an asset because that is the column your home is listed under. For example, let's say your home costs $100,000. You put $20,000 as a down payment and take out an $80,000 mortgage. The banker's balance sheet would then look like this:

BALANCE SHEET

Assets	Liabilities
🏠 $100,000	$80,000
	Net Worth
	$20,000

The difference between assets and liabilities is net worth—in this case, your $20,000 deposit. The balance sheet balances, the accountants and bankers are happy, and the new homeowner is happy.

For most people, this is all they want to know about accounting, and all they believe they need to know about accounting. Many people experience a lot of emotional comfort and pride because they feel that they are doing the right thing in purchasing a home. In their mind, they think it is an asset. The word *asset* sounds better than *liability*.

In teaching his son and me to be business owners and investors, rich dad often said, "If you want to be wealthy, you need to know more than the average person knows about accounting." Starting at the age of nine, he began pushing our financial education far beyond the financial education of most adults, and he did it in very simple language.

Rich dad said, "It is impossible to tell the difference between an asset and a liability just by looking at a balance sheet. To know that difference, you must also have an income statement. Without both an income statement and a balance sheet, it is impossible to tell the difference between an asset and a liability."

To make his point, rich dad drew the following diagram for his son and me.

INCOME STATEMENT

Income
Expenses

BALANCE SHEET

Assets	Liabilities

Rich Dad Poor Dad is really a book about the relationship between the income statement and balance sheet as much as it is the story of two dads and two sons. Without understanding the relationships, it is easy to be fooled.

A Most Important Lesson

Rich dad then said, "The most important words in business are the words *cash flow*." He went on to explain that rich people are rich because they can control cash flow. Poor people are poor because they cannot. "One of the most important life skills to develop is to learn to gain control of your cash flow. Most financial problems are caused by personal lack of control over cash flow." This is one of the most important lessons I learned as a nine-year-old boy.

To repeat Alan Greenspan's words: "Improved financial literacy would help prevent younger people from making poor financial decisions that can take years to overcome."

Rich dad's statement, "One of the most important life skills to develop is to learn to gain control of your cash flow," parallels Alan Greenspan's statement. When I saw the picture of that 58-year-old Enron employee on the front page of *USA TODAY*'s "Money" section, I saw a picture of a person who found out late in life that he had very little control over which way his cash was flowing. Alan Greenspan's reference to "making poor financial decisions that can take years to overcome" is especially prophetic here.

In March of 2000, millions of employees in America found out that they have no control over the cash flowing out of their retirement plans, what they were led to believe were assets. To rich dad and to me, that is one of the greatest flaws of these new DC pension plans. The worker puts money in, hoping that the money grows. But instead, what workers are finding out is that they do not have much control over their cash flow once their cash buys a stock, bond, or mutual fund.

Again, to repeat: "One of the most important life skills to develop is to learn to gain control of your cash flow. Most financial problems are caused by personal lack of control over cash flow."

This is one of the most important lessons I learned as a nine-year-old boy. As I grew up, I had to gain more and more control, not less, over my cash flow.

Kim and I were able to retire early in life because we took control over which direction our cash flowed. When the stock market went up, we made money because we had control over our cash flow. When the market crashed, we made even more money because we had control over our cash flow. We do not sit around watching our money flowing down the drain doing nothing as most people did after the March 2000 crash.

When I told the banker that *Rich Dad Poor Dad* was a book on accounting and accountability, I believe the word *accountability* was more important. The question from this Enron scandal is: How can workers be accountable for their own lives if they never learned to account for their money and they have no control over which way their retirement money flows? Millions, and I do mean millions, of people all over the world are in grave financial danger simply because they never learned accounting, how to be accountable, have little control over the cash flow in their retirement accounts, and hence have little-to-no control over their later lives.

Cash Flow Determines Whether It's an Asset or a Liability

Continuing on with rich dad's simple yet most important lesson, he said, "Which direction the cash is flowing determines if something is an asset or a liability."

He said, "Assets cash flow money into the income column. Liabilities cash flow money into and out of the expense column."

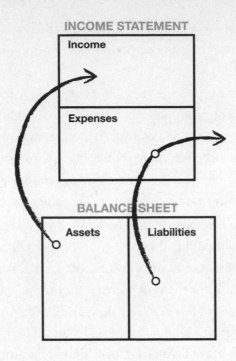

The lesson again is that it is the relationship of cash flow between an income statement and a balance sheet that tells if something is an asset or a liability. More simply stated, rich dad often said, "If you stop working, assets will put money into your pocket, and liabilities will take money out of your pocket." More graphically he said, "If you stop working, assets feed you and liabilities eat you."

After March of 2000, millions of people, not just Enron workers, found out that their arks, their retirement plans, were eating them alive, simply because they had no control over which way the cash was flowing.

A liability is anything that takes money from your pocket. That means a personal residence, the dream of the middle class, is more often a liability, rather than an asset. If a person rented out that home and the rental income was greater than all the expenses, then that same home would shift from the liability column to the asset column.

Personal Residence Turned into Rental Property

As a young boy, I learned that a house can be either an asset or a liability. That simple little lesson changed the direction of my life because I was less apt to be fooled into blindly believing my house is an asset. If not for that simple little lesson early in life, I am certain I would have wound up like my parents—buying a house, car, furniture, television sets, and jewelry—believing in my mind and in my heart that I was buying assets. My mom and dad truly believed in their hearts that they were buying assets. Instead, they were fooled by popular cultural myths, the financial myths of the middle class and poor.

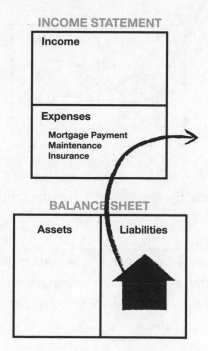

Now I can hear some of you saying, "What if I do not have a mortgage on my house? What if it is free and clear?" Or "What about all the appreciation my house has gained?" Or "What about my car? Isn't that an asset?"

In short, the answer is the same. It is cash flow that determines if something is an asset or a liability. In other words, a house without debt can still be a liability because it is not debt that determines if something is an asset or not. It is the direction of cash flowing between the income statement and balance sheet.

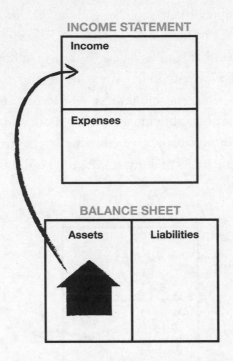

The point of this book is not to discuss the idea of your home being an asset or liability. It is to point out that millions of people have their retirement in jeopardy because they have been buying liabilities, not assets, for their retirement arks. Millions and millions of workers are opening their retirement account statements and wondering where the money went. In other words, which way did the cash flow? In millions of cases, the cash flowed out. They had invested in liabilities they thought were assets.

Facts versus Opinion

Many people think that accounting is dealing with facts, and in some ways, that is true. Yet, for the most part, accounting is based upon opinions, not facts. I promised those who have read my other books that I would go deeper into what rich dad taught me. This is where we go deeper. The point that accounting is made up of opinions rather than facts is a very, very important point to grasp.

Rich dad tells this story on how to find a good accountant. He said, "When interviewing the first accountant you ask him, 'How much is 1 + 1?' If the first candidate answers '2,' don't hire him because he is not smart enough. If the second accountant answers '3' to the same question, again don't hire him because he's stupid. If the third candidate answers the question with 'What do you want 1 + 1 to be?' hire him because you have found your accountant."

Is Your Retirement Account an Asset or a Liability?

I use this example to illustrate the point that accounting is primarily opinion rather than fact. When I ask people, "Is your retirement plan an asset?" most people will say yes. After all, they may have several hundred thousands of dollars or even millions of dollars in it. After pension reform, rich dad saw his employees' 401(k)s as liabilities, not assets, even though there was money, stocks, bonds, or mutual funds in the accounts. The question is: Who was right?

In February 2002, General Motors happily announced to the world that they would be posting a profit. Given the tough economic environment of 2001, that news was worth celebrating. Yet critics began to talk about GM's underfunded liability, their pension plan. As I watched a discussion on television, one commentator was calling the billions of dollars in General Motors' pension plan an asset. The second commentator was calling the same billions of dollars a major liability. Again, they were talking about the same billions of dollars, yet one expert called it an asset and the other called it a liability. The point here is that accounting is more often a matter of opinion rather than fact.

A major part of rich dad's financial education was to teach us to be critical thinkers. I use the word *critical* because I can hear some of the readers at this point being cynical, not critical. I can hear some of you saying, "Well, a billion dollars is an asset, no matter which way you look at it." In other words, that person is cynical rather than being simply critical, and there is a very big difference between critical and cynical.

Repeating Warren Buffett's statement: "When managers want to get across the facts of the business to you, it can be done within the rules of accounting. Unfortunately, when they want to play games, at least in some industries, it can also be done within the rules of accounting. If you can't recognize the differences, you shouldn't be in the equity-picking business."

Warren Buffett is advising a person to be a *critical* thinker, not a *cynical* thinker. He is saying, "If your mind cannot discern the finer differences, you can easily be fooled."

Millions of people believe their DC pension plans are assets. Another person can see those same pension plans as liabilities. The point rich dad would make is that to be a more sophisticated investor, you need to see it both ways. If you cannot see it both ways, as Buffett says, "you shouldn't be in the equity-picking business."

Assets Can Become Liabilities

Another vitally important lesson rich dad taught his son and me was that *all assets can become liabilities*. He said, "All assets have the potential to turn into liabilities in the blink of an eye. That is why you must be careful when you buy an asset, and be even more careful *after* you buy it."

Millions of people may have technically bought assets before March of 2000, but those same so-called assets quickly turned into liabilities after March of 2000. This sudden shift—from the perception that they had assets in their retirement accounts to the reality that they have purchased liabilities—causes millions of people today to feel uncertain about their retirement.

Today, millions of people want to know what a real asset is and what a real liability is. The real answer is that all assets can also be liabilities. That is why, if you want to build a rich ark, you must do as Alan Greenspan, Warren Buffett, Treasury Secretary Paul O'Neill, and rich dad recommend, which is to become financially literate. Financial literacy is essential to building a rich ark because, if you are not financially literate, you may spend years filling your ark with fool's gold, rather than real gold.

It's Time Now to Prepare for the Storm

This book is being written in the spring of 2002. Given the needs of the massive baby-boom generation—generally defined as the 83 million people born in America between 1946 and 1964—there should be another stock-market boom, a big one, when they are ready to start retiring.

Many of these baby boomers will be forced once again to enter the stock market through their DC pension plans. This last-chance gasp for some degree of financial security will cause the big boom before the big bust. This means that we all have to load our arks with good assets rather than bad assets,that will break loose in the storm and turn into liabilities. Of course, the big crash could happen tonight or tomorrow night. If nothing happens, the big bust may take until 2016, but the big bust will come. It will come simply because there are too many millions of baby boomers who are not in control of their arks, or don't have the financial education to be in control of their arks during rough seas.

This book is not so much about *predicting* the exact date as much as it is about *preparing*. The good news is that we all have time to prepare. I point out action steps to assist in your preparation for the coming perfect storm, a storm that will probably cause a giant boom and a giant bust. Remember rich dad's words, "If you want to become rich, start out by investing a lot of time before you begin investing a lot of money."

Build Your Ark

1. Review your financial statement. Analyze each item listed as an asset. For each, answer the question: Does it put money in your pocket?

     Yes ____   No ____

2. If the asset does not put money in your pocket, label it as "fool's gold."

3. How much of your income is from assets?
   In other words, is your money (assets) working for you?

4. Do you have assets that are not working for you today that you could turn into cash-flow-producing assets?

Additional Resources

If you are interested in learning how to take more control of your own ark and its cargo, the following games are designed to assist you in that learning process.

1. *CASHFLOW 101* and *CASHFLOW 202*

   I created these games in 1996 to teach the basics of both accounting and investing. As the names state, they are designed to teach people who want to be investors how to take control over the cash flow from their assets. They are not the easiest games, but once learned, people report that their lives are changed as the lights go on in their heads. Players learn how to turn their paychecks into assets and keep the cash flowing from those assets back into their pockets. Simply put, they are powerful life-changing games.

2. *CASHFLOW for Kids*

    This educational game is the simplified version of the adult version of *CASHFLOW 101*. The child's game is designed for children between the ages of six and twelve. Many parents find the kids' game a great place to start before going on to the adult version.

    This game was developed to teach young people how to avoid the glitter of all the fool's gold in the world and learn to take control of their own financial arks. *CASHFLOW for Kids* gives your children the opportunity to be the CFO of their lives. As Alan Greenspan, the chairman of the Federal Reserve Board, said, "Improved financial literacy would help prevent younger people from making poor financial decisions that can take years to overcome."

Chapter Thirteen

CONTROL #2: CONTROL OVER YOUR EMOTIONS

Warren Buffett often says, "If you cannot control your emotions, you cannot control your money."

A friend's wife said to me, "As a close friend, you're aware that we've recently made a lot of money. We've never had so much money. But now I'm terrified that we are going to lose it all." By the end of 2001, they had indeed nearly lost it all. What they were afraid would happen, did, in fact, happen. Their fear of losing became a self-fulfilling prophecy.

Rich dad said, "Money is an emotional subject. If you cannot control your emotions, your emotions will control your money." He also said, "When it comes to money, many people are financial hypochondriacs."

In the fifth grade, I began to read books on the great seagoing explorers such as Columbus, Magellan, Cortez, Cook, and others. It was because of their stories that I believe I wound up at the U.S. Merchant Marine Academy at Kings Point, New York. Although I went into the Marine Corps after graduation from Kings Point, my love of the sea has never left me.

One of the best books I have ever read about life on ships is *In the Heart of the Sea: The Tragedy of the Whaleship Essex*, written by Nathaniel Philbrick. The book is based upon a true story about the whaling ship *Essex*. In the early 1800s, the *Essex* sailed from Nantucket, 25 miles off the coast of Cape Cod, Massachusetts, around South America and out into the middle of the Pacific Ocean near the equator. It was supposed to be a voyage that would last two to three years. Unfortunately, the voyage came to a sudden end when a giant sperm whale rammed the ship and sank it.

If this story sounds familiar, it is because Herman Melville's *Moby Dick* was taken from the true story of the *Essex*. Having read both books, the story of *Moby Dick* pales in comparison to the real tale of what happened to the crew of the *Essex* after it sank. In fact, the story of *Moby Dick* ends after the ship is rammed. The story of the *Essex* begins after the ship is rammed.

As the *Essex* slowly began to sink, the crew of approximately 20 men climbed onto the three smaller whaleboats. Once provisions were transferred from the *Essex* to the whaleboats, the captain and the crew had to decide what they would do next. One option they discussed was simply raising their sails and letting the wind blow them to Tahiti, an easy trip they estimated would take about a week.

Suddenly, one of the crewmen said, "But the Tahitians are cannibals!" That was all it took. With that frightening thought, the mood of the crew in the three whaleboats changed, and they decided it was best they sail and row back to Chile, even though it was much farther away and it meant traveling against the wind. They chose Chile because they were familiar with Chile and felt they would be safer there than with the "cannibals of Tahiti." So off they sailed, straight into the wind.

More than 90 days later, one of the small whaleboats was sighted by another whaling ship from New England. As the captain of the whaling ship pulled alongside, he saw a man who looked like a skeleton in the bow of the boat and another man, just as skeletal, in the stern. In the middle of the boat was a pile of bones, the bleached bones of their fellow crewmembers. The men of the *Essex* had become what they were afraid of. Their fears had become a self-fulfilling prophecy.

The story of the *Essex* is much more than a gruesome story of cannibalism. It is also about a weak captain and a group of people who let their emotions do their thinking. It is about a group of men letting the thought of security determine their future. Instead of sailing to

Tahiti, they chose to sail back to what they felt familiar with, even though professionally they knew that sailing back to Chile was almost impossible.

It is also a story of assumptions. Remember assumptions from earlier in this book? Well, no one ever questioned the sailor who made the comment that the Tahitians were cannibals. All of the men were from New England. None had ever been to Tahiti. No one simply asked, "Have you ever been to Tahiti?"

Soon after the *Essex* tragedy, both Hawaii and Tahiti became paradise for whalers from all over the world. As a young boy, after reading about the great times whalers had in Tahiti, I used to dream of one day sailing a ship to Tahiti, a dream that came true in 1967. In fact, it was my dream of sailing to Tahiti that most inspired me to go to school in New York. In 1967 I sailed from Hawaii to Tahiti as a student on board an oil tanker. Instead of finding cannibals, I found a paradise far better than that of all my youthful dreams. I still dream of Tahiti and the beautiful people I met there.

Investing Is Paradise

For my wife, Kim, and me, investing is paradise. Investing means freedom, wealth, and security. There is risk in investing, just as there was risk in sailing to Tahiti, but the risk and the alternative are worth it. Sadly, many people take investment advice from so-called investment professionals who themselves have never been to paradise. Instead, many people assume that the people advising them know what they are talking about.

The underlying point is that when it comes to money, too many people allow their emotions to do their thinking for them. Our emotions are powerful forces, and emotional thoughts have the power to become self-fulfilling prophecies if not controlled. If you are to become captain of your own ark, one of the most important controls is the control over your emotions. When I heard my friend's wife say, "I'm terrified that we are going to lose it all," I then knew her emotions had taken over her life. Even though they had more than enough money to live in paradise, they never made it. Instead, their fear determined their fate, and indeed they nearly lost it all.

Three Levels of Controlling Thought

In explaining this phenomenon to his son and me, rich dad said there were three levels of controlling thought—lower, middle, and higher thought. When someone is speaking from their lower levels of thought, they often say things such as, "Investing is risky," or "What if I lose?" Rich dad explained by saying, "When it comes to money, most people never get out of the lower levels of thought." As usual, I did not fully understand what he meant, but as I grow older, I notice that many people are stuck in lower levels of thought, especially around the subject of money. I have dear friends who live in fear of investing, taking risks, and losing money. They cannot seem to shake these thoughts, and in some cases, these thoughts become self-fulfilling prophecies. Some of these friends have millions of dollars in the bank but live as cheaply as possible because they live in fear of losing that money. In many ways, they have already lost it, simply because they live like they do not have any money.

Teaching us how to get out of lower levels of thought, rich dad said, "If you decide that you do not want these lower-level emotions to run your thinking, you need both the middle level as well as the higher levels to pull you out." He was saying that it is our middle mind, the rational mind, that needs to learn the technical financial skills required. For example, when I was afraid of investing in real estate, rich dad suggested I take a course on real estate investing. By following that advice, my rational mind overcame my emotional mind and off I went to a weekend course on real estate investing. After the course, my fears were still there, but at least I felt better prepared to undertake the learning process that lay ahead. In 1973, that real estate course cost me $385, but over the years I have made millions of dollars from taking that seminar.

This is where the higher mind comes in. In spite of the fact that I have looked at thousands of potential real estate investments, have done nearly a hundred real estate transactions, and I consider myself successful at real estate investing, my lower mind's doubts and fears still kick in. My wife, Kim, and I are about to close on over $10 million worth of real estate this month alone. The nervousness and doubt from my lower mind are still with me. This is where the higher mind comes to the rescue. Because I have gone through the process of finding, buying, selling, and managing property so many times, when the fears of my lower mind act up, it is my higher mind that takes control. It comforts the doubts and fears of my lower mind and tells my middle brain to begin searching for the new information, advice, or education that my lower mind needs to feel more secure. Most non-investors do not have the technical skills in the middle mind, or the years of experience of the higher mind, to pull them out of the powerful grip of the emotions of the lower mind. That's why their lower mind ultimately runs the show.

One reason why financial education is so important is because, once you learn about finances, you can rely upon your middle mind to break the grip of fear and doubt in your lower emotional mind. When I look back upon my life, it was my rich dad playing *Monopoly*® with me and supplementing the game with real-world advice and experience, that helped me overcome those doubts and fears that we all have.

After he finished college, Warren Buffett invested $100 in a Dale Carnegie course. Reflecting on his investment he said, "I did not take the course to prevent my knees from shaking when speaking in public, but to do public speaking while my knees were knocking."

Kim and I invest even though we have fears and doubts. It is the challenges offered by our own personal fears and doubts that make investing so exciting. In other words, we do not let our lower mind run our lives. We use our doubts and fears to make our lives better.

That $385 real estate course in 1973 was important because the course and my rich dad's prior financial education provided the bridge to my higher mind. Even though I know that any piece of real estate can turn from an asset into a liability quickly, it is my higher mind that keeps me stable and thinking clearly through the challenges of being a professional investor.

Being skipper of your own ark does not mean you are free of doubts and fears. Being human means that we all have those doubts and fears. In fact, you would not be a good skipper if you did not have those worries. But if you are going to be a good skipper, you will need the help of your middle mind and your higher mind to guide your ark, especially if you want to get through the rough seas that lie ahead and still get to paradise.

Mutiny on the Bounty

As a young boy, I saw the movie *Mutiny on the Bounty* with Marlon Brando. I can still remember the scene where the *Bounty* pulls into a harbor in Tahiti and several outrigger canoes approach the ship, filled with beautiful Tahitian maidens, smiling, waving, and shouting, "Hi sailors." I know it wasn't possible back then, but if the crew of the *Essex* had seen that movie, instead of deciding to sail to Chile, they would probably have said, "Who cares about the cannibals? Let's go to Tahiti!" That's the power of a little education.

A Different World

It takes very little financial education to save money. As rich dad said, "I could train a monkey to save money." Similarly, it takes very little financial education to diversify. The reason most people save, and diversify if they invest, is because they lack the proper financial education of their middle mind. If they had that financial education, they might be more willing to venture out into the real world outside the chicken coop and find a world filled with opportunity and abundance. They will also find a world of crooks and liars, but after Enron, we know crooks and liars are also found inside the coop. The point is, without that financial education to their middle mind, staying inside the safety of the coop, saving money, and diversifying their mutual funds, are the smart things to do—and often the only things they can do.

Good Debt, Bad Debt

Many people inside the coop think it's smart is to be debt-free. Early in my life, rich dad pointed out that there is good debt and bad debt. He said, "Good debt is debt that makes you rich. Bad debt is debt that makes you poor." The reason so many people inside the chicken coop think all debt is bad and being debt-free is smart is because, in their world, the only kind of debt they know is bad debt. So again, in their world, being debt-free is smart.

If you are going to be the captain of your own ark, you will need to know the difference between good debt and bad debt. As students at the Merchant Marine Academy, we studied ship design extensively. One of the things we were taught was that small boats do not need ballast, the weight put in the bottom of the ship so that the ship will remain upright, and big ships do. For example, when large sailing ships went from Europe to the New World of America, most of the ships went over empty. If they did not put ballast in the holds of those ships, they would have capsized. A favorite form of ballast in the good old days of sailing ships was river rock. That is why today, wherever sailing ships are tied up in America, you can still find piles of river rock, which came over from Europe in the bottom of sailing ships. Once the ship arrived in America, the river-rock ballast was taken out, and the cargo bound for Europe took its place.

The point is, if you build a tiny ark, let's say an ark the size of an eight-foot rowboat, you do not need any ballast. In a small boat, the less ballast the better. But if you are to build a big ark, ballast is always a factor. In the world of the B and I quadrants, the science of using debt as leverage, good debt, is an important science. If you build a small ark, being debt-free or ballast-free is smart and you do not need to learn the science of managing good debt. In a small ark, any kind of debt is bad debt.

Early in my life, rich dad taught us how to borrow money rather than get out of debt. His reason for teaching us to be borrowers was so that we would someday be able to manage big arks. One of the most important lessons he taught us was that if you are going to acquire bad debt, a financial education or financial statements were not required. He said, "If all you want is bad debt, the banker will not require you to have a financial statement. All you need to buy a home, car, or receive a credit card is a simple credit application. But if you want good debt, debt that makes you rich, the banker will require you to have a financial statement. Before letting you have good debt, the banker first wants to see your financial report card, your financial statement, to find out if you are smart enough to handle good debt."

I now more fully understand and appreciate rich dad's lessons on the differences between good debt and bad debt. I know that bad debt comes at higher interest rates. If a person does not have a financial statement, the banker assumes the person is not financially educated and naturally charges a higher rate of interest for the risk of loaning money to someone without much financial training. Yet, if I come in to borrow money for a business or investment real estate, he will require a financial statement. In this case, the banker wants to see my financial report card before he risks lending money at a lower interest rate.

Good Interest, Bad Interest

The same is true for people who save money. If you lack a solid financial education, the banker will pay you the lowest interest rate possible. If you are financially savvy, there are many programs that will pay far higher interest rates. An example of this is the 2 percent taxable interest versus the 7.75 percent tax-free interest I wrote about in an earlier chapter.

The fear of the lower mind is very expensive to people who save. So if you want to be the captain of a big ark, you need to know the difference between good debt and bad debt, as well as good interest and bad interest.

Mandatory Education

Referring to the CASHFLOW Quadrant, if you live in the world of the E and S quadrants, you do not need financial statements. If you live in the world of the B and I quadrants, financial statements and a good financial education are mandatory. Many times, a financial statement is required by law in the B and I quadrants. In most instances, the law does not require them for people in the E and S quadrants.

ERISA and its subsequent amendments resulted in millions of people moving from the E and S quadrants into the I quadrant—without the proper financial education. Because they lack this financial education to their middle mind, millions of people have become financial prisoners, held hostage by the doubts and fears of their lower mind.

Analysis Paralysis

Some people are not good investors because they are too well educated and become trapped in a world of analysis paralysis. They live in what rich dad called, "the world of what-if." What if this goes wrong? What if that goes wrong? In the world of investing, the term "can't pull the trigger" often refers to someone who knows all the answers, but just cannot bring themselves to put money on the table. They come right up to the brink of investing, but their lower mind overpowers their middle mind and they do not go through with the investment and enter the real world. These people are best staying with the pat formula—invest for the long term, dollar cost average, and diversify, diversify, diversify. Their fear and doubt are in control.

Warren Buffett says, "If you have to go through too much investigation, something is wrong."

Education Reduces the Fear

It was the financial education I received from rich dad starting at the age of nine that helped me control the fear of investing. I still have fear, but through education and experience, I was able to start building my ark. One of the biggest surprises in my life was to finally become financially free. I had always thought that once I had enough money, I could retire, sit on my ark, and take life easy. In 1994 at the age of 47, I finally completed the ark. Then I found out how boring life was just sitting on my ark. That is why I created the *CASHFLOW 101* board game in 1996.

I created the *CASHFLOW* game to share the lessons I learned from my rich dad and from real-life investments I have made. Some have been very successful, and others have been failures. The *CASHFLOW* game also teaches the important vocabulary of money. Best yet, by simply playing it, your fears about money and investing will start to disappear.

Chapter Fourteen
HOW I BUILT MY ARK

The *CASHFLOW* game not only teaches the basics of financial literacy. It also points out the four different levels of investing found in the real world. In building our ark, Kim and I followed the real-life investment plan found in the game itself.

The Four Investment Levels

Level #1: Small Deals

On the *CASHFLOW* game board, small-deal investment cards and big-deal investment cards are found. When most investors start out, they start out with small deals. Of course there is always the egotist, just as in real life, who wants to start with a big deal, even though they do not have any money.

In real life, in the early 1970s, I purchased my first piece of investment real estate. It was an $18,000 condominium on the island of Maui. Even though I did not have much money, I was able to buy three of those $18,000 condominiums by raising investor money for the down payment. I then sold them for $48,000 each in less than a year, netting me $90,000, which was split between myself and my investors. I made more that year from my investments than I did from my job at Xerox. From that point on, I was hooked on learning to become a better investor.

In real life, Kim purchased her first investment property in 1989. It was a two-bedroom, one-bath rental home that sold for $45,000. It took a $5,000 down payment, and she made approximately $25 a month positive cash flow. Although Kim was very nervous, she gained a tremendous amount of experience that serves her well today.

Today, we continue to do a few small deals. I wrote earlier about investing in municipal mortgage REITs which pay a 7.75 percent tax-free return on our money. While most people are receiving less than 2 percent taxable interest from their banks, we receive nearly a 12 percent effective return on our money. In order to play this investment, you must watch stock-market trends and the short-term interest rates dictated by the Federal Reserve Bank. That means every time someone like Alan Greenspan talks, you had best listen.

Level #2: Big Deals

Once a *CASHFLOW* player has made some money from investing in small deals, they are now ready to take on bigger deals.

Kim and I did this in real life. After we had purchased nearly 12 small properties, we were ready to sell them through a tax-deferred 1031 exchange, which means we did not have to pay the capital-gains tax that stock investors often have to pay. After we sold our 12 small deals, we were ready to move on to bigger deals. With the proceeds from those small deals, we purchased two larger apartment houses and were able to retire in 1994. In other words, it took Kim and me less than five years to move from small deals to big deals and retire.

After we retired, we capitalized on our experience by looking for other big deals.

Here are some examples of our big deals:

PREPs: Private Real Estate Partnerships

Kim and I like to invest in private real estate partnerships, or what we call PREPs. (No one else calls them that.) It is simply a code name we gave to this form of real estate investing. A PREP is more often called a *real estate syndication* and is simply a private partnership that is formed to buy a large real estate investment.

The following is an example of a PREP. In an earlier book I wrote about wanting to buy a new Porsche for $50,000. Instead of wasting my money on the Porsche, which is a liability, Kim and I pooled our money with nine other investors to raise $500,000 equity. We then purchased a mini-storage warehouse by financing the mortgage through a bank.

That warehouse paid each partner approximately $1,000 to $1,400 a month in cash flow. I do not know what the other partners did with their monthly cash-flow check, but Kim and I used our checks to make the monthly payments for the Porsche. After three years, the mini-storage warehouse was refinanced. We then got our initial $50,000 back, which we reinvested in another PREP. Since the rents went up on the mini-storage warehouse, we continue to receive our monthly cash flow which has grown to approximately $2,000 a month. If the property were sold today, we stand to make an additional $100,000 to $200,000 from capital gains—and I still have the Porsche. This is an example of an asset buying our liability and helping us with our early retirement. Since we no longer have any money in the investment and we still receive our $2,000 a month, what is our new ROI (return on investment)? Infinite.

Kim and I invest in one or two of these types of PREPs a year. Our average returns are 15 percent to 25 percent cash-on-cash returns, *plus* the offsetting depreciation deductions, which are not really losses but phantom cash flow. This can easily put our returns in the 50 percent-or-more range. Try doing that with most mutual funds.

We like these investments because the risk is shared with other investors, we use our banker's money, the investment is secured to real estate, we receive monthly cash flow, there is a strong potential for capital gains if the property goes up in value, the income is tax-advantaged, and the capital gains are tax-advantaged at the time of sale. Most stocks and mutual funds do not offer such tax advantages, steady cash flow, or security.

The latest PREP Kim and I invested in was a 240-unit apartment building that pays a 15 percent tax-advantaged return, which is comparable to a 30 percent taxable return, with capital gains potential. We are in this partnership with three other investors.

Best of all, in a little over three years, we will have all of our initial investment back, we will still own the property, still receive the monthly cash flow, and then be able to go out and use the same initial investment money to do it all over again on another property!

Triple Net Leases

A similar big deal, but a slightly different investment, is called a *triple net lease*. Kim and I like these investments for many reasons.

- Triple-net-lease investments are often in excellent commercial locations, such as a street corner of a busy intersection.

- The tenant is often a public company such as a major drugstore, fast-food franchise, or national retail chain. That means the cash flow is often steady and secure.

- The tenant is responsible for everything. *Triple net* means that, in addition to their lease payment, the tenant pays for the maintenance of the building, the insurance, the taxes, and structural repairs. For those who hate the idea of managing and maintaining real estate, these triple-net investments are the best. The problem is, these investments require a rich investor.

In these types of investments, the steady cash flow is excellent, the risk is low, and the tax advantages are great. But the main reason Kim and I invest in such properties is to own the land at the corner of the intersection. Once the lease is up in 15 to 20 years, that corner land at the busy intersection should have increased tremendously in value. One of the reasons McDonald's is such a rich company is not only because it sells a lot of burgers, but also because it owns the land at some of the best intersections in the world.

A friend of mine took an early retirement and cashed in his 401(k) with $3 million in it, prior to the crash of 2000. He took $1 million and purchased a publicly traded famous hamburger franchise (not McDonald's) triple-net-lease property. He did not take out a loan. He simply paid the $1 million price and retired. His $1 million investment pays an 8.5 percent annual return, which means he receives approximately $85,000 a year tax-advantaged cash flow, which increases every five years. In other words, his 8.5 percent tax-advantaged return is similar to receiving a 17 percent return from the stock market each and every year.

The difference is, because he can count on this money regardless of whether the stock market goes up or down, he sleeps well. Each month the money is wired to his bank account. At the end of 20 years, he will own a great piece of real estate he can pass on to his children and grandchildren. While 8.5 percent is not a great return to me, for him it is a smart and secure return. I do not know what he did with the remaining $2 million, but I think most went to pay taxes and to pay for his new boat.

If you are tired of the ups and downs of the stock market and wondering how the rich feel secure, just drive to a busy intersection and look at the commercial buildings on each corner. Chances are that the buildings (including the drugstore, the supermarket, and the fast-food franchise) are all owned by a single investor. They do not own the business, just the building and often the land under the business. They don't have the headache of running the business or maintaining the property. Instead, each month while millions watch the ups and downs of the stock market, that triple-net investor is having a check wired to his or her bank account each month. To me, that makes much more investment sense.

The beauty of this type of investment is that you receive the monthly cash flow, your tenants pay for the debt on the property, and in the end, you own the underlying real estate so you also benefit from the appreciation during the term of the lease.

There are two issues with triple-net-lease purchases. One is that they usually require a substantial down payment. The second problem is that most financial planners who sell mutual funds and insurance do not recommend them because they do not make a commission on such investments. I have heard financial planners say that these real estate investments are risky, and instead they recommend a diversified mutual fund portfolio, which to me is extremely risky. To invest in triple-net-lease investments, you will need to find an experienced commercial real estate broker with at least five years of experience. Do not be afraid to ask to speak to satisfied clients, if he or she has any. As with any investment, there are good and bad triple-net-lease purchases.

An Investment We Turned Down

The following is an example of an investment I recently looked at, but turned down because it did not return enough money.

The real estate was a newly built supermarket in the Midwest. The tenant is a public company with excellent credit. The company does $15 billion in sales, it has 3,000 grocery stores and 2,000 convenience stores.

Purchase price	$6,600,000
Down payment	1,600,000
Mortgage	5,000,000
	Positive cash flow:
Years 1-2	$198,000 (11%)
Years 3-8	$240,000 (14%)
Years 9-10	$282,000 (16%)

Although this was a very safe and secure investment, Kim and I turned it down because it was not a great investment. We turned it down because we can find investments with higher returns sitting on better pieces of real estate. The location of this property was not as solid as we like to see in a triple net lease. If you have a prime location, even if your tenant defaults, you should have an easier time leasing the property again.

The Starting Point

A point to remember here is that both Kim and I started with small deals. As our wealth grew, so did our experience and hence the size of the investments, the security, and the higher returns. In other words, education and experience ultimately make a person richer and richer. Kim and I tend to add two such investments to our ark each year so our passive income increases each year. That is the power of education and experience. Many mutual fund investors would love to receive $200,000 passive income each year for 20 years, rather than sweat the ups and downs of the stock market. If you can do just five of these big deals in your lifetime, you could easily earn over $1 million a year for as long as you live.

Level #3: The Fast Track

As many of you know, the *CASHFLOW* board game has two tracks. One is the Rat Race. The second is the Fast Track. In real life, investments on the Fast Track are by law reserved only for the rich.

The following are some real-life examples of investments Kim and I have added to our ark since our retirement in 1994.

Private Placements

As entrepreneurs, we like investing in small start-up companies that have the potential to go public. Along the way, we have invested in two oil companies, one silver company, a gold company, and a consumer-products company. One oil company ran into trouble when it failed to strike oil and ran out of money. The other oil company discovered gas and is now being acquired by a publicly listed company. The silver company was acquired by a company listed on the Toronto Stock Exchange in 2001 and is beginning to attract investor attention. It is in production and has cash flow from the ore it sells. The gold company has secured rights to an advanced exploration project with a resource of 3 million ounces of gold. It is set to go public in 2003 through an IPO. The consumer-products company is also set to go public in 2002 through a reverse merger.

Most of these small start-up companies have taken four to five years to develop in order to get them ready to bring to the market. I wrote about this process of starting companies and getting them ready for the public markets in book number three, *Rich Dad's Guide to Investing*. I remember that after the book came out in 1999, a few people commented that I was wasting my time starting gold, silver, and oil companies. The reason was because the high-tech boom and dotcom boom were on. Today, due to changes in market conditions, gold, silver, and oil are coming back into favor. Again, an entrepreneur must have vision and be able to build a company for a market five years out.

Going Public

The advantage to building a company and taking it public is that the founders receive the largest blocks of shares at very favorable prices, as low as two cents a share to 25 cents a share. An entrepreneur may be able to buy a substantial percentage of the company at that price. After the stock goes public—and let's say the share price hits $3 a share—the founders can begin to sell a few shares to recoup their initial investment and go on to reap the benefits of a growing public company. Of course, these are the riskiest of all investments in the stock market and only the very rich or the very savvy should invest in such companies. This end of the stock market is where most of the crooks and con men hang out. That is why, if you should venture into this market, your business and investment training must be the best.

If your business and investment skills are limited, you may fall prey to these crooks and con men or, even worse, become one of them.

Level #4: CASHFLOW 202

After a person has their millions securely stored in their ark, they are ready to move on to *CASHFLOW 202*, the game that introduces the fundamentals of technical investing. Although many people who are not rich play the options market with paper assets, I chose to follow my rich dad's advice and waited until I had a steady source of cash flow before playing this high-speed game.

I personally feel picking stock and mutual funds is the riskiest of all investment strategies. I would rather have steady cash flow from a business and real estate or use options to protect my positions in volatile markets. But that is just my opinion.

One of the benefits of playing both *CASHFLOW 101* and *202* multiple times is that you can begin to see the four different levels of investments and find out how you too can learn to invest for greater returns, steady income, and with far less risk. Of course, to invest in the four levels will require that you commit to studying for a number of years to gain your education and experience. If you are not willing to invest in your education, then investing in mutual funds or picking stocks is much safer for you than the four other levels of investments.

Warning!

When you look at my *CASHFLOW* board game, you'll notice that there are two tracks. The small circular track is fondly called the Rat Race, which is where 90 percent of all investors are. The larger outer track is called the Fast Track. Kim and I invest primarily in investments from the Fast Track. They are not investments for the average investor. If you talk to most financial advisors, they will say that the investments that Kim and I invest in are far too risky and should not be invested in. I agree. They are too risky for the average investor. Yet they are not risky if you educate yourself and gain experience in the B and I quadrants. If you do gain the necessary education and experience, you may find that these investments are the safest, highest-yielding, most exciting investments in the world, but you must do your part. Over the years, Kim and I have lost money in businesses and in other types of investments. We have had businesses not succeed, and we have invested in private-investment partnerships that failed. In the last five years, we have lost approximately $125,000 in such ventures. We have also made tens of millions of dollars during that same period of time. So our education and experience continue.

The point in sharing our investments is not to brag, but to encourage and inspire some of you to begin your journey to greatly improve your financial education and find your way to financial freedom. While we agree that these investments are too risky for most people, with the proper education and experience, we have found these pathways to actually be the safest and most secure. It is not the investment that is necessarily risky. In most cases, it is the investor who is risky.

Start a Part-Time Business

If you do not have the money to invest in these investments, then I often recommend you keep your daytime job and start a part-time business. The greatest fortunes have been created through building businesses. If you do not have the money to start a business or lack the experience, then join a network-marketing company that has a great training program that will give you the opportunity to gain the money to invest with.

When people say to me, "I don't have the money," I often reply with, "Then start a part-time business." Some do, but most would rather continue to say, "I don't have the money."

Build Your Ark

1. Analyze your level of thought when it comes to money:

   - Do you fear that you'll lose money?
     Yes _____ No _____

   - Do you fear you won't have enough money?
     Yes _____ No _____

   - Do you find yourself saying, "I can't afford it," instead of, "How can I afford it?"
     Yes _____ No _____

   - Do you want to develop a higher level of thought when it comes to money?
     Yes _____ No _____

2. Analyze your personal financial statement.
   Label each liability and expense as either good debt or bad debt.

3. Will you commit to start with a small deal?

   Yes _____ No _____

4. Start jotting down your negative thoughts about:
   - a part-time business
   - real estate
   - stocks

Now analyze those negative thoughts. Are they based on fact or fear?

Chapter Fifteen

CONTROL #3: CONTROL OVER YOUR EXCUSES

Rich dad said, "Excuses are the words coming from the loser in you."

Time to Grow Up

A few years ago, I was speaking to a group of about a hundred people about investing. They were between the ages of 25 and 35. Bright and well dressed, most had college degrees and good jobs. For a group that seemed to have everything going for them, they whined about whatever I had to say. For example, when I said, "I usually look at a hundred properties before actually acquiring one," immediately a young woman raised her hand and said, "A hundred properties? Who has time for that? Besides, I think I'm too old to begin investing in real estate."

Letting that comment go, I continued with my discussion on financing a property. I explained that I sometimes used a larger down payment just to keep my debt-to-equity ratios in line. Immediately a hand went up, and this time a young man said, "But what if you don't have any money for a down payment? I still have student loans to pay off."

Before I could say anything, another young man stood up and said, "Real estate won't work for me. I have credit problems."

With that, I stopped the class. "Look," I said, "I know this was advertised to be a talk on investing in real estate. But before I go on, I want to offer you a lesson far more important than making money with real estate. I'm going to share with you a very important lesson from rich dad."

I turned and wrote a question on my flip chart: What do you want to be when you grow up? Turning to the group, I then asked, "How many of you have ever been asked this question?"

All of the hands in the room went up.

"Who would like to say what they wanted to be when they grew up?"

"I wanted to be a medical doctor," said one of the women, "and I became one."

"Good," I replied. "Anyone else?"

"My dad wanted me to go into business with him, but after college I opened my own business," said a young man.

"Okay," I replied. "Now when rich dad asked his son, Mike, and me that question, he was not talking about what professions we wanted to become when we grew up. He was asking us if we wanted to grow up to become more honest or less honest, more reliable or less reliable, to have more integrity or less integrity. That was what he wanted to find out when he asked that question."

There was a long, silent pause. Finally, someone asked, "You mean honesty and integrity really are important in investing?"

"Well, I can't speak for everyone, but to me they are," I replied. "But I am not just talking about investing. I am asking if honesty, reliability, and integrity are important to you."

"Well, of course they are," replied a young woman in the front row.

"Then let me pass on a lesson from rich dad," I responded, "a lesson far more important than investing, but a lesson that will make you a better investor nonetheless."

Turning to my flip chart, I wrote in quotes: "Excuses are lies you tell yourself."

Putting my marker down, I turned back to the group and paused awhile. I wanted to let the words on the flip chart sink in. Finally, I began again by saying, "Today I heard people saying, 'I don't have time,' 'I don't have money,' and 'My credit is bad.' Are those lies or truths?"

"Well, I don't have the money," shouted the young man who had used that excuse. "That's a fact. That's not a lie."

"And who has time to look at a hundred stupid properties?" said the young woman who had told us she had no time. "Do you know how busy I am? I have a business to run and kids to feed. When I say I don't have time, I don't have time. I'm busy. I'm not lying."

"My student loans are a mile high," said the young man who mentioned his debt problem. "That is a fact, not a lie."

"All right, rich dad's lesson on growing up is about to begin," I said, smiling. "Rich dad told me years ago that if I wanted to grow up to be an honest person, I had to become more and more honest, not stay the same. In other words, I had to be tougher on myself by being more honest with myself. For example, when I personally use the excuse, 'I have no time,' a more honest and truthful statement would be, 'I am not willing to make the time.'"

"So instead of making an excuse, you become more honest with yourself?" asked one of the participants.

"Exactly," I said. "Years ago, rich dad taught his son and me that all excuses are lies."

Upon hearing that, the young man sat back in his seat and said quietly, "I get what you're saying. So growing up means not using the facts of our lives as excuses for our lives. If we do that, we become more honest."

"You're getting it," I replied. "In sports, a person might say that the referee calls the game tighter. That means the referee is demanding a higher standard of play from the players. What rich dad was saying is that, as you grow up, it's important to call your own game tighter. Be more honest with yourself. Raise the standards on yourself. If you don't, your life stays the same."

"But what about me? I am busy. I really don't have any time, especially to go looking at a hundred properties."

I noticed she had dropped the excuse about being too old. Since she didn't bring it up, I wasn't going to either. "Then just be honest about it," I said. "Just say, 'I'm not going to make the time.'"

"So all you are saying is to stop whining, complaining, and acting like babies."

"That's a great way of saying it," I said. "Grow up, and stop acting like babies. Every time you make an excuse, you're acting like a baby."

"Well, not everyone is rich like you with all the free time and money in the world," said someone from a back row.

The room groaned with that remark.

Smiling, I said, "I would not have the free time and money if I had let excuses be truths instead of lies. I too started without any money. I too had mountains of debt, nearly a million dollars. And I too am busy."

"And you would still have those problems if you had used those problems as excuses," said the woman with no time. "I get what you are saying. Excuses hold us back. No one else holds us back."

"That's correct," I said. "Rich dad often said, "Excuses are the words coming from the loser in you.'"

"So by being more honest with your excuses, that honesty allows the winner in you to take over," said the woman with no time. "If you are truthful with your excuses, then the loser shuts up and the winner can be heard."

"Exactly," I said. "And the more the winner in you speaks, the more you grow up. But first, you need to be willing to call your game tighter and raise your own standards."

"So how can I find more time?" asked the woman with no time.

"Great question," I said with a big smile. "The winner in you is now talking."

"It is? I am?" said the woman with no time.

"Sure. Instead of complaining to me that you have no time and letting the loser in you speak to you, the winner in you is asking me how I found the time. If the loser speaks, you learn nothing. But if the winner speaks, you might learn something."

"So that is how you find the money even when you have no money," said the man with no money.

"You got it," I said. "Look, we all have the same amount of time. We all have 24 hours in a day. A winner just finds ways of making better use of that time. A loser lets not having enough time be the excuse for not getting things done. Rarely have I ever invested in a piece of property when I had enough money. And I often have credit problems because I always want to borrow as much as possible when I find a great real estate investment."

"So how do you find the time to look at a hundred properties?" asked the woman with no time.

"Another good question," I replied with a smile. "I estimate that I look at approximately 300 to 500 properties a year. I may not buy anything that year, yet I still look. Sometimes looking at a property may be simply looking only at the sales flyer the real estate agent puts out on the property. The analysis might take less than five minutes of my time. Sometimes I will spend three months chasing one deal and then have it fall apart. So time is relative. The point is, I am always looking. Regardless if I am in New York, Sydney, Paris, Singapore, or Athens, I always stop and look at properties. Regardless of how busy I am, I always look. I'm always looking for a good deal to put into my assets column. I'm looking at the same time I'm running my businesses and leading a normal life."

"So you don't always buy," said the man without money.

"No. In fact, rarely do I buy, but it costs you nothing to look. Just as it costs you no money to walk into a department store and look around, it costs you no money to look at property, businesses, or stocks."

"Oh, I go shopping all the time when I'm on business trips, especially between appointments," said the woman with no time. "You and I just shop in different places."

"So how do you find the money when you find a deal, especially when you do not have any money?" asked the man with no money.

"Well, that is where right-brained creativity comes in. Not having money after finding a great investment is how I gained most of my financial education. You'd be surprised how intelligent you become when you must use your creative mind to solve financial problems. Solving financial problems or challenges increases your financial intelligence. I have money today simply because I didn't let not having money be an excuse. Even though I had no time, I still looked at property, even if it was only for a few minutes. Every time I looked at a property, even if only from a sales information sheet, I would analyze the deal to see how I could turn this piece of real estate into an asset that put money in my pocket. That is what made me rich. Money did not make me rich. Investing time when I had no time and investing money when I had very little money are what made me rich."

"So excuses don't make you rich. Excuses keep you poor," said the young woman in the front row.

"Well said," I replied with a great big smile. The class had gotten a lesson far more important than how to invest in real estate. I could tell that most of them got the lesson about the importance of growing up to be more honest and more truthful with themselves.

Developing Your Sixth Sense

In a previous chapter, I wrote about the lower, middle, and higher mind. Excuses generally come from the lower mind. With a little financial education of the middle mind and a little dedication, the higher mind can develop. After looking at and analyzing thousands of properties, the process is much easier because I have all three minds working together, rather than just one or two.

Finding a good deal is almost a psychic experience. Many times, I have intuitively known without much research that a certain property was a great deal. Something just goes off inside me, and I become like a bloodhound on the trail. But this sixth sense would not have been developed if I had allowed my excuses to run my life.

The same is true with developing a sixth sense about people. Operating outside the chicken coop, I have met characters with all sorts of deals. I have done business with some less-than-honest characters, not because I knew they were less-than-honest, but because I simply lacked enough real-world experience. I was not able to tell the con artists from the more honest people.

Today, the sixth sense from my higher mind plays a very important role in detecting the phonies, liars, con men, flakes, and others who operate outside the boundaries of the chicken coop. I am still not always right, but I learn from my mistakes and get better each time. I believe that without rich dad's lesson on growing up to be more honest, I might have easily become one of those phony con men, operating outside the coop.

One of the reasons my real dad lost all his savings in his ice cream franchise was not because of the franchise, but because of the people he went into business with. His partners were not crooks, but his partners were all schoolteachers just like my dad—teachers without much real-world business experience. None had much financial training to the middle brain, and none had much real-world business experience. When the business started going bad, instead of admitting they knew nothing, the group began making excuses and blaming each other for the problems. Once that happened, the business fell apart, and my dad lost everything. They went into the ice cream business as adults and wound up acting like a bunch of kids. So bad things can happen to good people, especially if they are not willing to face their own truths and call their own game tighter.

After the ice cream franchise and swearing on a stack of Bibles that he would not do business with schoolteachers again, my dad entered into two more outside-the-coop business ventures, this time with people he thought were businesspeople. Again, the same things happened. The businesses did not perform as expected, sales dropped, money was lost, and adults began behaving like children.

The same things have happened to me and I have behaved in the same way, sometimes even worse. Many times, things did not go as expected on several real estate deals and on my first two major business ventures. Each time things went bad, I too found myself acting like a kid. If not for my rich dad's advice on being more truthful and growing up and not making excuses or blaming someone else, I think I would still be a kid.

Unfortunately, my father did not have a person like my rich dad to talk to each time a business venture went bad. Instead of becoming more truthful to himself, he sank deeper into his lower mind, becoming angrier with his ex-partners, harder on himself, and less confident about his future. After the third business failure, he gave up. In my opinion, he retreated to his lower mind and stayed there. To me, that is the price of not having the proper education for the middle mind and not allowing the wisdom of the higher mind to develop.

Fortunately for me, rich dad taught me about my lower, middle, and higher minds. He reminded me to return to my higher mind and begin to assess what things my middle mind could learn from these experiences. Instead of blaming others or being hard on myself, he asked me to search for deeper truths and more meaningful insights so I could find out more about me.

Just to recap, rich dad started my investing career at the age of nine, simply by playing *Monopoly*®. I purchased my first property in my mid-twenties. My first failure in real estate came at the age of 26. I started my first real business, the nylon-and-Velcro wallet business, at the age of 27. That business and the business that followed both went bust. My third business and most of my subsequent businesses have done very well. In 1994 at the age of 47, I started my options-trading education after I was financially stable. I have made a lot of money, but I have also lost a lot of money. The point is, each time I failed, I retreated into my lower mind, the place where fight or flight occurs. I too acted like a kid and sometimes like a baby. But after I got through with my thumb-sucking retreat, it was my rich dad's lesson on not making excuses, not blaming, being more honest with myself, and seeking more information and education that pulled me out of my funk and allowed the wisdom of my higher mind to develop. Without that guidance, I do not know where I would be today. Without that guidance, I doubt if I would have grown up, a process I am still actively involved in today.

The point is, too many people give up too early. If they are disappointed, lose a few dollars, or have their feelings hurt, most people retreat back to the world of the lower mind. I believe this is one of the primary reasons why so few people attain great wealth, even in the richest country in the world. I also believe it is the reason why so many people choose security over freedom.

Lessons Learned

I learned two very important lessons from this process. The first lesson is that once I developed some real-life experience, it was easier for me to remain calm, even if things were not going my way. For example, in real estate or business, if things were going bad, I could remain calm because the emotion from my higher mind would kick in. That emotion is love, the love of the game. Today, regardless of what is happening in business or real estate, winning or losing, I remain happy because I have learned to love the game, and love comes from the higher mind.

The second lesson I learned was that when I find myself thrashing around in my lower mind, ready to fight or run, I remember the rule: "Silence is golden." Instead of lashing out and saying something I will regret later, I do my best (I don't always succeed in this one) to remain silent and ask my higher mind to think of a higher thought. If my higher mind does kick in, I am then able to find a better way of saying the same thing—without all the blame, anger, or self-justification.

At the academy, in flight school, and in the real world of business and investing, one of the most important lessons for me to learn was to remain calm, think from my higher mind, and focus on the mission—regardless what is happening with the ship.

If you want to be the captain of your ark, then the buck and the excuses all stop with you.

Build Your Ark

1. Are you lying to yourself?

2. What do you want to be when you grow up (even if you think you are already grown up)?

3. Do you make excuses about not having enough time or money?

4. Excuses are lies you tell yourself. Make a sign with this saying and post it where you will see it daily: "Make an effort, not an excuse."

5. Review your negative thoughts in the exercise from Chapter 14 and decide if any of your negative thoughts are really excuses.

6. Challenge yourself to find a minimum of five hours a week to devote to building your ark.

7. Make the five-hour exercise a personal commitment or a family activity.

   • Walk, bike, or drive neighborhoods looking at real estate.

   • Visit a real estate broker to inquire about investment properties.

   • Spend dinner one night a week discussing new business ideas.

   • Attend franchise shows in your area.

   • Attend local seminars on real estate, building businesses, or investing in the stock market.

8. Decide which asset class you want to start with: business, real estate, or investing in stocks and/or options.

Case Study

A couple of years ago, Chuck and Denise took a trip to visit Denise's sister in California. She had started a part-time furniture business out of her home that was fairly profitable. Denise and Chuck recognized the potential of creating a large company around a similar business model and decided to go for it.

Chuck and Denise had been playing the *CASHFLOW 101* board game for several years and had read all of the Rich Dad books which enabled them to recognize the business opportunity for their furniture business and gave them the courage to take action. As they built a successful business, they learned the difference between an S and a B business owner as described in *Rich Dad's CASHFLOW Quadrant*. They are now able to leave their business management to others and the business still makes money—a true B business. They have even started branching out into new states through joint ventures to create more assets instead of trying to do everything themselves.

Ironically, Chuck and Denise used to judge their success on the number and quality of the doodads they owned. By understanding the Rich Dad definition of assets, they have now focused on buying or building assets, not liabilities or doodads. If they want doodads, they first buy assets that will generate the cash flow to pay for the doodads. After they pay for the doodad, they still own the asset which continues to generate additional cash flow each month. This was a big distinction for them and helped them set their own investment rules.

They have taken an idea, a business opportunity, and built a very successful multimillion-dollar business in just a couple of years. They have taken control of their financial ark and are filling it with assets.

Chapter Sixteen

CONTROL #4: CONTROL OVER YOUR VISION

In the 1970s, poor dad would often drive by a shopping center near Waikiki and say, "When I was in college, I could have bought all that land for $5 an acre." The next time we would drive by it, he would say, "Did I tell you about the time a salesman offered me that land for $5 an acre?"

The kids would reply, "Yes, Dad, you told us many times."

My dad was in college in the 1940s. At that time, the land he pointed to was a swamp. By the 1960s, that same piece of land was one of the largest shopping centers in the world. I estimate that a $500 investment in the 1940s is today worth at least $500 million. The person who did purchase the land was the same age as my dad. The difference between their personal fortunes is a difference in vision.

Paraphrasing something Warren Buffett once said, "If history made you rich, then librarians would be billionaires."

Rich dad said, "Many people go through life driving their car by looking in the rearview mirror." He also said, "These are the people who often say, 'I would have, I should have, I could have.'"

Recently I was looking at a small house that was listed for $160,000. A person who lived next door came forward and said, "I've lived here for 20 years. I remember when that house cost $11,000."

"You should have bought it back then," I said.

"Oh no," the neighbor said. "Eleven thousand dollars was too much money back then. It wasn't worth the price."

"Maybe you should buy it now," I replied.

"Oh no," the neighbor said. "One hundred sixty thousand dollars is way too much money for this house. It isn't worth the price."

Lower-Mind Thinking

Rich dad used to say, "When it comes to money, many people are financial hypochondriacs." Their thinking comes from the lower mind which blurs their vision of the future. These are the people who often drive their car by looking into the rearview mirror. Their fear of losing causes them to not take action when once-in-a-lifetime opportunities are placed right in front of their eyes. Later as they drive down the highway of life, you hear them saying, "I would have, I should have, I could have." As many wise people have said, "Hindsight is 20/20." Rich dad said, "If you want to be rich, it is best to be farsighted."

A Very Bright Future

When I caution people about the coming stock-market crash, I am not pessimistic about the future. I am very optimistic about the future. Warning people about the coming stock-market crash is the same as warning a friend about a road up ahead that is washed out. If the person will take another route, they can still get to their destination safe, sound, and on time.

As captain of your own ark, one essential skill is to develop your vision. Rich dad's definition of *vision* is "seeing with your *mind* rather than with your *eyes*." In order to develop this vision, it is important to first train your middle mind and then go out in the real world and allow your higher mind to develop its natural wisdom, often called *intuition* or *instinct*.

The Future Will Be Different

Things are changing far too quickly to attempt to see the future through your rearview mirror. Regardless of how old you are, stop for a moment and think of all the changes that have happened in the last few years. Thinking back upon my own life, I remember when a golf club called a *wood* really was made out of wood. Today, the new woods are made out of new composite materials I have never heard of. In other words, the game remains the same, but the tools used to play the game have changed dramatically. That is true in many areas of life. Today when someone says, "Let's stay in touch," it could be via foot, car, bus, plane, telephone, fax, regular mail, or email.

If you go further back in time, you will see that just a hundred years ago, not even kings, queens, or the richest people in the world were flying on planes because there weren't any. Almost anyone can afford to fly today. A hundred years ago, only the rich had cars. Today, cars are everywhere. A hundred years ago, you needed to know Morse code to communicate over the telegraph. Today, people all over the world carry cell phones. I do not know too many people today who know Morse code. In 1990, the world did not know what the World Wide Web was. Today, the Internet is changing the future of the world faster than any other invention in history.

How Do You See the Future?

In August of 1981, I traveled to a ski resort in the mountains between California and Nevada to attend a conference entitled "The Future of Business" with Dr. R. Buckminster Fuller. At the time, Dr. Fuller was considered one of the world's leading futurists. Even though I knew a little of his fame and reputation, I was still somewhat skeptical that anyone could teach you to see the future without a crystal ball.

However, that week with Dr. Fuller was a turning point in my life. It was not an easy turning point, but I believe it was a turn for the better.

The method Dr. Fuller used to predict the future was based on a principle he called *ephemeralization*. Without getting into too much mind-numbing detail, I will use the story of the *Titanic* as a simple example of ephemeralization.

Centuries before the *Titanic* was built, humans first learned about the possibility of ships by clinging to a log and floating downstream.

Soon, humans dug the log out and created a dugout canoe. Next came lighter boats using planks and rib construction. The wooden ships got larger and larger until the battle of the *Monitor* and *Merrimac*, the first ironclad warships. Once steel construction was introduced, ships grew into giants of the seas, carrying passengers, freight, and armaments throughout the world. Businesspeople began investing in bigger and bigger ships until the *Titanic* disaster. Soon after the *Titanic* sank, the golden age of ships ended. That is an overly simplified example of ephemeralization, one of the principles which Fuller used to predict the future.

Simply put, ephemeralization is the process of starting small, growing bigger, becoming too big, then small again, suddenly disappearing, or becoming invisible, as in the case of wireless communications. On occasion, the end of growth is marked by a disaster, as in the case of the *Titanic* and the giant airship, the *Hindenburg*. Fuller would say that the technology simply grew too large. In the case of the *Titanic* and similar ships of that size, they grew too large to maneuver, men operating the ships believed they were un-sinkable, and a new technology was on its way—the airplane. The airplane was in its infancy stage, starting small and then growing bigger and bigger.

Think of It as a Hotel

I was in New York soon after the World Trade Center disaster. Walking down Fifth Avenue, I stopped to purchase a news magazine with the picture of the burning World Trade Center towers on the cover. Two things hit me from that magazine. One was how the two twin towers stood out, especially looking at them across the water from the shores of New Jersey. Although I had been to New York many times, it never occurred to me how much those towers dwarfed the other buildings.

The second item that caught my attention in the magazine was a full two-page ad for a new aircraft. The headline for this aircraft ad read, "Don't think of it as an aircraft. Think of it as a hotel." The double-page ad showed the interior of the aircraft with hotel suites instead of seats, a shopping center, and a small bar and restaurant. In many ways, it looked like a set from the *Titanic* movie.

Standing on the New York street corner, my mind drifted back in time to 1981, to the ski resort on a warm summer's day listening to Dr. Fuller talk about the symbolism of the *Titanic*. Did the attack on the World Trade Center signal the end of the golden era of airlines? Had giant skyscrapers, symbols of the Industrial Age, suddenly become dinosaurs? Had big business become too big? Did the attack on the Pentagon represent the end of American economic and military leadership? And if the attack did symbolize all those things, the question is: What comes next? Could anyone now see the future?

During the 1981 event, Dr. Fuller mentioned that after 1957, the year the Russians launched the first satellite, all new technological breakthroughs would be invisible to the unaided human eye. Fuller explained that after the *Titanic* disaster, we could still see with our eyes the new technology that replaced the old technology—in this case, the airplane.

But after 1957, the new technology that would replace the airplane would be invisible. That is why, while standing on that street corner in New York, gazing into the future, I was reminded to begin seeing the changes with my mind, not with my eyes.

Long before September 11, 2001, Buffett advised investors to join AA, which stood for Airlines Anonymous. Buffett said that ever since the Wright brothers, the airlines had never been a very profitable industry. After 9/11, the airline industry and all the businesses that support that industry, like hotels and rental cars, could be industries in decline. While there will be airlines, hotels, and rental cars for years to come, a new technology is about to change things for all of us.

Although Buffett did not invest in major airlines, he did invest in a company prior to September 11 that operated small private corporate aircraft. I seriously doubt if Buffett ever met Fuller, yet the two men followed very similar principles. Fuller added that if the technology did not disappear and go invisible, the technology would get smaller, as it did in the case of the smaller business jets.

Instead of the example of smaller business jets, Fuller used the example of computers. Not very long ago, computers were physical monsters, requiring a large dedicated room, many people to run it, massive amounts of electric power, and limited computing capacity. Today, computers are smaller, much less expensive, and have much more computing power than the larger mainframes of old. That is another example of ephemeralization, the ability to do so much more with so much less.

Again, these examples are overly simplified. Dr. Fuller went into much more depth with his explanation of this important principle, one of the principles he used to predict the future. The main point is that things start out small, grow, and soon become big, sometimes too big.

The other point is that after 1957, the new technology would be invisible. Today, not only do we have the business of smaller business jets booming, but video conferencing is also finally beginning to be accepted. Video conferencing is the growth industry that is taking away business from the larger airline industry. Video conferencing is one of the invisible technologies of the Information Age that is replacing the need for giant aircraft.

Mutual Funds Are Too Big

Since the late 1980s, the mutual fund industry took off. There are more mutual fund companies than public companies. Some mutual fund companies are even larger than many of the companies they invest in. The question is: Have some mutual fund companies become too big? I'll leave that answer for you to decide. The fact remains that more and more people are becoming independent stock market investors because a little investor can be far more maneuverable than a large mutual fund.

There has also been an explosion in people investing in hedge funds rather than mutual funds for the same reason Warren Buffett would invest in a small jet company rather than in the major airlines. The reason is, when things become too big, they are less maneuverable and often think they are unsinkable.

How to Improve Your Vision to See the Future

One way for you to see the future is by watching things getting too big. Then watch for something small or invisible to replace it. For example, soon after the attack on the World Trade Center, Chevron and Texaco, two giant companies, announced that they were merging to become a giant of an oil company. On the same page of the business section, a smaller company announced a breakthrough in fuel-cell technology, a new technology that has the potential of taking a lot of business away from big oil companies.

Bill Gates and Steve Jobs became very rich young men by seeing what big companies could not see. Bill Gates got the software contract for IBM's PCs because IBM did not see the spread of powerful and smaller computers. Steve Jobs became a rich man by using a technology that Xerox did not know how to market, a technology that helped create the Macintosh computer.

Invisible Skyscrapers

When I returned to New York for the second time after September 11th, I met a friend who had moved his office from the Empire State Building to a smaller office building. He said, "My staff were quitting because they did not want to sit in the next target." After he made that comment, I realized that we had officially entered the Information Age, the age where being invisible is better.

The network-marketing industry is an Information-Age business because it is an invisible business. Because it is an invisible business, it is often hard to describe the business's benefits to people who think with Industrial-Age minds and who still try to see the business with their eyes, rather than with their minds.

It would be hard for a terrorist to attack the network-marketing industry simply because the business offices are also invisible. Most network-marketing offices are hidden in homes throughout the world.

People are running massive, invisible businesses from their homes. If you could see their business, it would look like invisible skyscrapers rising from neighborhoods all over the world.

The Invisible Economy Is Strong and Growing

Dr. Fuller predicted that we would soon witness the death of the Industrial Age. He also predicted that it might be difficult for people to see the dawn of the Information Age simply because the changes would be invisible. Dr. Fuller died in 1983 and did not live to see many of his predictions come true, but they did.

Just look at the Internet and you will see that the world of the invisible is here. This invisible economy presents a growing problem for governments because governments are by-products of the Industrial Age. The government is trying to collect taxes and define borders for the invisible economy of the Information Age. This problem for governments will grow if the invisible economy becomes too big, and government cannot collect taxes or define borders. If this happens, the currency of the country will eventually weaken, simply because the power of a country's currency is linked to its ability to collect taxes. So have governments gotten too big too? Will there still be government, as we know it, in the Information Age? Can government become invisible?

Dr. Fuller believed governments were obsolete. He believed that humanity was about to evolve or disappear because of government's diminishing powers. Fuller believed that humans had to choose between the two Utopian worlds of greater personal integrity or bigger government. Otherwise, humanity, as we know it, would disappear. In other words, we as individual human beings need to solve more problems rather than turn those problems over to the government.

Lookouts on the Bow

For centuries, captains of ships have always posted a lookout on the bow of the ship as well as in the crow's nest. As captain of your own ark, you too will need to post lookouts on your bow and in the crow's nest. Metaphorically that means you will need to do the following.

Keep your word.

Dr. Fuller said that we were entering the age of integrity. *Integrity* simply means "whole or complete." That means that your thoughts, your words, and your actions need to be the same. If you will do that, the future is yours.

Keep an open mind and your ears tuned for change.

Since changes are now invisible, you will have to see more with your mind than with your eyes.

Learn to read financial statements.

Regardless if you invest in companies, stocks, real estate, government securities, or yourself, a financial statement allows the mind to see the true financial condition of the investment, government, or person in question. Always remember that a banker wants to see neat and complete financial statements. Many times a banker decides to lend or to not lend you money in the first three minutes. If you do not have neat and complete financial statements and are not articulate in explaining your financial position, then chances are that the only kind of debt you will be granted is bad debt at high interest rates.

Use technology.

Computer programs now allow the individual to see what before only the rich or powerful could see. I have friends who trade stocks or options. They now have charts and software that give them the same power to search for investments that giant investment firms have. The individual investors have the same power as the big firms because of these new tools of the trade. Similar advances in technology are available for businesses and real estate. As stated earlier, the game of golf remains the same, but the tools have changed.

Watch for bigness.

There is a saying in the investment world that when someone becomes famous enough for the front cover of national magazines, their career is over. Not long ago, in the Industrial Age, a blue-chip company may have been a leading company for 60 years or more. Today, with advances in technology, the life expectancy of a company is much shorter. In other words, the moment something or someone becomes too big, they are about to decline and be replaced by something or someone new. That same observation tends to be true for mutual fund companies, real estate, and careers. There is always something or someone new coming along to take the place of the leader. Your job is to be aware of people or things becoming too big and then watch for the replacement.

Watch for changes in the laws.

Rich dad was forever watching for changes in the laws and the effect the laws had upon our future. ERISA and its subsequent amendments are an example. The law that created Social Security has created a problem that will have to be solved one way or the other. I suggest you watch how government ultimately decides to handle this massive mess. As rich dad said, "Changes in the law change our future."

Watch out for inflation.

Just as markets go up and down, so does inflation. Right after September 11, 2001, the Federal Reserve Bank flooded the world with U.S. dollars to provide economic stability and liquidity. The long- term effect of all this printed money may lead to inflation, which means the U.S. dollar will go down in value. If inflation sets in, anything of questionable value will lose value, while things of value—assets such as real estate, gold, silver, and utility stocks—may greatly increase in value.

Governments do five basic economic things:

1. Collect taxes
2. Print money
3. Spend money
4. Push problems they cannot solve forward into the future
5. Control the economy through interest rates

During the 1990s, two reasons stock prices went so high were low inflation and low interest rates. When inflation goes up, the government often counters it by raising interest rates. When interest rates go up, stock markets usually come down. So during periods of high inflation and high interest rates, mutual funds generally take a beating or fail to increase in value.

Those of us old enough to remember the late 1970s may remember when inflation went through the roof, interest rates hit all-time highs, and the stock market went down. I am not saying that such a time will come again, but I would be vigilant. If we enter a period of high inflation and high interest rates, people counting on their DC pension plans and mutual funds may find themselves in serious financial trouble. If inflation rears its ugly head, savers will be punished and debtors will be rewarded, just as in the late 1970s.

Pay close attention to government's handling of its social programs.

It is not news that Social Security, Medicare, Medicaid, and other government programs are in trouble and the problem is getting worse. As stated earlier, government is not solving these problems. It is just pushing these problems forward onto future generations. Sometime around 2016, all this pushing the string forward is about to come to a head. Pay close attention to how the growing problem is handled. If governments begin raising taxes excessively, be prepared for anything, and be prepared to act quickly. Today, money can literally move at the speed of light.

The problem is becoming more and more serious. As I write, 28 states have spending overruns and lower-than-expected revenues. Medicaid is the leading reason for overspending. The problem is only going to get worse as more and more people grow old and require medical care they cannot afford. We all need to watch how the handling of this growing problem unfolds.

The future will be different. It is more important than ever to see what others cannot or do not want to see.

Build Your Ark

Get together with friends who encourage you in your efforts to build your ark. Discuss the following goals as outlined in this chapter:

- Keep your word.
- Keep an open mind and your ears tuned for change.
- Learn to read financial statements.
- Use technology.
- Watch for bigness.
- Watch for changes in the law.
- Watch out for inflation.
- Pay close attention to government's handling of its social programs.

With these concepts in mind, review these eight changes listed in Chapter 9, "The Perfect Storm," with your group. How can you turn these negatives into business opportunities?

1. Millions will be left destitute in old age.
2. Medical care will get even more expensive.
3. Terrorism will increase.
4. Japan, currently the world's second largest economy, is on the brink of financial collapse and depression.
5. China will become the world's largest economy.
6. The world population will continue to age.
7. Wall Street is obsolete.
8. Big corporations are losing the public trust and failing.

By reviewing these items regularly and brainstorming possibilities for business opportunities, your financial awareness will improve dramatically. Challenge each other to set and achieve goals.

Chapter Seventeen
CONTROL #5: CONTROL OVER THE RULES

As students at the academy, we spent a lot of time learning about driving ships, loading cargo, and tying knots. We also spent a lot of time studying the different laws a ship's officer needed to be aware of. Although we were not being trained to be lawyers, we needed to be familiar with the different laws that affected the running of a ship on the water. The laws we studied in depth were:

- *Admiralty law*—the law of the seas

- *Business law*—contracts and other legal documents used in the business of shipping

- *Labor law*—how to deal with crews that are members of labor unions

- *Rules of the road*—laws that govern the safe operation of a ship upon the water

There were also classes on the laws involving war as well as how to deal with pirates, a problem that is growing in the twenty-first century.

We needed to know that the rules for navigating on rivers were different from the rules on the ocean. There was also extensive study of channel markers such as buoys. We also had classes on the different laws of the different ports of call in different countries. For example, we needed to know the difference between the rules for bringing a ship into New York versus bringing a ship into Hong Kong.

One of the more extensive and toughest sets of rules we were required to study were the rules of the road. These were the international rules on the shipping lanes throughout the world. The reason this was one of the toughest sets of rules to study was because many of the rules had to be memorized and written verbatim for the U.S. Coast Guard licensing exam. The rules were fascinating because they were written to amalgamate the changes in technology upon the high seas. For example, Rule 16 referenced the introduction of radar into the world of shipping. The rule states that a ship which detects the presence of another ship without visually sighting it must stop its engines. In other words, if you could see a ship via radar but not with your eyes and a danger of collision existed, the engines had to be stopped and the rules had to be followed to the letter. There were many times at sea when our ship could see small fishing boats ahead of us on our radar, but we could not see them through the fog with our eyes. Immediately, we stopped our engines. After we stopped our engines, we were then directed by the rules to guide our ship cautiously until danger of collision was over. All ships are still required to follow that rule.

Another set of rules which were created because of changes in technology are the rules between a sailing ship and a ship powered by an engine. Upon the high seas, a ship powered by an engine must always give way to a ship powered by sail. The exception is if the ships meet in a restricted channel or harbor. Then the ship that is more maneuverable must give way to the less maneuverable and often larger ship, regardless if sail or engine propels it. These rules were required to be memorized because there was often not enough time to call an admiralty attorney and ask for an opinion. A ship's officer had to know the rules, and the rules were different for different situations.

Rules of Engagement

As military pilots, we were also trained to be very aware of the rules. When flying from one country to another, we were briefed as to distance and altitudes over beaches, altitudes over cities, rules for different airports, and many other rules. In war zones, we were also taught the rules of engagement. Even though we may have been coming under enemy fire, we were still required to follow the rules before firing back.

Rich Dad's Rules

Rich dad was also very aware of the rules. He too required his son and me to know that there were different rules for different people and different situations.

When he drew his CASHFLOW Quadrant for Mike and me, he often discussed the different rules that guided the different quadrants.

In 1943, the Current Tax Payment Act was passed. This law basically made it possible for the government to get paid before any employee got paid. When people say, "Pay yourself first," that statement technically does not apply to anyone in the E quadrant because in the E quadrant, the government always gets paid first. There is very little an accountant can do to help a person in the E quadrant pay less in taxes.

Up until 1986, the people in the S quadrant enjoyed many of the same tax loopholes that people in the B quadrant enjoyed. But after the 1986 Tax Reform Act, anyone who was a licensed professional—such as a doctor, lawyer, engineer, accountant, or architect, as well as some employees—could no longer use the same loopholes as those in the B quadrant and I quadrant. That 1986 change in the law led to the crash of the real estate market, the stock market, and the end of many savings and loans. Banks, big business, and well-advised businesspeople and investors gained, while many others lost tax advantages because of this law change.

In 1933, Joseph P. Kennedy, head of the newly founded Securities and Exchange Commission and father of President John F. Kennedy, supported a law that in essence keeps the poor and middle class from investing in the same paper-asset investments of the rich. As a result, people who are not millionaires or people who earn less than $200,000 individually or $300,000 as a couple—which is less than 5 percent of the U.S. population—are often unable to invest in some of the best investments in the world.

When you look at the game board of *CASHFLOW 101*, you see two different tracks.

How To Get Out Of The Rat Race

The *CASHFLOW 101* game board reflects the 1933 SEC ruling. The smaller circular track is the Rat Race. That is where the poor and middle class invest. The larger track, the track known as the Fast Track, is where the rich invest. Not only is the game different on the different tracks, but the rules are different as well. Rich dad insisted that Mike and I know the differences between the games and the rules.

Rules of the Quadrants

I want as little money as possible coming to me from the E quadrant. I do not have, nor do I ever want, any income as a specialist such as a doctor, lawyer, or accountant from the S quadrant. Today, 90 percent of my income comes from the B and I quadrants. Why? The answer is because the rules for getting rich are better in those quadrants.

If you are to become the captain of your own ark, you may need to be very aware of the different rules for the different quadrants. That does not mean going back to school to become an accountant or attorney. It simply means you will need control over competent advisors, a subject covered in the next chapter. The reason you want to be aware of the different rules for the different quadrants is simply because, as skipper of your ship, you need to know the differences.

At the academy, a very important course of study was labor law. The reason we had to study labor law was because, as ship's officers, we had to deal with unions, union labor, and union rules. If we as ship's officers were not aware of those rules, we would not have been effective leaders.

On a similar note, rich dad had his son and me pay particular attention to the rules of the E quadrant. Once we understood the rules that govern workers in the E quadrant, Mike and I knew which quadrants we wanted to be in. The following are a few simple examples of some of the differences and the reasons why, as captain of your ark, you too want to know the differences.

- **Saving Money versus Borrowing**

  As covered earlier, most people think that saving money is smart. Yet, if you look at the tax laws governing each quadrant, you will see that saving money in the E quadrant is a losing proposition. For a person to save a dollar in the E quadrant requires that the worker earn nearly $2 since taxes take nearly 50 percent of a worker's earnings. When looking at the taxes a person in the E quadrant pays on the interest from those savings and the loss of value to inflation, saving may be a good habit, but it is not a financially smart way to drive a ship.

In the I quadrant, I would rather *borrow* money than *save* money. In fact, the more money I borrow and the less of my own money I put into the real estate investment, the higher my ROI (return on investment). In other words, the more I borrow, the harder my own money works, and the higher my returns—if the investment is a good investment. Using an overly simplified example, if I purchase a $100,000 property and put 20 percent, or $20,000, down and borrow $80,000 at 8 percent interest and net $200 a month income after all expenses, my return on investment, or ROI, is roughly 12 percent.

If all things stay the same and I only put $10,000 down, or 10 percent, borrow 90 percent, or $90,000, at 8 percent interest, my monthly net income drops to approximately $130 a month but my return on my $10,000 investment jumps to approximately 15 percent. That 3 percent difference is more than the interest rate banks are paying savers today.

If all things could be held equal and I could find a similar investment, I would be better off buying two properties, putting less down, and earning more money by borrowing more money. If there were capital appreciation on both properties, then my return on capital would be even greater.

Again, this is an overly simplified example. But the point is, if the investment is a sound investment, the more I borrow, the higher my returns. That is why I would rather borrow than save, while most people think it smart to save and get out of debt. The difference is a difference of quadrants and rules, a difference in basic financial education, and a difference in experience.

Taking this example further, if you factor in depreciation, the returns go even higher; depending upon which quadrant you are in. (If you are a doctor or lawyer in the S quadrant or an employee in the E quadrant, the following example may not work for you.)

There are many times when Kim and I will earn a 15 percent return on our cash just from rental income. Because of the rules, we can also earn an additional 30 percent or more from depreciation, which is also known as phantom cash flow. So what appears on the surface as a 15 percent return may actually be a 45 percent return. For example, on a $10,000 down payment on a rental property that returns $1,500 in net rental income, there can be an additional $3,000 in reduced taxes from depreciation, or a total of $4,500 cash flow per year from the $10,000 down payment.

If you correctly structure your corporate entities in which you hold title to your properties, that $4,500 in real money can stay virtually tax free as long as you follow the rules. Try getting that kind of return from $10,000 in savings from your bank. At the bank down the street from me, if I had $10,000 in savings, I would be earning $200 a year and paying approximately $100 in taxes, netting me $100 instead of $4,500 per year on the same amount of money. That is why I do not save money and would rather borrow.

Years ago, rich dad taught me that investing in real estate through a business generates four types of income.

1. Rental income

2. Depreciation

3. Appreciation

4. Tax advantages

That is why he played the game of *Monopoly* with his son and me for hours and hours. It went far beyond simply making money. One of the main reasons was to teach us the rules of the B and I quadrants. When all four types of income are factored into the simple example above, the $100 received from the bank is losing value, as is the $10,000 due to inflation. The $4,500 has a good chance of increasing due to rental increases. The chances of additional capital appreciation of not only your $10,000 but also the bank's $90,000 is good, if the investment is a sound investment.

In other words, if the property increases in value, the bank continues to receive only 8 percent on the $90,000, and you get the rest. If the property goes up in value, let's say from $100,000 to $200,000, I can go back to the bank and borrow an additional $75,000 or more tax free. Or I can sell the property through an exchange, putting the additional $100,000 to work without having to pay taxes on the capital gains at that moment. In other words, the more financial education you have and the more you know about the rules of the quadrants, the more money you can make.

This simplified example just scratches the surface of what is possible if you understand the rules of the B and I quadrants. In other words, the actual returns can be even greater if you know what you are doing and have competent advisors. I will not go into the more technical information because I do not want to go beyond the scope of this book. If you have questions on the above example, you may want to talk to an accountant or a real estate agent who specializes in investment real estate. They may give you greater insight into the different rules of the I quadrant.

Caution: For these numbers to work, a person should have several years of real estate investing under his or her belt. If a person does not have that experience, I would not recommend using your banker's money to get ahead financially. Debt as leverage can be very dangerous on a ship with a green captain. Warren Buffett says, "When you combine ignorance and borrowed money, the consequences can get interesting."

- **Owner of a Business versus an Employee of a Business**
  As the captain of your ark, you will need to know the differences between an owner of a business and an employee of a business.

  When you compare the financial statements of an employee to those of a business owner, the differences speak for themselves.

  As an employee, all expenses are after-tax expenses. As a business owner, you have some degree of control of what you spend with pre-tax dollars versus the employee's after-tax expense dollars.

EMPLOYEE	BUSINESS OWNER
INCOME STATEMENT	INCOME STATEMENT
Income	**Income**
Expenses Taxes Mortgage payment Real estate taxes Car payment School loan payment Credit card payment Food Clothing Other expenses	**Expenses** Mortgage payment Real estate taxes Car payment School loan payment Credit card payment Food Clothing Other expenses Taxes
BALANCE SHEET	BALANCE SHEET
Assets / Liabilities	Assets / Liabilities

As captain of your ark, you want maximum control over the use of the different rules of each of the quadrants. Because an ark consists of all four quadrants, you need to know the rules for each quadrant.

Taking Control of the Rules

One of the reasons I want as little income as possible from the E quadrant is simply because I have the least control over the rules. In the E quadrant, the government controls the rules. Even when it comes to an employee's so-called tax-free retirement plan, the government still makes the rules.

In America, the government allows an employee to place a limited amount of money into their DC pension plan. However, the income is usually pulled out at the highest tax rate possible, the tax rate of the E quadrant. In other words, even though employees today are "investing," in many ways, ERISA forces them to invest into the rules of the E quadrant rather than the rules of the I quadrant. I do not like the rules of E quadrant because the rules of the E quadrant limit the amount I can invest and often limit me to savings, mutual funds, and stocks—the investment vehicles of choice for the middle class. People who invest in only these investments often have small arks. If you want to have a large ark, you need to invest in the investments of the rich. To do that, you first need to take control of the rules.

When you look at the I quadrant, you see the date 1933. The 1933 act required that all offers and sale of securities become registered, unless they fall within certain exemptions. This resulted in a difference between paper-asset investments for the rich and for everyone else.

Rich dad said to me, "One of the problems of ERISA is that it confines investors to the paper-asset investments of the middle class. Those are the riskiest investments with the lowest level of returns." The reason he said they were the riskiest is because the investor has very little control over the ups and downs of the markets. They provide the lowest level of returns because most mutual funds are diversified. Rich dad said, "When you diversify your mutual funds, you are diversifying something that is already diversified. Diversifying mutual funds is like taking a high-octane gasoline and adding water and then orange juice to it. Why would you advise someone to diversify something that is already diversified? Why not just tell them to keep their money in the bank? The net return will be about the same in the long run, and it's probably less risky." As a side comment, rich dad said, "Diversification keeps the stock market floating at unrealistic values. Because a mutual fund is a diversified fund, many stocks are purchased instead of just one good stock. That gives the less valuable companies a higher-than-realistic valuation." In other words, mutual funds inflate the stock prices of average companies, which cause a bubble that will eventually burst.

If you will look deeper into the I quadrant, you may notice that there are more investments than just paper assets. In the world of investing, the three main asset classes are businesses, real estate, and paper assets. By investing in paper assets through your retirement plan, by law, you can only invest in the paper assets of the middle class. But if you invest in the other assets such as businesses and real estate, you can use the same rules the rich use and gain the same advantages of the rich. To me, that makes more sense.

Using the Rules of the Rich

When a person realizes that their DC pension plan is not going to carry them the distance and they ask me what to do, I say the same thing rich dad would say, which is, "Stop using the rules of the middle class and start using the rules of the rich." I then offer the following suggestions and remind the person that they are only suggestions. I would not force anyone to do what I recommend unless they really want to do it and are willing to invest time into study and real-life experience.

Build Your Own Ark

Suggestion #1
Keep Your Daytime Job and Start a Part-Time Business
This suggestion immediately gives you the following advantages:

- *Tax advantages of the rich*
  Comparing the income statement and balance sheet of an employee and a business owner illustrates this advantage.

- *Time to practice learning the skills and the rules required for the B quadrant*
  You have to start preparing now because the years of greatest change are still coming. Starting a part-time business now will give you a number of valuable years to gain priceless experience.

- *More control over your life*
  Rather than being downsized or forced to retire before you can afford to, starting a business gives you a certain degree of control over your future.

- *Business and trade continue even if the market goes down*
  When the stock market crashes, business goes on. In 1950, the economy was booming while the stock market stayed depressed. It was only when Charles Merrill, one of the founders of Merrill Lynch, introduced store-front retailing of stocks that the stock market took off again.

  Warren Buffett says, "I never attempt to make money in the stock market. I buy on the assumption that they could close the market the next day and not reopen it for five years."

  The stock market is not really attached to the smaller but real economy. Even when the economy is depressed, business will go on. Businesses such as food stores, dry cleaners, gasoline stations, insurance agents, real estate sales, pest control, retail stores, professional services will continue. Big business may be hurt, but small legitimate real businesses will do okay.

- *Potential for small businesses to grow into large assets*
  For example, let's say someone starts XYZ Small Juice
  Company with a $10,000 initial investment. Ten years later,
  the company has no debt and nets $100,000 in earnings.
  Using a ten-times-earnings formula, if that company were
  sold, it would be worth $1 million to the owner.

  If ABC Big Juice Company comes along and licenses the use
  of XYZ Small Juice Company's secret formula, that license
  alone could possibly be worth millions of dollars in royalty
  payments if ABC Big Juice Company markets XYZ Small Juice
  Company's products worldwide. That licensing transaction is
  invisible but very profitable.
  It is also intellectual property.

  Every successful business has intellectual property. Intellectual
  property includes patents, trademarks, copyrights, trade dress,
  reputation, licenses, goodwill (reputation), and much more.
  As the future becomes more invisible, intellectual property
  has never been more important. It is the key to great wealth
  now and in the future.

- *A higher rate of return*
  DC plans are forecasts based on an average 8 percent to
  9 percent gain. Small business owners, if they are good, can
  get a significantly higher rate of return. Rather than invest
  a dollar into a DC retirement plan, a dollar invested back
  into your own business could easily get you a 40 percent to
  100 percent return, with tax advantages, if you are a good
  business operator.

Quoting Warren Buffett: "A lot of great fortunes in the world have
been made by owning a single wonderful business. If you understand
the business, you don't need to own very many of them."

Getting Started

If you have decided to buy or build a business, there are many
decisions to make. The following is adapted from *Rich Dad's Choose to
Be Rich program* (available at RichDad.com).

Build Your Own Business

Of all the business options, starting your own company is the most difficult because you'll be developing every system on your own. However, it is also potentially the most rewarding. In choosing a business, it is always best to solve a problem or serve a need. When you have decided on the type of business, here is a partial list of the next steps to follow:

- Name your business.

- Begin to seek funding sources.

- Search for outside advisors.

- Select your business entity and form it.

- Obtain any necessary licenses and permits.

- Set up a relationship with your banker.

- Protect proprietary information (intellectual property).

- Write a business plan.

- Select your location.

- Form your manufacturing or procurement or service procedures—i.e., how you will manufacture and deliver your goods or services.

- Plan ahead for bookkeeping, accounting, and office systems.

- Decide on pricing strategies.

- Determine employee needs.

- Prepare your marketing plan.

- Seek insurance coverage.

- Address legal issues.

- Fine-tune your cash-flow budget.

- Set up your office.

- Hire employees.

- Announce your business.

Buy an Existing Business

If you want to avoid the headaches of starting a business from scratch, you may decide you want to buy an existing business. Here are some pros and cons to consider:

Pros
- No long, risky start-up period

- All systems in place

- Existing customer base

- Faster route to profitability than with a start-up

- Existing goodwill of the business

Cons
- The danger of buying a lemon

- Skeletons in the closet

- Sticky personnel issues due to the transition

- Potential competition from the seller

- Existing ill will of the business

Buy a Franchise

If you want to buy a ready-made business system that offers a support structure, you may want to consider a franchise.

Pros
- Tried and proven business systems
- Licensed trademark and recognition of brand
- Training program
- Operations manual
- Specifications, quality standards, and blueprints
- Ongoing assistance in systems and operations

Cons
- Expensive
- Restrictive—must conform to the operations manual

Join Network Marketing

You may want to join a network-marketing company where the entry cost is low and there are training programs to help you succeed. The companies are typically based on direct sales with home-business opportunities.

Pros
- Minimal start-up costs
- Comprehensive training
- Can be either full- or part-time
- Can work at home
- Work with a national or international brand
- Build passive and residual income
- Develop communication and leadership skills

- Automated order processing, distribution, and accounting systems which prevent many of the headaches associated with traditional start-ups

Cons
- Low start-up fees can mean low commitment
- Need self-discipline
- Need to deal with rejection

Suggestion #2
Invest in Small Real Estate Properties

Investing in small real estate properties gives you:

- *The ability to use your banker's money to invest*
  Instead of trying to save money for retirement, if you learn to invest in real estate, you can borrow money to become richer faster.

  In an earlier illustration, I used the example of a 15 percent return using 90 percent borrowed money. On top of that, if you know what you are doing, you can gain an additional 30 percent in real phantom cash flow.

Rich dad taught me six steps to become a good real estate investor. The six steps are important because if one or more of the steps is missing, the real estate investment will go sour.

1. Decide to become a real estate investor. You have to make a commitment and set your goals.

2. Find an area to concentrate on. If you're just starting out, stick with an area you're familiar with or that is nearby.

3. Find properties that meet your criteria. By learning how to analyze properties, you'll be able to tell good deals from bad ones.

4. Negotiate the deal. After analyzing the numbers, you are ready to make offers, negotiate, and reach an agreement.

5. Put the deal together. From due diligence to financing and settlement, it's important to stay on top of all the technical details.

6. Manage the property. It is not as much hassle as you think, and it is one of the best ways to make the most of your investment and get the cash flowing.

- *The awareness that real estate is real business*
  When you look at your tenant's financial statement, you will see why the property you rent to him is so important.

Tenant's Financial Statement

INCOME STATEMENT

Income

Expenses
Taxes
Rents
Food
Clothes
Transportation

BALANCE SHEET

Assets	Liabilities

Looking at the financial statement, you can easily see that rent is a high-priority expense for your tenant. Rent for many people is more important than their DC pension plan.

I often hear people say, "Many people have lost a lot of money in real estate." I reply, "That is true. But the facts are, more people have lost a lot more money in the stock market through their retirement plans."

Another comment I hear is, "Real estate is not as liquid as stocks and mutual funds." I reply, "Every month, Kim and I receive tens of thousands of dollars in rental income as well as income from tax advantages. That is the kind of real liquidity we want."

If you are concerned about your DC retirement plan and do not want to make a large commitment to real estate, you may want to consider owning four houses. You have one house to live in, and three houses to provide you income when the stock market crashes.

John Maynard Keynes, the famous economist, once said, "The markets can remain irrational longer than you can remain liquid." Small real estate properties can provide you liquidity until the market crash is over, regardless how long the recovery takes.

Suggestion #3
Plan on Becoming Rich Rather Than
Becoming a High-Income Person with a Lot of Money

In other words, use the rules of the rich, which are the rules of the B and I quadrants. Many high-income people—such as doctors, lawyers, and high-paid executives—are severely penalized for their high income. By utilizing the rules of the rich, a high-income person can gain more control over their money and become rich faster, safer, and more efficiently. In other words, a DC pension plan, a Roth IRA, Keogh, and other plans really do not help the high-income wage earner.

Suggestion #4

**Understand How Professional Investors
Protect Themselves from Market Crashes**

When I purchase a piece of real estate, my banker requires me to insure my investment. The same is true for my businesses. When professional investors invest in stocks, many use insurance to protect their assets. But most people with DC pension plans have no insurance from catastrophic loss. When the market crashes, they find out they have no control. As captain of your own ark, anything you invest in must be insured.

In *Retire Young Retire Rich*, I wrote about how to use options to insure your paper assets. Find out how to use options as insurance, and you will discover how experienced options traders make fortunes with very little risk and much higher returns. Once you know how options work, you may never want to purchase a share of stock or mutual funds again. The advanced game *CASHFLOW 202* teaches technical trading in a fun and risk-free environment. However, you must master *CASHFLOW 101* before you tackle the advanced version.

Suggestion #5

Don't De-Worsify—Diversify

When I hear people say they are diversifying, I ask them what they mean. Many simply diversify into more paper assets such as sector funds, large cap funds, bond funds, and money funds. This is not diversifying. This is de-worsifying. All a person is investing in is more and more paper assets, often more mutual funds. Instead, I recommend investing in different types of asset classes and truly spreading the risk, but also improving your chances of higher returns.

My rich dad taught me to build businesses and then invest the profits from the business in real estate. I have followed this formula over and over again.

Case Study

Scott is a dentist and real estate investor in Seattle, Washington. He became a dentist because his father, a lifelong employee, encouraged him to be his own boss. A couple of years ago, he took the time to analyze where he was in designing and building his financial ark. He owned two practices as well as the buildings for both practices. Even with this setup, he realized he would still have to work for the rest of his life. The major portion of his income was still from his physical labor as a dentist. He also knew he did not want to join the typical Rat Race of buying a big house and bigger car, supporting wife and kids, and so on.

At this point, Scott read *Rich Dad Poor Dad* and realized that, while he had built a successful practice, he needed to diversify more into real estate. Following the Rich Dad philosophy, Scott developed and took control of his own set of investment rules. He started saving 20 percent of the dental revenues weekly and put it toward real estate investing. After starting with small properties, he used his time and discipline to invest in bigger and bigger deals. He has now invested in warehouses, gas stations, strip malls, and other commercial properties. In fact, he owns one warehouse that generates $17,000 every month in cash flow. He also invests in real estate contracts, which are paper assets that pay him 14%. He attributes his success in moving to the right side of the CASHFLOW Quadrant to the lessons he learned from *Rich Dad Poor Dad*. Today, he even passes out copies of the book to his friends.

Scott has built a financial ark full of business assets, paper assets, and real estate assets and has prepared himself to be able to profit during the next down as well as up market.

Chapter Eighteen

CONTROL #6: CONTROL OVER YOUR ADVISORS

One of the most painful, costly, yet priceless mistakes I made early in my business career was to think that my accountant knew more than I did. In fact, rich dad told me my business had financial cancer because the three of us thought our accountant knew what he was doing.

After the nylon-and-Velcro wallet business got into trouble, the first thing the accountant did was cut back on our sales and marketing budget. He said, "We need to trim our expenses and pay our creditors." Not knowing any better, we let him do that. After the company crashed, I discovered that the creditors he paid off were his friends who invested in our little company. In other words, he left the company without any debt to his friends, and the rest of us were left holding the bag.

After this learning experience, rich dad said, "Always remember that you are the entrepreneur, the visionary, and the leader. Never let your advisors run your business. When business begins to slow down, spend a lot of money on promotion. After business has picked up, then you can cut back and pay off some of the bills that came from the promotion." He also said, "When business slows, too many people cut back on promotion rather than spend more on promotion. When business picks up, they spend instead of cut back. That is one reason why so many small businesses stay small.

They cut back when they should *spend*, and *spend* when they should cut back. This is also true of big businesses."

After September 11, I noticed many companies began to cut back on their sales, marketing, and promotion budgets. That is a sign that the company is run by accountants and advisors rather than the captain of the ship.

The Betrayed Investor

A recent cover of *Business Week* read, "The Betrayed Investor." The cover-story article interviewed three investors who had been betrayed: two attorneys and one accountant.

The story of the accountant read like this:

James J. Houlihan Jr.'s plan to retire at 50 is gone. In the last two years, he lost about 30% of a portfolio invested in such stocks as EMC, Lucent Technologies, and WorldCom. Now, the 41-year-old must work harder to rebuild his four children's college funds. "I just don't understand how a business can appear to be so strong and in six months become a fraction of its value," laments Houlihan. "There are people who know what's going on, and then there's the rest of us." He'll save more and spend less—but he's not counting on stocks to make up for what's lost. He and his brother run an accounting firm in Fort Wayne, Indiana, so it's not as if he doesn't understand analyst reports. But now, he says, "I don't pay them any credence. It's complete B.S. It's gotten to the point where you don't know who you can rely on."

The story of one of the attorneys read like this:
Until three years ago, 31-year-old Manhattan attorney Heather E. Barr had no interest in the stock market or planning for retirement. At the urging of a co-worker, she finally signed up for one of three Salomon Smith Barney Inc. funds offered by her company's 401(k) plan. It also happened to be at the peak of the market. For a while, the account did fairly well, but by last year, she had lost a third of her money. The last time she looked, the account was worth less than $2,000. She has since stopped opening her statements. While she still puts an automatic $50 a month into the plan, she's not holding out hope for a rebound.

"I don't have any faith in the stock market," she says. "Everyone says you have to ride it out and be in for the long haul. Maybe that's true, but putting money in a shoe box would have landed me more."

You're the Captain

The point is not to put down accountants, attorneys, or any other highly educated professional. The article's choice of an accountant and two attorneys illustrated the point that there is more to being the captain of an ark than having the financial literacy of an accountant or being well versed on the rules like an attorney. Accountants and attorneys are highly specialized professionals. More often than not, they are from the E or S quadrant. Being the captain of your ark requires you to operate in the B and I quadrants, which requires you to be far more generalized than specialized. A specialist knows a lot about a little, while a generalist knows a little about a lot. One of the hardest lessons I had to learn is to listen to my advisors, trust my instincts, and live with my decision, right or wrong, good or bad. As rich dad said, "You are the captain of your ship, not your advisors."

A Lesson Relearned

Recently, I had to painfully relearn the lesson that I am still the captain of my own ark and financial statement. Kim and I had purchased a property in December of 2001. After our accountant and tax advisors had blessed the investment, we then turned the finalization of the agreement over to the seller's attorney and our attorney. Two months and thousands of dollars in attorneys' fees later, the investment fell apart. What seemed like a simple transaction had turned into an expensive nightmare.

Stepping back into the negotiations, I found out that the two attorneys were now personally at war with each other, rather than professionally and objectively putting the deal together. The negotiation broke down over points that did not matter. All the attorneys could do was focus on what was wrong with each other, rather than what was right for the deal. The strong positive points of the investment had been forgotten. The investment objectives—

cash flow, appreciation, depreciation, and tax-free gains—were not important to the attorneys. Being right was more important to them. Two months of time and tens of thousands of dollars were lost because I let my advisor run the ship. I could hear rich dad saying, "Just because someone is smart and went to a good school does not mean they know anything about the real world of business or investing."

Rich dad surrounded himself with very smart people. He was an active listener and treated each advisor with respect. Yet at the end of the day, he always remembered that he was still the captain of his ship. The final decision was still up to him.

Be the Captain

Many of the recent losses in the stock market were caused simply because too many people let advisors run their arks. If you are going to be the captain of your ship, you need to be in control of your advisors.

Again quoting Warren Buffett, "You don't need to be a rocket scientist. Investing is not a game where a guy with the 160 IQ beats the guy with a 130 IQ. Rationality is essential."

Build Your Ark

- Do you have a team of advisors?
  Yes ____   No ____

  Business and investing are team sports, and you need competent advisors.

- Meet regularly (monthly) with your advisors.

- The only silly question is the one you don't ask.

- Make the final decision.

- Forgive yourself for making mistakes.

- Learn from your mistakes.

Additional Resources

Genius comes in all forms. The following are two books I have enjoyed reading and have learned a lot from and recommend that people read.

The first book, *When Genius Failed* by Roger Lowenstein, offers brilliant insight into what happens when people forget that geniuses are human. When Genius Failed is about how a group of approximately 100 people nearly bankrupted the United States in the late 1990s.

The second book, *At Work with Thomas Edison* by Blaine McCormick and John P. Keegan, is about America's first high-tech entrepreneur.

Both books will give you potent insights into the world of two different types of genius. These books are important because the two different types of genius are for two different eras of history. *When Genius Failed* is about the type of genius that was respected during the era of corporate America's dominance in the world. The book on Edison is about the world prior to corporate America's rise. In other words, in different periods of time, different types of genius are required.

Chapter Nineteen
CONTROL #7: CONTROL OVER YOUR TIME

Rich dad said, "One of your greatest assets is time. One of the reasons most people do not become rich is because they do not make good use of their time. Most people work hard making the rich richer, but fail to work hard making themselves rich."

In 1974, I began working at the Xerox Corporation in downtown Honolulu. For those of you who have read my other books, you already know that I chose the Xerox Corporation because the company had an excellent sales-training program. Rich dad recommended I learn to sell if I was going to become an entrepreneur in the B quadrant. He said, "The number-one skill of a business owner is the ability to sell." He also said, "When I find a business that is struggling financially, it is often because the owner cannot sell."

However, only a year later, I was on probation with the Honolulu branch of Xerox because I could not sell. My shyness and fear of rejection put me at the bottom of the list of new sales trainees. If my sales performance did not improve quickly, I was going to be fired. Again I turned to rich dad for advice.

On a hot summer day, I met rich dad at a restaurant near his office, and he reminded me again of one of his core philosophies. After listening to my tale of woe, my poor sales performance, and my fear of rejection, he asked, "So what are you going to do about it? How many times do I have to remind you that you do not get rich at work? How many times do I have to remind you that you get rich in your spare time?"

Getting Rich Faster

A few weeks later, after leaving my office at Xerox, I walked up the street to a nonprofit charity and sat on their phone bank dialing for dollars. The reason I did this was to gain more sales experience—faster. Three to five nights a week, I would make ten to thirty phone sales pitches, asking people to donate money to this worthy cause. In a three-hour period, I was making as many sales presentations as I was making in a month pounding the streets for Xerox. In other words, I was getting rich faster. I was getting rich because I was gaining a skill that would enrich my life forever. By late 1975, I was no longer on probation at Xerox, my sales were improving, and so was my income. By 1976, I was one of the top sales representatives. When my sales manager asked me what the secret to my success was, I simply said, "I made more sales calls faster." He smiled and I never told him I made my sales calls for a charity, and did them in my spare time.

About the same time, rich dad encouraged me to begin investing in real estate. That is why I took a real estate investment course before I got out of the Marine Corps. Rich dad always said, "I *make* my money in my business. I keep my money in real estate."

When I reflect on my life, I appreciate rich dad's wisdom of getting rich in your spare time. Today I am financially free because of what I did in my spare time, rather than what I did at work. Today, if you are working hard on somebody else's ark, you may want to set aside some spare time to build your own ark.

I Love My Work!

People often say to me, "But I love my work. I love what I do." To those statements, I reply, "Congratulations. Loving what you do is very important." Yet silently, I ask this question, "Is what you love doing providing everything you need?"

The point is, many people love their work, but their work will not provide for their long-term needs. For example, Kim and I have a friend who is a great interior designer, and her husband is an executive in a manufacturing company. They both love their work and make a lot of money, but neither of them has anything to fall back on. When they asked for advice, one of the first questions I asked them was, "How much can you sell your job for?"

Both replied, "Nothing. We cannot sell our jobs."

I simply sat there in the silence and let them listen to their own words. Finally, the silence became deafening. "So what are you saying?" asked the wife. "Quit our jobs?"

Again, I said nothing and the squirm factor became higher. "Look, we've come to ask for help. The least you can do is say something. Are you saying we should quit our jobs? Is that what you're saying?"

Once again, I sat quietly, letting them respond to the silence.

My silence was met by their silence. Finally, the husband took a deep breath and rocked back in his chair as I sat at my desk. His wife, our friend the interior decorator, was still leaning forward, hoping for an answer from me. After about 30 seconds of silence, she too rocked back in her chair and sat there in silence.

"How much can we sell our jobs for?" asked the husband as he rocked back and forth, listening to the question I asked initially that he was now asking in his own words. "How much can I sell my job for?" he suddenly asked, but this time in a much louder voice. I could tell he was hearing his own question, not my question.

"Well, the answer is nothing," he said, answering himself. "Absolutely nothing."

"But it provides us income," said his wife in a defensive tone. "We earn money to put a roof over our heads, feed the kids, and provide for the future."

"I know, I know," said the husband. "I know all that. But that is not the question being asked. The question is, 'How much can we sell our jobs for?'"

"So you say we're working for nothing?" asked the wife.

"No," I replied, breaking my silence. "I just asked a question, a question I wanted you to ask yourself."

"So we're working at something we cannot sell," said the husband. "What do you suggest?"

"Well, how about investing time to work for yourself? Why not work just as hard to make yourself rich as you do to make someone else rich?"

"So invest some time in ourselves," said the wife.

I went on to tell the story of my dialing for dollars for the charity and investing in real estate. "When I look back upon those years, my job did not make me rich. What made me rich was what I did after my job. What are you doing?"

"Truthfully, nothing," said the husband. "We work hard for our clients, we work hard to pay bills, we work hard to set a few dollars aside for our retirement, and we work hard for our kids and their future education."

"So you invest in your kids' future?" I asked.

"I know, I know," said the husband. "I got the message. It's time we invested some time in our future."

Investing in Becoming Investors

Today it is no longer enough to be professionally competent. We all need to be professionally and financially competent. Earlier, I wrote that many people today are investing, but very few are becoming investors. The couple I just mentioned fell into that category. After the market crash, they realized that they might be better off becoming investors rather than trusting their money to people they hoped and prayed were investors.

The couple attended some Rich Dad investing courses and then commented afterwards, "I cannot believe how fast a person can make money from their investments. Why would anyone want to put money in mutual funds and hope for a 10 percent-per-year taxable return? Why would anyone want to take the risk of having their mutual funds wiped out in a market crash? Why not learn how to make money when the market is going up as well as coming down?

The point is that you can gain more control over your time if your money can work at a higher rate of return. For example, it is relatively simple to use your banker's money rather than your own money to generate 50 percent or more in returns per year.

Rich dad taught his son and me that if you can increase the velocity of your money, you could gain valuable time. For example if you earn 5 percent per year on your investment, it takes you approximately 20 years to get your initial investment back. If your money earns 50 percent per year, you get your investment back in two years. If you can earn 100 percent per month, you get your money back in one month, or 12 times each year. These returns are possible with the appropriate financial investment education. In other words, a small investment in your financial education can gain you massive amounts of financial time.

Health and Wealth

Rich dad often said that there was a strong correlation between health and wealth. I define wealth as the number of days you can survive without working, while still maintaining your standard of living. More specifically, *wealth is measured in time more than money*. For example, if you had $5,000 in savings and your monthly expenses were $1,000 a month, your wealth would be 5 months.

The same is true with health. If you are healthy, you have years ahead of you. But if your health begins to deteriorate, then your time on this earth diminishes. So health and wealth can be measured relative to time.

Another measurement of health and wealth is recovery time. For example, if you go for a physical examination, the medical examiner may ask to take your resting heart rate and then put you on a treadmill to get your heart rate up. After attaining an elevated heart rate, the examiner then measures how fast it takes your body to recover to the resting heart rate. That is called recovery time. The same is true with surgery. If a person is healthy, the recovery time is short. If the person is physically weak, the recovery time may take longer.

Wealth can be measured in the same way, relative to time. If a person is a true investor with the proper education and experience, if they lose everything, their recovery time can be quick. But if a person is like the 58-year-old Enron employee on the front page of the "Money" section of *USA TODAY*, the financial-recovery time may take longer than that person has years of work left. He may be healthy, but his wealth is anemic.

Rich dad encouraged his son and me to learn to build businesses and become investors. That is why I went through sales training and learned about property. Today, I make my money in business and store my money in real estate.

Four Kinds of People

There are four kinds of people.

1. People who must be right

2. People who must win

3. People who must be liked

4. People who must be comfortable

I can place my friends and family into each of the four categories. I would say Kim and I are definitely in the category that needs to win. One of the reasons we could retire young and retire rich is because winning was more important than any of the other three categories. By having the return on our money pick up speed, we could retire far earlier than most people and win our private race to financial freedom—and financial freedom means having more free time.

As captain of your own ark, one of the ways you can increase the speed of your ark and gain more time is by investing some time in your financial education.

Earlier in this book, I wrote about educating the middle mind. As captain of your ark, after you gain that education, it is still up to you to turn that middle-mind education into higher-mind wisdom. One of the more frustrating things about learning is investing the time to convert knowledge into wisdom. When I was struggling financially in the 1980s, the hard part of life was knowing what to do mentally, but not being able to do what I knew I had to do. The benefit of investing the time first into education and then into live practice is that a person begins to learn to love the game. For example, I did not like building a business when I was failing at it. Today, I love the process. When I was losing at investing in real estate, I hated real estate. Today, I love the game of real estate and the properties Kim and I own.

As captain of your ark, I strongly urge you to learn to love your cargo. Today, I love my businesses and my real estate. I learned to love these assets and skills because I first invested time into educating my middle mind and then invested time in teaching my higher mind to love the assets.

A Little Education Means Less Time, Less Money, Less Risk, and a Higher Standard of Living

A friend of mine just told me that his 401(k) lost over $350,000. At 53 years old, he is now concerned that he can never retire. He realizes that diversification will not deliver the returns he wants or the long-term protection he needs. When he asked me for some advice, I said, "Why don't you take your $30,000, buy three rental houses for $100,000 each, and let your tenants pay down your mortgage as well as give you income? By the time you're 65, you should have a steady stream of income, if you have invested wisely."

His response was, "All I need is $30,000?"

Nodding, I said, "All you really need is $15,000 to buy three rental properties. The federal government has loan programs, if you qualify, that allow individuals to only put 5 percent down on certain properties."

"So are you saying I could retire with only $15,000? And the bank will lend me the rest?"

"I believe so," I replied. "If market conditions remained the same and I had five to ten years before retiring, I am quite certain that I could retire with only $15,000 invested."

"What about people who live in expensive cities such as New York or San Francisco? Won't it be hard for them to find inexpensive rental properties?"

"In the heart of the city, yes, it would be hard. But if you go an hour out of most cities, you can find affordable properties. All you have to do is find an area that is going up in value. Over time, your property should appreciate. If inflation hits, you can raise your rents. By the time you retire, those three houses should be paying you a steady income, a far more secure income than income from mutual funds."

"And with far less money," he added.

"That's correct," I replied. "With a little education and experience, you can retire using less money, less risk, higher returns, and contribute to society by providing much needed housing."

"But what if everyone begins to invest in rental real estate?" he asked.

"Then we help the government provide housing at lower prices and hopefully raise the standard of living for those who cannot afford to buy a house. If there is more supply, then rents come down. If there are more owners competing for tenants, then competition will improve the quality of housing."

"How long do you hold your property before you sell?" he asked.

I replied by quoting Warren Buffett, "My time frame for holding a stock is forever."

"So you hold forever?"

"Most of the time," I said. "But every now and then I sell. I usually sell when I made a bad investment and I just want to get rid of it. But generally I follow Warren Buffett's idea of investing in what I love and holding on forever. I love the real estate and the businesses in my asset column."

"And I do not have to stop with three houses?"

"No, you don't," I replied. "It's just like playing *Monopoly*. If you have four green houses, you can then buy a red hotel. The government loves you, your banker loves you, and your future is more secure. One reason you feel more secure is because real estate can protect you from one of life's greatest financial threats, which is the threat of inflation.

"As inflation increases due to taxes, excess government spending, the government's printing of money, increasing costs of materials, rising interest rates, and the rising cost of insurance, you can pass those increases on to your tenant. Mutual funds often lose value during periods of high inflation and high interest rates, but a good property can increase in value during the same period. If you have purchased your real estate early enough and have a fixed interest rate, you have greater control over your investments as long as you do not invest in cities with rent control. As long as the rents are allowed to increase, inflation can actually be your friend. The same is true if you understand how stock options work. If inflation goes up, and stock prices fall, you can make more money on the way down, while those in most mutual funds will be losing money and losing time."

"So I would have a lot more control," said my friend. "By investing some time in financial education, I gain more time, I take greater control over my assets, use less of my hard-earned money, control my income for life, improve my returns, and lower my risk—all with a little education."

Agreeing, I said, "All with a little education."

Invest in Yourself

One of the ways to gain more control of your time is to invest some time in learning to create assets that return your money at a higher rate of speed. Just as a race car driver must increase their training if they want to handle higher speeds, so an investor must invest in their education if they want to handle investments that return more money in less time and at higher speeds.

Education requires three steps, and each step requires an investment of time.

1. **Invest some time finding the long- and short-term reasons why you want to learn something.**
   You may want to sit down and write down your goals and the reasons you want to achieve your goals. These reasons will give you the energy to move forward.

2. **Invest some time in learning the technical knowledge required to achieve your goals.**
   For example, I still invest time going to classes on how to build businesses and invest in real estate. The investment in technical knowledge saves me time because it gives me guidance, tells me what I must learn once class is over, and gives priceless insights from the instructor.

3. **Invest some time learning through real-life trial and error.**
   Right after your technical classes are over, it is important to go out and gain some of your own experience and wisdom. The reason I recommend starting small and using a small amount of money is simply because you will make mistakes. In the real world, humans learn by making mistakes. In traditional schools, humans are punished for making mistakes. That is why you may need to forget some of the bad habits school teaches you and go out and make mistakes and learn from them. The more wisdom you gain, the greater financial challenges you can take on.

If you follow this three-step process, you may find that your wealth goes up as your confidence and experience increase. When wealth and experience increase, you gain greater control over your future and expend less time getting richer.

Why a DC Retirement Plan Is a Waste of Time

To me, the great waste of time with pension reform was that it failed to encourage people to learn to manage their own money and their own investments. The plan basically said, "Turn your money over to people who are smarter than you are." The problem is, you may have noticed that many of the people you thought were financially smarter than you are not.

Warren Buffett says this about students coming out of our current MBA and finance programs:

It has been helpful to me to have tens of thousands [of students] turned out of business schools taught that it didn't do any good to think. Current finance classes can help you do average.

In other words, one reason he does well in the markets is because graduates of business schools run most of the large fund companies, and they are not good investors.

Simply put, the biggest problem with saving money and investing in mutual funds is that you do not gain much real-world investing experience. To me, that is a massive waste of time and money. Without real-world investing experience, it takes a lot of time, greater risk, tons of money, and constant financial insecurity all for a small financial return that may not be there when you need it. If you're over 45 years of age and have been wiped out or are just starting out, investing in a diversified DC pension plan will probably not work. In most cases, time is a real challenge for a person over 45.

There are many ways to gain greater control over your time. One way is via education. Rich Dad puts out different products in different formats because people learn differently. For example, some people learn by reading, yet many others do not. Some people learn well in traditional schools, but unfortunately, traditional schools teach little about the game of investing. Some people learn by doing, which is why we have created games for people to learn by playing. And still others learn by attending intensive seminars that concentrate the learning process into a short period of time.

In addition to our regular products such as books, audios, videos, and games, some of the intensive coaching and seminars we offer cover the following subjects:

- Stock options investing

- Real estate investing

- Building a business

Our education is designed for people who are looking for real-world investing education rather than getting an education for a college degree. Real-world investors coach and teach our seminars, and they don't have the time to waste your time. There is too much money to be made and too much fun to have in the real world of business and investing.

Build Your Ark

- Go back to Chapter 10 and review your answers:
  How many years before you reach 65?_____
  How many years before 2016?_____

- Have you committed the minimum five hours per week?
  Yes_____ No_____

- Make a commitment to a business or real estate investment today.
  Write it here: _____

Case Study

Allen is an attorney and was a partner in one of the premier international law firms. The more successful he became, the less time he had to spend with his family and friends. He was paid exceptionally well, but his income was still based on the hours he physically invested in each project.

After reading *Rich Dad Poor Dad* and *Rich Dad's CASHFLOW Quadrant*, Allen realized he was a "Super S" on the left side of the CASHFLOW Quadrant. After practicing law for over 25 years and seeing an ever-increasing demand for his time from his clients, he knew he had to make a change. Even though Allen had accumulated a significant amount of wealth in savings, he realized the bulk of his time was still being spent making others rich.

Allen changed his association with the law firm so he could be more flexible in the way he did business with his clients. Now he can choose the clients he wants to work with and he has the ability to exchange services for equity. Instead of just working for an hourly rate, which would keep him in the S quadrant, he can now invest his time in exchange for ownership in the companies he advises and has shifted to the B quadrant. He is using his time to build equity for himself, an asset in the B quadrant of the CASHFLOW Quadrant.

While Allen had already filled his financial ark with paper assets through savings plans and 401(k) plans, his wealth was closely tied to the stock market and out of his direct control. He realized just how out of control he was when he saw the value of his paper assets decline significantly in the last market downturn.

By changing how he spends his time, Allen is now building business assets and real estate over which he has more control. This change adds stability to his financial ark and make it less susceptible to fluctuations in the stock market. He currently owns an equity interest in a number of different types of companies including an Internet-marketing company, a medical-imaging company, an environmental company, a gold company, and oil and gas companies. He has invested money directly in some companies while he has exchanged his services for stock in others.

His financial statements now include three asset classes: paper, business, and real estate. By focusing on moving to the right side of the CASHFLOW Quadrant, Allen has succeeded in escaping the Rat Race while also building stability for his financial ark.

Chapter Twenty

CONTROL #8: CONTROL OVER YOUR DESTINY

Drawing Out the Rich Person in You

According to Webster's dictionary, the word *education* comes from the Latin *educo or educe*, which means, "to draw out or lead out." By choosing to attend the U.S. Merchant Marine Academy in New York, I was choosing to have the sailor in me come out. By attending the U.S. Navy Flight School in Florida, I was choosing to have the pilot in me brought out. By deciding to follow in my rich dad's footsteps rather than my poor dad's, I was choosing to have the rich person in me come out.

In 1974, I had to make a decision as to which dad I would follow. I knew that if I followed my own dad's advice of, "Go back to school, get your master's degree, and then get a secure job," I would wind up like him. I also knew that if I followed in my rich dad's footsteps, there were no guarantees as to where I would wind up. By 1974, I was old enough to know that rich dad's path had no guarantees. I could wind up broke and destitute just as well as wind up rich. By this time, I had seen many of rich dad's friends who had started on the journey with rich dad, but had not made it to their destination. I knew I had to make a choice between a guaranteed destiny or an uncertain destiny. As you know, I chose the destiny that was uncertain.

My decision to choose an uncertain destiny—to build my own ark rather than build one for someone else—had little to do with the destination and everything to do with the *process*—the road to the destination. Many of us have heard the saying, "The easy road becomes hard, and the hard road becomes easy." In 1974, I decided to take the hard road, the road without guarantees. The decision was easy. It was taking that first step that was hard. Five years later, in 1979, I had to make that decision again. Pulling myself up and out of a giant hole I had dug for myself was one of the most difficult things I have ever done, yet it was one of the best things I have ever done. I can honestly say that I have learned more from my failures than from my successes, and I have learned more from my stupidity than from my intelligence.

I recommend people keep their daytime job and start a part-time business or start investing in a small income property, simply because it takes a few years to learn the basics. The journey out of the chicken coop only begins with the first step. There are many steps that follow.

If rich dad's prophecy comes true, and I believe it will, the next few years will be boom years in the stock market. It will be the big boom before the big bust. The baby boomers will be pouring money into their last chance for retirement. Happy days will be here again. But instead of acting like drunken sailors on shore leave during this period of financial euphoria, I suggest you begin to methodically build your ark. Invest your time and some money in education and in experience. Be willing to make mistakes, but make sure they are small, and then learn from them. After learning from each mistake, congratulate yourself and step forward again. Although you may not necessarily be gaining financially, you will be gaining priceless experience, personal self-confidence, and more control over your destiny. Most importantly, you will be calling more and more for that rich person inside of you to come out.

Sir Isaac Newton once said, "I can measure the motion of celestial bodies, but I cannot measure human folly." He said this after personally losing a fortune during a period of financial euphoria known as the South Sea Bubble, a bubble that burst in 1720. Even a genius became a fool once he lost control of himself, his emotions, his excuses, his vision, his rules, his advisors, and his fortune.

I am quite certain that once the stock market recovers and begins its climb, people will once again forget the past and be heard once again saying, "This time it's different!" But sometime after 2012, things really will be different. Things will be different because this time, the past will catch up with the future. So prepare yourself and your ark to do well during the good times, and to do even better during the bad times. Study, read, attend classes, and practice as if your life depends upon your ability to invest—because it does. If you can do that, you will have called out the rich person inside you to become the captain of your ark.

Rich Dad Was a Tough Dad

Both my dads were tough men. Maybe that is why I found the discipline at the academy and in the Marine Corps fairly easy. Rich dad was especially tough on Mike and me when it came to money, business, and investing. After all, he was turning over his fortune to his son, and he was training me to acquire my own fortune.

Warren Buffett was also tough on his children. His partner had this to say about how Buffett treated his kids: "Warren is just as tough on his children as he is on his employees. He doesn't believe that if you love somebody, the way to do him good is to give him something he's not entitled to."

Warren Buffett calls inherited wealth, "food stamps for the rich." He goes on to say, "All these people who think that food stamps are debilitating and lead to a cycle of poverty are the same ones who go out and want to leave a ton of money to their kids."

When his son Howard ran for county commissioner in Omaha, voters falsely assumed that with his surname, his campaign would be well financed. That was not the case. Buffett senior explained, "I asked him to spell his name in lower-case letters so that everyone would realize that he was the Buffett without the capital."

Money Does Not Make You Rich

The other day I was in a store buying some clothes. The clerk asked me what I did. I replied, "I'm an investor."

As he rang up my purchase, he said, "That takes a lot of money, doesn't it?"

Shaking my head, I replied by saying, "No, it doesn't. In fact, money has very little to do with investing. Like many other people, I started with nothing."

"But you went to a good school then, didn't you?"

"I went to a good school, but what I learned had very little to do with investing or becoming rich," I replied. "And besides, money does not make you rich."

"So how did you become rich?" asked the clerk. "How did you find the money to invest?"

"I studied, I read a lot, I started small and made many mistakes, and I have good advisors and mentors. It's what I learned on the streets that made me rich," I replied as I signed my credit-card receipt.

"That sounds like a lot of work," said the young man.

"It is," I replied, "but so is what you are doing."

Not Having Money Makes You Richer

As you already know, rich dad never did finish school and, because of this, his speaking and writing skills were limited. Yet because he had to face the real world at the age of 13, his financial adversity caused him to develop his financial abilities and become one of the smartest persons I have ever known. When his son, Mike, and I get together these days, we continually discuss what we learned about business, investing, money, and life from his dad, my rich dad. We often comment, "Because he had no money, he became rich. Because he had no education, he became a genius. And because he had no security to fall back on, he found freedom."

What Do You Want to Be When You Grow Up?

One of the more important words to rich dad was the word *fiduciary*. Webster's dictionary defines *fiduciary* as "held in trust, generally referring to financial matters."

Rich dad said, "Regardless whether you wind up rich or poor, I always want you to be a person people can trust. Your word is your bond. If you wind up as a poor man and find yourself flat broke, if you and your family haven't eaten in days and there is a $100 bill sitting on someone's desk, I want you to be trustworthy enough to let it sit there. If you are poor, I want you to be a person who can be trusted to protect your family and your limited wealth, allowing both to grow with safety. If you are poor, I want you to be generous with your time, your wealth, and your wisdom. If you wind up rich men, you are to do the same things as a trustworthy poor man. That is what I want you to grow up to be. Regardless whether you grow up to be rich or poor, I want you to grow up to be people who can be trusted."

Inside each of you is a rich, poor, and middle-class person. Living in a free country means we all have the choice to decide which person we want to be. Start today by taking control of your education and your destiny.

Build Your Ark

- Are you in the middle of self-doubt?
  Yes _____ No _____

- Do you want a recipe or quick-fix answers?
  A recipe _____ Quick-fix answers _____

- Reevaluate which level of thought you have about money.

- To be in charge of your own ark, you must design it with your personal goal in mind. Take action and start building it today.

- Review the "Build Your Ark" sections at the end of each chapter.

- Ask yourself, "What is holding me back?" _____

Conclusion

A PROPHET'S HOPE IS TO BE WRONG

Rich dad often said, "I hope I'm wrong."

He believed that by giving his son and me enough of a warning, we would have the time to prepare, just in case he was right. He said, "The question is not whether I am right or wrong. The question is: Are you prepared just in case I am right?"

The good news was that rich dad's prophecy motivated me to prepare, rather than remain complacent. In preparation, Kim and I built our ark. Building our ark led to increased financial education, experience, and financial freedom. So even if the great flood never comes and rich dad was wrong, our preparation has led us to a more financially secure position in life.

A giant stock-market crash is coming, but the market crash is not the problem. Predicting a market crash is not a big deal. All financial markets go up, and all financial markets come down. Market cycles are a part of life. Predicting a market crash is like predicting the coming of winter.

The issue is that the next market crash will reveal big problems. The next crash will be especially hard because three generations have pushed a bigger problem forward—the problem of how people support themselves once their working days are over. That is an unprecedented problem that grows bigger every day.

Warren Buffett says, "It's only when the tide goes out that you learn who's been swimming naked." The next market crash will reveal who has been swimming naked, and one of those groups could be the government itself. For too long now, the government has made promises it knows it cannot keep. But broken promises are not really the problem.

The real problem is a society that is naïve enough to actually believe the promises. Too many people believe the government is responsible for saving them from their own inadequacies. Many people believe the government is like their fairy godmother, a mythical person who can wave a magic wand and all their financial problems will disappear. A society that believes in fairy tales is not a mature society.

In the real world of business and investing, the fairy godmother is the Federal Reserve Board. The fairy godfather is the government. In financial terms, they are called, "the lenders of last resort." Right after September 11, 2001, the Federal Reserve flooded the economy with money as any grandparent would, hoping to ease the pain of their grandkids. When airlines got in trouble after the attack, the federal government stepped forward as the lender of last resort to save some of these airlines. This was like the kindly old grandpa stepping forward to rescue one of his adult children who also happens to have kids. My question and concern is whether the federal and state governments can afford to be the lender of last resort for much longer.

Like it or not, within a few years, millions of baby boomers in America will start turning 70 years old. The question is: How many of them will have enough to afford to live for the rest of their lives? How many will look to the state and federal governments to be the fairy godparents?

The message of this book is that sometime soon people will begin to realize that neither the government nor the stock market can save them.

The Bad News

The bad news is that the next stock-market crash will reveal a level of poverty in America that will shock the world. The world will ask how the richest country of all time can suddenly have so many poor people.

Even worse, economic anger and frustration are on the rise worldwide, which means we will need to solve these problems globally as well as nationally.

As Warren Buffett says, "In the event of nuclear war, disregard this message."

The Good News

The good news is that when times are bad, people are often at their best. Right after the September 11 attack, millions of people found it in their hearts to do something positive and find the hero within themselves. I believe that the coming financial disaster will also bring out the best in people. Rather than complacency, despair, and depression, I believe people will rise up and work together to solve our problems.

Earlier in this book, I wrote that there are three types of education.

1. Academic

2. Professional

3. Financial

In America today, I would grade our ability to teach the basics of reading and writing as a C, or average. I would rate our ability to train people professionally as an A, or excellent. America has great professional schools.

But when it comes to financial education, I would give the American school system an F for failure. This deficiency needs to be corrected immediately if we are to continue as a world power.

In the Industrial Age, all a person needed was academic and professional education. In the Information Age, those two levels of education are no longer enough. In the Information Age, a person needs to be financially competent as well as academically and professionally competent. A high-paying job is not enough. We need to know how to survive when our working days are over. That will require financial education on a large scale.

Two Professions

In the Industrial Age, all we needed was a good job or profession. In the Information Age, we will need two professions. One profession is how we make our money. The second profession is how we invest our money. In order to have the second profession, financial literacy is mandatory.

It's Your Choice

Noah could see the future, and he prepared for it. If you see a future similar to the one rich dad did, you too may want to prepare while there is still time to prepare. Hopefully, of course, the giant stock-market crash will not come. Maybe someone will wave a magic wand, and we will live happily ever after.

But I do not think a stock-market crash can be averted. Nor do I think that millions of baby boomers will suddenly save enough money to care for themselves for as long as they live. I think we will face an emergency, and out of this crisis, a new financial world will emerge. Of that I am confident, and I look forward to it. The coming stock-market crash will reveal problems that we, as a society, have been pushing under the rug for too long. The good news is that once these problems are exposed and the truths are told, we have a chance to solve them once and for all—not just for ourselves, but also for the world.

Beyond the Bulls and the Bears

With the promotion of the 401(k) plans, the U.S. government, and other governments throughout the world offering similar plans, required millions of people to invest without first requiring them to become investors. As non-investors entered the market, most were simply told that on average the stock market goes up. With that assumption, the boom in mutual funds was on.

The truth is that real-world investors know that all markets—regardless whether they are stocks, bonds, real estate, heating oil, pork bellies, crude oil, mutual funds, or interest rates—move up, down, and sideways. A real-world investor would not invest in an asset that only did well in one direction, or in a program that did not allow you to exit when necessary.

But that is just what the 401(k) plan does. It pushes people into assets that they have no control over and doesn't allow them to exit without some sort of penalty. That is like handcuffing a swimmer and throwing him into the deep end of the pool.

Due to their lack of education, most investors in DC pension plans have had to buy into the optimistic, Pollyanna point of view, the point of view of an eternal bull market. Real-world investors know that each market is made up of both bulls and bears. For those of you who want to take greater control over your financial destiny, you may want to go beyond just being a bull or a bear. If you want to be a real-world investor, you may want to develop your financial education, experience, and instincts in order to become a person who can see beyond the ups and downs of any market and always see the brighter future that lies ahead.

Noah knew that he had to take action because a catastrophe was about to take place. Being a man of vision, he could see beyond the darkness to a brand-new world at the end of the flood. Although he knew he could not save everyone, he knew he could bring life to the new world. He took action, not only because of the impending disaster, but also for the brighter future he knew lay ahead.

Being a real-world investor means being in tune with the real world. Optimists love the idea of buying, holding, diversifying, and praying. But if you plan on taking control of your future, you need to have real-world skills to see the better world beyond the storm clouds. If you become a real-world investor, you will not care if markets go up or markets go down because you will do well in all markets. You will not get caught in the debate of whether the bulls or the bears are in control—a debate that most short-term investors get caught up in, buying or selling with every turn of the market. If you become a real-world investor, you will simply see the ups and downs of markets as one of the games of life.

Obviously, we are living in very chaotic times. Obviously, we as a global society have many challenges ahead. One of the challenges is the growing poverty, not only in the third world, but also in first-world countries such as America. The gap between the haves and have-nots must be narrowed.

Teachers hold the key to the future. Teachers hold the key because they are the people who prepare our children for the future. My poor dad, a teacher, often worried that schools focused too much on ancient history rather than the future. He would say, "If I could see the future, I would know what to teach our kids." Teachers must have the courage to offer their students the educational skills required for the future. If more teachers would teach these financial skills, my rich dad's prophecy can be proven wrong. And that is the job of a prophet—to provide enough of a warning so that his prophecy will be wrong and the actions taken will lead to a better world for us all.

This book is not meant to be a doom-and-gloom book. This book is written to inspire you to gain the skills you need to see the bigger and brighter picture of life, the life beyond the brewing storm clouds. The future will be very bright for those who are prepared, but being prepared also means having faith as Noah did—the faith to see a better world beyond the storm.

Rich dad often quoted the saying, "The darkest hour is the hour just before dawn." That was his way of reminding us to continue to improve our skills, to keep our faith strong—especially in the darkest of hours, and to have the courage to step forward while others are running backward.

You have the opportunity to take control of your financial life. By building your own ark full of assets that work for you, you can prepare yourself to prosper, no matter how the market performs.

Thank you for reading this book.

About the Author
Robert Kiyosaki

Best known as the author of *Rich Dad Poor Dad*—the #1 personal finance book of all time—Robert Kiyosaki has challenged and changed the way tens of millions of people around the world think about money. He is an entrepreneur, educator, and investor who believes the world needs more entrepreneurs who will create jobs.

With perspectives on money and investing that often contradict conventional wisdom, Robert has earned an international reputation for straight talk, irreverence, and courage and has become a passionate and outspoken advocate for financial education.

Robert and Kim Kiyosaki are founders of The Rich Dad Company, a financial education company, and creators of the *CASHFLOW*® games. In 2013, the company will leverage the global success of the Rich Dad games in the launch of a new and breakthrough offering in mobile and online gaming.

Robert has been heralded as a visionary who has a gift for simplifying complex concepts—ideas related to money, investing, finance, and economics—and has shared his personal journey to financial freedom in ways that resonate with audiences of all ages and backgrounds. His core principles and messages—like "your house is not an asset" and "Invest for cash flow" and "savers are losers"—have ignited a firestorm of criticism and ridicule... only to have played out on the world economic stage over the past decade in ways that were both unsettling and prophetic.

His point of view is that "old" advice—go to college, get a good job, save money, get out of debt, invest for the long term, and diversify—has become obsolete advice in today's fast-paced Information Age. His Rich Dad philosophies and messages challenge the status quo. His teachings encourage people to become financially educated and to take an active role in investing for their future.

The author of 19 books, including the international blockbuster *Rich Dad Poor Dad*, Robert has been a featured guest with media outlets in every corner of the world—from CNN, the BBC, Fox News, Al Jazeera, GBTV and PBS, to *Larry King Live*, *Oprah*, *Peoples Daily*, *Sydney Morning Herald*, *The Doctors*, *Straits Times*, *Bloomberg*, *NPR*, *USA TODAY*, and hundreds of others—and his books have topped international bestsellers lists for more than a decade. He continues to teach and inspire audiences around the world.

His most recent books include *Unfair Advantage: The Power of Financial Education*, *Midas Touch*, the second book he has co-authored with Donald Trump, and *Why "A" Students Work for "C" Students*.

To learn more, visit RichDad.com

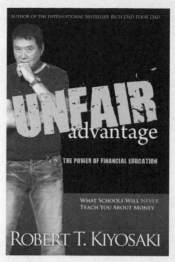 

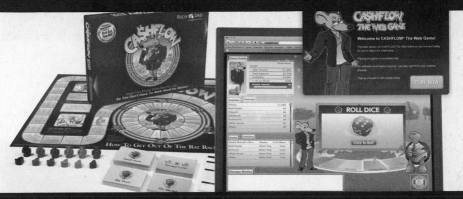

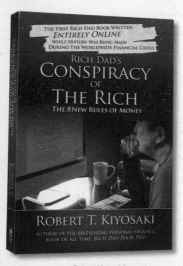